INTERNET
AND THE LAW

Legal Fundamentals for the

Internet User

T0198067

Raymond A. Kurz

with

Bart G. Newland

Steven Lieberman

Celine M. Jimenez

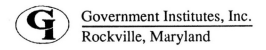
Government Institutes, Inc.
Rockville, Maryland

Government Institutes, a Division of ABS Group Inc.
4 Research Place, Rockville, Maryland 20850, USA
Phone: (301) 921-2300
Fax: (301) 921-0373
Email: giinfo@govinst.com
Internet: http://www.govinst.com

03 02 01 00   7   6

Library of Congress Cataloging-in-Publication Data

Kurz, Raymond A.
Internet and the law: legal fundamentals for the Internet user / Raymond A. Kurz with Bart G. Newland, Steven Lieberman, Celine M. Jimenez.
       p.   cm.
Includes index.
ISBN: 0-86587-506-5
1. Information storage and retrieval systems--Law--United States.
2. Internet (Computer network)   I. Title.
KF242.A1K87   1995
343.73099'9--dc20
                                    99-49563
                                    CIP

Printed in the United States of America

Table Of Contents

Page

FOREWORD AND ACKNOWLEDGEMENTS x

ABOUT THE AUTHORS xi

INTRODUCTION xiii

Chapter 1

INTELLECTUAL PROPERTY OVERVIEW 1

Copyrights, Trademarks, And Patents
Are Not Synonymous 1

Constitutional Basis For Protecting
Patents, Copyrights And Trademarks 2

What Do Patents, Copyrights And
Trademarks Protect? 3

Chapter 2

COPYRIGHTS 6

Works Are Protected Upon Creation 6

The Creator Of A Work Is Presumed
To Be The Owner Of The Copyright 7

Works Made For Hire Are An Exception
To The Rule That The Creator Is The
Presumptive Owner Of The Copyright 8

Certain Commissioned Works May Also

Be Works For Hire 10
Joint Works 12
Subject Matter Of Copyright 12
Requirement Of Originality And Creativity 14
Copyright Does Not Extend To Ideas 19
Government Works 21
What Are The Copyright Rights? 21
  The Right To Reproduce A Work 23
  The Right To Make Derivative Works 23
  Exception To The Exclusive Rights Of The
      Copyright Holder Regarding Computer Programs 24
  Compulsory Licensing For Phonorecords 25
  Fair Use 26
  Additional Rights In Copyrighted Works 27
Copyright Notice 29
Restoration Of Copyright And Works
  That Have Fallen Into The Public Domain
  For Failure To Display Appropriate Notice ... 32
Copyright Registration 33
Duration Of Copyright 36
Infringement And Liability Issues 37
  Who Is Liable For Copyright Infringement? 39
  Remedies For Copyright Infringement 41
  Recent Cases Involving On-line Services 41
Assignment And Licensing 42
Copyright Searching 43
International Considerations 44

Chapter 3

TRADEMARKS 49
Trademarks, Service Marks And Trade Names . . 51
The Value Of Trademarks 52
Considerations In Choosing A Trademark 53
Availability 54
Subject Matter Of Trademark Protection 56
Colors As Trademarks 58
Scope Of Protection 59
Generic Terms 59
Descriptive Terms 60
Suggestive Terms 61
Coined Or Arbitrary Terms 61
Why The Categories Of Trademarks Are Important . . 62
How Trademark Rights Are Obtained 64
Use Is King 64
The Trademark Registration Process And
Advantages Of Federal Registration 66
The Trademark Application Process 68
Use Of The Trademark Symbol 72
Maintaining A Trademark 73
Use And Registration Of Domain Names 78
Trademark Infringement 79
Assignment And Licensing 82
International Aspects 83

Chapter 4

UNFAIR COMPETITION 87
Wrongful Acts Proscribed By The Lanham Act . . 88
Protection Of Unregistered Trademarks 89
False Or Misleading Advertising 90
Remedies Under Section 43(a) Of The Lanham Act 91
Infringement Of Rights Of Publicity 92
Other Causes Of Action 92
Dilution Of Trademarks 93

Chapter 5

PATENTS 96
Introduction 96
Patent Law Basics 98
What Is A Patent? 98
How Is A Patent Obtained? 100
How Is A Patent Enforced? 104
How Can Patent Rights Of
Others Be Investigated? 105
Patent Protection For Computer Software 106
Avoiding Patent Problems On The 'Net 110

Chapter 6

TRADE SECRETS 113
Introduction 113
The Requirements Of A Trade Secret 113

A Trade Secret Must Not Be Commonly Known 117
A Trade Secret Must Be Kept Secret 117

Enforcement Of Trade Secret Rights 120

Protecting Trade Secrets By Contract 122

Reverse Engineering 124

Protecting Trade Secrets On The Internet 125

A Sample Form Confidentiality Agreement 127

Chapter 7

ASSIGNMENT AND LICENSING 131

Introduction 131

Definitional Aspects Of Assignments
And Licenses 133

Recordation 134

Licensing Of Copyrights 135
Are Copyright Rights Involved? 136
Identifying The Rights-Holders 136
Common Provisions In Licenses
Involving Copyrights 140

Shareware 142

Licensing Of Multimedia Works 144

Shrinkwrap-Type Licensing 146

Licensing Of Trademarks 148
Common Provisions In Trademark Licenses 149

Licensing Of Patents 151

Digital Signatures 156

Chapter 8

DEFAMATION 160
Scenario: 160
An Overview Of General Defamation Principles .. 161
Liability Of Owners And Operators Of On-line
Services For Statements Uploaded
By Subscribers 165
Current Case Law On The
Publisher/Distributor/Common Carrier Issue .. 165
Analogous Case Law 170
Practical Advice To Owners And Operators
Of On-line Services 172
Where A Suit Based On An Internet
Message May Be Maintained 178
When Must A Libel Action Arising
From An Electronic Publication Be Brought? . 185

Appendices

Appendix 1 192
Sample Form: U.S. Copyright Office Forms:
Form TX 192
Sample Form: U.S. Copyright Office Forms:
Form SR 196
Sample Form: U.S. Copyright Office Forms:
Form VA 200
Sample Form: U.S. Copyright Office Forms:
Form PA 204

Appendix 2 208
  U.S. Patent And Trademark Office Form:
    Application For Federal Registration 208

Appendix 3 210
  International Classification Of Goods/Services 210

Appendix 4 214
  Sample Form: Assignment Of All Rights In
    Works, Including Copyright Rights 214

Appendix 5 217
  Sample Form: Assignment Of Trademark Registration 217

Appendix 6 219
  Sample Form: Basic Trademark License Agreement 219

Appendix 7 225
  Sample Form: Work Made For Hire/Assignment
    Clause In Independent Contractor-Type
    Agreement For Artwork 225

Appendix 8 226
  Sample Form: Confidentiality Agreement 226

Appendix 9 229
  Proposed [PTO] Examination Guidelines
    For Computer-Implemented Invention 229

Index 239

FOREWORD AND ACKNOWLEDGEMENTS

This book is intended to introduce the reader to some of the significant legal issues involved in conducting business on–line. It is not intended to be relied upon as legal advice nor is it in any way a substitute for consultation with competent counsel.

Internet And The Law: Legal Fundamentals For The Internet User was the result of a team effort by the attorneys, paralegals and secretarial staff of Rothwell, Figg, Ernst & Kurz. In addition to the contributing authors, for their efforts in writing their chapters and reviewing the chapters of other contributors, special appreciation is extended to the following individuals.

G. Franklin Rothwell, for his review of and comments to the book and for his guidance and experience over the years which formed the foundation of the pages which follow.

Celine M. Jimenez, for her special efforts in assisting with the editing, organization, and logistics of the book.

Joseph A. Hynds and K. Denise Hoefler, for their careful review of and comment to the book.

Colleen Vann, for going above and beyond the call of duty in typing, formatting and otherwise preparing the book for print.

Raymond A. Kurz
Editor/Author
Rothwell, Figg, Ernst & Kurz
555 Thirteenth Street, N.W., Ste. 701–E
Washington, D.C. 20004
Tele.: (202) 783–6040 Fax: (202) 783–6031
Internet: rakur@rfek.com

ABOUT THE AUTHORS

Raymond A. Kurz – Editor and principal author, is a shareholder at the firm of Rothwell, Figg, Ernst & Kurz, specializing in intellectual property litigation, counseling and Trademark and Copyright Office practice. He represents clients in diverse fields ranging from electronics to consumer goods, as well as, copyright and trademark interests in a variety of computer software fields including, communications and network management, financial institutional trading, and interactive educational and multimedia software. Mr. Kurz was coordinator and host of a recent conference on European Community Trademarks and has also lectured on intellectual property law issues.

Bart G. Newland – Author of the chapter on Patents, is a shareholder at Rothwell, Figg, Ernst & Kurz, and his practice centers on patent law and related licensing, litigation, and client counselling. His experience includes both private and in–house corporate intellectual property practice. The primary focus of Mr. Newland's practice is chemical and biotechnology patent law. He has significant expertise and interest in the areas of computers and telecommunications, and Mr. Newland serves as the firm's in–house expert on Internet matters, law firm automation and other computer–related issues.

Steven Lieberman – Author of the chapter on Defamation, is a shareholder at Rothwell, Figg, Ernst & Kurz and specializes in intellectual property litigation and First Amendment law. Previously, Mr. Lieberman was with Cahill Gordon & Reindel where he worked extensively on media law issues with Floyd Abrams. Mr. Lieberman is chairman of the Defamation and New Technologies Subcommittee of the Committee on Media Law of the New York State Bar Association and a member of the Libel Defense Resource Center ("LDRC") Cyberspace Committee. Mr. Lieberman is a co–author of the District of Columbia Section of the LDRC's annual <u>50–State Survey of Media Privacy and Related Law</u>, has written on the subject of on–line defamation and is currently editing a collection of articles on that subject for the New York State Bar Association and the LDRC.

Celine M. Jimenez – Author of the chapters on Trade Secrets, and Assignment and Licensing, is an associate with Rothwell, Figg, Ernst & Kurz and specializes in intellectual property litigation, computer law, licensing and counseling. She has litigated patent and trade secret cases in the electronics, communications and mechanical fields, and litigated a variety of trademark and copyright matters. Ms. Jimenez' practice also focuses on licensing and copyright protection of computer software with a special emphasis on telecommunications, network management and multimedia software.

INTRODUCTION

Your environmental regulation compliance newsletter group has decided to spread its wings and make its presence known on the Internet (thereby improving your group's present method of exchanging information from a newsletter with a circulation of one hundred and seventy–five to a potential community of twenty–five million and growing). You have therefore decided to establish an interactive environmental compliance World Wide Web site through an Internet access provider. In anticipation of this momentous occasion, you have decided that your present group name "Environmental Compliance" is not intriguing enough to catch the attention of your new worldwide audience. After weeks of consideration, you have arrived at the most clever name that you can think of, "The Envi–Check," and you have decided to reserve your source of contact with the world at large by registering "Envi–Check.Com." as your domain name with InterNIC, the Internet Network Information Center, which assigns domain names in North America.

Your debut communication on the Internet is well thought out. In an obscure Usenet newsgroup, you have found an extremely interesting article written by the president of a small widget manufacturing company, Acme Widget Corp., regarding an obscure OSHA regulation carrying draconian penalties for lack of compliance. You believe that this report is worthy of sharing and you download Acme Widget Corp.'s report and incorporate the downloaded report into your Web site. Your unintentional adventure into the legalities of Cyberspace has begun.

Three weeks later, you receive a letter from Acme Widget Corp.'s lawyer charging you with a violation 17 U.S.C. § 106 *et. seq* (copyright infringement). You receive a second letter from a lawyer representing "Envi Checker Corp." charging you with a violation of 15 U.S.C. § 1114 and 15 U.S.C. § 1125(a) (trademark infringement and federal unfair competition), and a third letter arrives from a lawyer representing Mr. Smith, the President of Acme Widget Corp., charging you with libel for the portion of your debut Internet piece in which you had suggested that Mr. Smith must have had below average intelligence for failing to recognize that it was an OSHA violation to manufacture widgets between 2:00 p.m. and 2:05 p.m. on days when there is a full moon (in view of the high incidence of accidents in the manufacturing of widgets which occurs at that particular time). You have now been charged with various counts of trademark infringement, unfair competition, false designation of origin, copyright infringement, libel and, as all three letters said, "*inter alia.*"

This scenario, while fictitious, highlights just a few of the potential legal land mines which await those who wish to take advantage of the tremendous communications potential of the Internet. The explosion in the use of the Internet has thrust unsuspecting, unwary, but well-intentioned groups, companies, organizations and individuals into potential legal nightmares. However, there are steps which can be taken and actions which can be avoided so as to minimize the chances of becoming an unwitting litigant and to assure that your rights as an Internet user are protected against encroachment by others.

The purpose of this book is to <u>acquaint</u> Internet participants and users with the legal landscape within which they operate. This book is <u>not</u> intended to be a treatise delving into the details of the jurisprudence which is discussed in the succeeding chapters. Rather, it is intended to make the reader aware of the basics of laws which relate to the new medium in which the reader may wish to express himself or herself. More specifically, this book will explain basic principles pertaining to laws of copyright, trademark, trade secret, patent, libel/defamation and related issues as well as touch upon basic principles of contract law and licensing.

It is hoped that this book will provide the reader with a basic understanding of how to navigate through and avoid the legal morass within cyberspace and that it will allow the readers to become familiar with the issues involved in achieving adequate protection of their intellectual and commercial endeavors and to guard against abuse by others.

Raymond A. Kurz
Rothwell, Figg, Ernst & Kurz

INTERNET

AND THE LAW

Legal Fundamentals for the

Internet User _____

Chapter 1

INTELLECTUAL PROPERTY OVERVIEW*

Copyrights, Trademarks, And Patents Are Not Synonymous

A first step in understanding the basics of the intellectual property issues involved in participating in Internet exploration and utilization is an understanding of some of the basic legal terms. Everyone has heard the terms "copyright," "trademark" and "patent." However, relatively few have taken note that one does not copyright an idea, trademark an invention or patent the name of business' goods or services. Although these terms are often used by even sophisticated companies interchangeably, each of these three concepts is distinct. They are sometimes collectively referred to as "intellectual property."

The phrase "intellectual property" generally denotes the product of one's intellectual endeavors. For example, inventing a new and improved widget would be an intellectual endeavor. The invention would be the "intellectual property" of the inventor and may be subject to protection under the patent laws. Similarly, an article written by Mr. Smith, the President of Acme Widget Corp., represents the expression of Mr. Smith's intellectual and creative endeavors and, thus, represents his "intellectual property," protected by way of the copyright laws.

Although trademarks have often been referred to as "intellectual property," it is perhaps more accurate to view trademarks as <u>commercial</u> property considering the Constitutional basis for trademark protection (which is discussed in the succeeding section) and the commercial identification function performed by trademarks. The name ACME, which Acme Widget Corp. affixes to its widgets to identify and

---

*Chapter written by Raymond A. Kurz, Rothwell, Figg, Ernst & Kurz.

distinguish their widgets from widgets made by other companies, is a trademark protected by trademark and unfair competition laws.

Constitutional Basis For Protecting Patents, Copyrights And Trademarks

Copyright protection and patent protection find their origins in a specific provision of the United States Constitution which provides that Congress has the power "To promote the Progress of Science and useful Arts, by securing for limited Times to Authors and Inventors, the exclusive Right to their respective Writings and Discoveries."[1] The reference in the Constitution to "writings" gave rise to protections enacted by Congress by way of the copyright laws, and the reference to "discoveries" gave rise to the protections enacted by Congress by way of the patent laws. Thus, from the simple concept of protection of authors' and inventors' "writings and discoveries," there has evolved a great body of case law and complex statutes and rules relating to copyright and patent protection.

In contrast to the specific provision in the U.S. Constitution for protecting "writings and discoveries," trademark protection, while also based on powers granted to Congress in the United States Constitution, is founded in a less direct manner. The United States Constitution contains a Commerce Clause which gives Congress the power "To regulate Commerce with foreign Nations, and among the several States, and with the Indian Tribes."[2] It is this power to regulate commerce which constitutionally supports the great body of law and associated volumes of statutes and rules relating to trademarks and unfair competition.

What Do Patents, Copyrights And Trademarks Protect?

In very basic terms, patents protect products, machines, methods or compositions as they are embodied in utilitarian inventions (utility patents), or aesthetic designs (design patents). Patents can protect new and better utilitarian objects as diverse as computer hardware and software, an improved potato or tomato, a better mousetrap, and even a better mouse. Patents also can protect the methods of making the objects and methods of using them, such as for the treatment of disease. Methods of doing business, theoretical scientific discoveries and mathematical algorithms (see, however, the chapter on Patents for further information concerning algorithms) are not patentable class of subject matter. New and improved products and machines embodying them, however, often are patentable.

Trademarks protect words, symbols or other forms of expression which identify the source of the goods or services provided by a person or entity. Trademarks have been granted for designs, fanciful expressions, common words of the English or foreign languages, letters, numbers, colors or color combinations, the configuration of products and product packaging, sounds and even smells. Trademarks do not protect generic terms, functional aspects of utilitarian objects or merely informational statements.

Copyrights protect the creative endeavors of authors as those endeavors are particularly expressed in "writings" fixed in some tangible medium. Works protected by copyright include literary works, artwork, sculpture (loosely interpreted to constitute a "writing"), photographs, music, and computer programs. Copyrights do not protect titles, single words or short phrases. Copyrights also do not protect ideas (rather, they protect only the expression of ideas as set forth in a tangible medium).

In the context of cyberspace, computer programs, being the product of the creative efforts of their authors, have usually been protected by the copyright laws, while computer hardware has always been the subject of patent protection. In recent years, patent laws have been adapting to recognize that computer programs are also protectable as "inventions" (in addition to being protected under the copyright laws).

If one were to create the latest preschool educational computer game, calling it WARRIOR VILLAINS, the result of that endeavor might be the subject of trademark, copyright and patent protection. More specifically, the catchy phrase, WARRIER VILLAINS, created to get the attention of the youngest members of our society (and to assure that these consumers know what to tell their parents to buy them for Christmas), is a trademark. The computer program itself, being the "writings" of an author, would be the subject of copyright protection (as discussed in a succeeding chapter, copyright laws provide for a broad view as to what is sufficiently "creative" to warrant copyright protection). The computer program (or elements of it) might also be the subject of patent protection if it provides a new and non–obvious method of controlling some operation of the computer.

These concepts, along with other basic forms of legal protection and potential liability are discussed in more detail in succeeding chapters.

Endnotes

1. U.S. Const. Art. 1, § 8, Cl. 8.

2. U.S. Const. Art. 1, § 8, Cl. 3.

Chapter 2

COPYRIGHTS*

The Internet is a unique medium in which copyright issues arise, as the types of works which may find their way onto the Internet (and the copyright issues attendant to those works) are as varied as the universe of works which may be subject to copyright protection. Thus, it would be a mistake to focus attention solely on so–called "computer law" issues when considering the law of copyright as it relates to the Internet. While computer copyright law issues are discussed, the focus of this chapter is the entire range of subject matter found on the Internet. Indeed, the copyright status of such traditional works as written works, works of art, audiovisual works, and other works such as computer programs must be considered when navigating and working within the medium known as the Internet. This chapter highlights some of the basic copyright issues which pertain to all copyrightable works as well as issues related in particular to posting and interacting with such works on–line.

Copyright issues are perhaps the most misunderstood of all intellectual property issues. While seemingly simple in many respects, copyright law can be completely counterintuitive. Several underlying concepts help in understanding basic aspects of the copyright laws and go a long way to aid in understanding some of the more intricate details. These concepts are explained below.

Works Are Protected Upon Creation

Works of authorship, i.e., the universe of copyrightable works, are protected upon creation. That is, as soon as such a work is "fixed in any tangible medium," including computer–readable formats such as computer software, the work is immediately subject to copyright

---

*Chapter written by Raymond A. Kurz, Rothwell, Figg, Ernst & Kurz.

protection. While formalities, such as registering one's claim to copyright and using appropriate copyright notice may be very valuable in protecting and enforcing one's copyright, these formalities are not needed in order for copyrights to arise. It is absolutely fundamental to the present copyright protection scheme that works are protected upon creation. As soon as an author puts pen to paper, brush to canvas, or fingers to a computer keyboard, an author has created a work which is potentially subject to protection under the copyright laws. The reason a work is characterized as "potentially" subject to protection is that in order to be subject to copyright protection, the work also must pass threshold standards of "creativity" and "originality" to be considered to be a work of copyrightable "authorship." These concepts are discussed in succeeding sections of this chapter.

The Creator Of A Work Is Presumed To Be The Owner Of The Copyright

In addition to the concept of a work being protected upon creation, another basic underlying aspect of the copyright protection scheme is that in most circumstances (with the most notable exception being an author who creates a work within the scope of his or her employment), the creator of the work is the owner of the copyright in the work. This aspect of copyright law seems to many to be counterintuitive as there is often a misconception that if Party A pays Party B for creating a work for Party A, Party A should be the owner of all rights to the work created by Party B. This is not the case and this aspect of copyright law has caused more problems and potential problems than can be imagined. Unless there is a specific agreement assigning the copyright (or unless other very specific conditions are met, which will be discussed in succeeding sections), the party who pays for the work owns only the tangible copy of the work, while the creator of the work owns the copyright in the work.

Works Made For Hire Are An Exception To The Rule That The Creator Is The Presumptive Owner Of The Copyright

While the creator of a work is most often the owner of the copyright in a work, there is one major exception involving "works made for hire." Under the copyright laws, a work made for hire can arise in two situations. First, where an employee of a company prepares a work within the scope of his or her employment, the employer is considered to be the author of the work as a work made for hire. The law regarding works made for hire has evolved over the years. Relatively recently (in 1989), the United States Supreme Court applied the work–for–hire doctrine by taking into account the circumstances which govern the traditional employer/employee relationship, such as:

(1) The level of skill required to create the work.

(2) The source of the instrumentalities and tools used to create the work.

(3) The location of the work (e.g., was the work performed at the "employer's" place of business).

(4) The duration of the relationship between the parties.

(5) Whether the "employer" has the right to assign additional projects to the "employee."

(6) The extent of the "employee's" discretion over when and how long to work.

(7) The method of payment.

(8) The "employee's" role in hiring and paying assistants.

(9)   Whether the work is part of the regular business of the "employer."

(10) Whether the "employer" is in business.

(11) The provision of employee benefits.

(12) Tax treatment of the "employee."[1]

Thus, in most cases, it is the traditional employer/employee relationship which will trigger the "work made for hire" exception to the rule that the creator is the owner of the copyright in a work.

This traditional employer/employee relationship is to be distinguished from the relationship which arises when a party hires another as an independent contractor. The independent contractor may be specifically hired, paid and directed to perform a particular task, e.g., write computer software or create artwork. However, under the copyright laws, this situation does not necessarily give rise to a work being considered to be a "work made for hire." Instead (unless very specific conditions can be met), the independent contractor who created the software or artwork will be the copyright owner, rather than the party who hires the independent contractor.

Today, there are many companies who, unbeknownst to them, are not the copyright owners in various computer programs and other works which were created by independent contractors. This could have dire consequences should the independent contractor seek to enforce his or her rights of copyright and can greatly restrict what the company that paid for the software (or other work) can actually do with it.

Certain Commissioned Works May Also Be Works For Hire

While, generally, works created by an independent contractor are not considered to be works made for hire, there is a narrow class of works created by independent contractors known as "specially ordered or commissioned works" that may constitute works made for hire.[2] For these "specially ordered or commissioned works," copyright vests in the party who specially ordered or commissioned the work. It is emphasized, however, that this class of works is very narrow, and requires that <u>two</u> conditions be met.

First, the work must fall into one of the following categories of works, namely, works specially ordered or commissioned:

(1) as a contribution to a "collective work" (a "collective work" is a work, such as a periodical issue, anthology or encyclopedia in which a number of contributions constituting separate and independent works in themselves are assembled into a collective whole);

(2) as part of a motion picture or other audiovisual work;

(3) as a translation;

(4) as a supplementary work prepared for publication as a secondary adjunct to a work of another author (for the purpose of illustrating, explaining, revising, commenting upon or assisting in the use of another work such as forewords, afterwards, pictorial illustrations, maps, charts, tables, editorial notes, musical arrangements, answer material for tests, bibliographies, appendixes and indexes);

(5)   as a compilation (i.e., a work formed by the collection and assembling of preexisting materials or of data that are selected, coordinated, or arranged in such a way that the resulting work as a whole constitutes an original work of authorship; the term "compilation" includes collective works);

(6)   as an instructional text;

(7)   as a test;

(8)   as answer material for a test; or

(9)   as an atlas.[3]

Second, in addition to falling into one of the foregoing categories, in order for a specially ordered or commissioned work to be considered to be a work for hire, the parties must expressly agree in writing that the work is considered by the parties to be a work for hire.[4]

Only if the work falls into one of the nine enumerated categories of works <u>and</u> is the subject of a written agreement between the parties specifically indicating that the work is a work for hire (or if the work being created is created within the scope of one's employment), will the work be owned by the party paying for the work or employing the creator rather than the creator.

It is therefore incumbent on those who hire others to create copyrightable works and who wish to own the copyright in those works either to:

(1)   assure themselves that they are an employer of the creator of the work in the traditional sense of the word (or that the work

definitely meets <u>both</u> criteria for a specially ordered or commissioned work); or

(2) obtain ownership by way of a written assignment of the copyright in the work from the creator.

Assignments and the form of assignments (including a sample form of assignment) are addressed in a later chapter of this book. For purposes of this chapter, however, the reader should simply remember, if in doubt, obtain a written assignment of copyright from the creator of the work.

Joint Works

Joint works are works to which two or more authors contribute copyrightable subject matter with the intention of merging the contributions into inseparable or interdependent parts of a unitary whole.[5] Each joint author is entitled to exploit the entire work. However, each joint author must also "account" to all other joint authors. This means that if one author exploits the work and receives remuneration, that author must share that remuneration with all other joint authors. The division of that remuneration is sometimes subject to controversy, depending on the respective contributions of the parties. It is, therefore, best to reduce to writing any agreement between joint authors to more explicitly set out the various rights (and remuneration) between or among the joint authors.

Subject Matter Of Copyright

Generally, copyright protects all works of original authorship which are sufficiently creative, and which are fixed in a tangible medium of expression (the concepts of "originality" and "creativity" are discussed in succeeding chapters). These copyrightable works are classified in the following eight categories:

(1)   literary works;

(2)   musical works, including any accompanying words;

(3)   dramatic works, including accompanying music;

(4)   pantomimes and choreographic works;

(5)   pictorial, graphic and sculptural works;

(6)   motion pictures and other audiovisual works;

(7)   sound recordings; and

(8)   architectural works.[6]

Computer software code is generally considered to constitute a "literary work" which is defined in the Copyright Act as "works, other than audiovisual works, expressed in words, numbers, or other verbal or numerical symbols or indicia, regardless of the nature of the material objects, such as books, periodicals, manuscripts, phonorecords, film, tapes, disks or cards, in which they are embodied."[7] Thus, computer software is protectable as would be any other "literary work."

Obviously, however, the subject matter which may find its way onto the Internet includes not only computer software code, but various works that fall into the other categories of protectable subject matter, such as musical works, pictorial and graphic works, motion pictures and other audiovisual works, sound recordings, depictions of architectural works, and so forth. Therefore, copyright protection for works which appear on the Internet must be considered according to the category into which they fall.

The determination of what category applies to a particular work is not merely an academic exercise taken on as amusement by copyright professors. Rather, these categories of copyrightable works may very well determine the scope of protection and the exceptions to protection which pertain to a given work. For example, there are certain provisions of the Copyright Act that specifically concern the scope of copyright protection for pictorial, graphic and sculptural works, for sound recordings, for musical works, for architectural works, and for other types of works.[8] These provisions are numerous and complex, and will not be discussed in detail here. Certain of these provisions, however, are discussed in succeeding sections of this chapter.

Requirement Of Originality And Creativity

The concept of originality as used in this book means only that a work must be original as to the author in order to be protected by copyright.[9] This is different from the concept of novelty as may be found in the patent laws which means that an invention must be new or novel *vis-à-vis* the rest of the world. Under the copyright laws, a work may be identical to another work created by another party and still be subject to copyright protection if the party that created the second work did not copy it from the earlier existing work. If, for example, an author could prove he or she were on a desert island from birth and had not had access to War and Peace while on the desert island, and by some miracle created a work identical to War and Peace, the desert island author himself or herself would be entitled to copyright protection to the newly created, "original" to the desert island author, War and Peace.

In order to avoid later charges that a work is not original to the author (e.g., that the work was copied from an earlier work), it is often advisable to document the creative process involved in preparing a work. This practice has found particular utility in the context of computer programming, especially where a computer program is being created to perform the same function as a prior existing program. This practice, often referred to as "clean room" creation of a work, involves careful documentation of the lack of access the programmers had to the prior existing program (i.e., they create the new program in a "clean room"), as well as the creative steps undertaken to create the newer program.

This "clean room" practice should be considered in contexts other than computer programming and may be especially valuable in various other situations where a party wishes to create a work (or hire another to create a work) that will perform the same function or embody the same idea as a prior existing work (as already mentioned and as discussed below, ideas themselves are not subject to copyright protection).

In addition to being original, in order to be subject to copyright protection, a work must be sufficiently "creative." The copyright laws do not protect completely trivial works devoid of creative authorship, works which are "merely" ideas, or works which are purely functional or utilitarian. For example, the Copyright Regulations specifically set out that the following material is not subject to copyright protection:

(1)   words and short phrases such as names, titles and slogans; familiar symbols or designs; mere variations of typographic ornamentation, lettering or coloring; mere listing of ingredients or contents;

(2)   ideas, plans, methods, systems, or devices, as distinguished from the particular manner in which they are expressed or described in a writing;

(3) blank forms, such as time cards, graph paper, account books, diaries, bank checks, scorecards, address books, report forms, order forms and the like, which are designed for recording information and do not themselves convey information;

(4) works consisting entirely of information that is common property containing no original authorship, such as, for example: standard calendars, height and weight charts, tape measures and rulers, schedules of sporting events, and lists or tables taken from public documents or other common sources; and

(5) typeface as typeface.[10]

The Copyright Statute also specifically provides that copyright does not extend to "any idea, procedure, process, system, method of operation, concept, principle, or discovery, regardless of the form in which it is described, explained, illustrated, or embodied in such work."[11] Simply stated, copyright does not protect ideas or utilitarian aspects of works, nor does it protect works which do not have a sufficient threshold of creativity.

A recent illustrative case regarding the subject matter of copyright is Lotus v. Borland which concerned Lotus' menu commands.[12] In March of 1995, the United States Court of Appeals for the First Circuit held that the Lotus 1–2–3 menu command hierarchy is uncopyrightable subject matter and that Borland was thus not liable for copying it into its Quattro and Quattro Pro products. The court based this decision on the conclusion that the command hierarchy is a "method of operation" of a computer. Thus, where a development concerns the way in which a computer operates, copyright protection may not exist.

Drawing the distinction between where the utilitarian aspect of a work ends and where the copyrightable subject matter begins and determining just what is considered to be sufficiently "creative" generally, is the subject of much debate.

The seminal legal decision regarding copyright protection in works which happen to be utilitarian objects concerned the design of a lamp.[13] In that case, the U.S. Supreme Court upheld the copyright in the design of a lamp base which was in the form of a statue. The Court essentially held that copyright in a work is not lost merely because the work happens to be embodied in a utilitarian object or "useful article." However, works which are completely utilitarian in nature, i.e., where it is not possible to separate out the utilitarian aspect of the work from the creative aspect, are not subject to copyright protection.

At one time, it was believed that artwork created solely for advertising and promotional purposes might not be sufficiently creative to constitute copyrightable subject matter. However, in a landmark case, Justice Holmes of the U.S. Supreme Court held that a promotional circus poster was indeed sufficiently creative to constitute copyrightable subject matter.[14] While we may take it for granted today that advertising and promotional posters and the like should be considered to be subject to copyright protection as "works of art," such was not always the case. In the circus poster case, Justice Holmes was careful to point out the danger of judges "trained only in the law" being arbiters of taste and creativity. Nevertheless, significant disputes can and do arise as to whether particular works are sufficiently creative so as to warrant copyright protection.

Today, the Copyright Office routinely rejects copyright applications which, in the eyes of the copyright official considering the application, are for works insufficiently creative to warrant copyright protection.

One class of works which is commonly found on the Internet are databases and other compilations of information. Questions often arise as to whether such compilations are sufficiently original and creative to satisfy the threshold requisites of copyright protection. At one end of the spectrum are works in which the creator has selected and arranged the material of the compilation in a creative and imaginative way. In these circumstances, even if the material in the compilation is not itself subject to copyright (e.g., perhaps because it consists of titles, short phrases, etc., or perhaps because the material consists of works in which copyright which has expired), copyright protection will nevertheless arise from the creativity involved in the selection and arrangement of the noncopyrightable elements.

At the other end of the spectrum are compilations of information for which not only is the underlying material not subject to copyright, but the selection and arrangement of that material is without sufficient originality or creativity, e.g., the subject matter is arranged alphabetically or numerically. In those circumstances, copyright protection may be denied in its entirety. Case law has vacillated regarding the copyrightability of such simple compilations. Some cases essentially protected the "sweat of the brow" of the researcher. Other cases denied protection for works which consisted primarily of the researcher's "sweat of the brow."

In 1991, the Supreme Court apparently settled the issue by unanimously deciding that there was insufficient creativity in arranging listings in a telephone book in alphabetical order so as to warrant copyright protection.[15] Nevertheless, the issue of whether there is sufficient creativity in the selection and arrangement of elements of compilations, where the underlying information itself is not subject to copyright protection, has been inconsistently dealt with by the courts even after the 1991 Supreme Court decision. The controlling factor in all such cases is whether there is sufficient creativity in the selection of the material which is the subject of the compilation. Where good arguments can be made that a database or other compilation is not mere "sweat of the brow," but rather is the subject of the creativity of the compiler, the work should be protected by copyright.

Copyright Does Not Extend To Ideas

As mentioned in the previous section, copyright protection does not extend to ideas. It protects only specific expressions of ideas.

As one could imagine, it is sometimes difficult to determine whether a work is a "mere" idea which is not protectable by copyright or, in fact, an expression of an idea which is protectable by copyright. This problem is the focus of many cases involving computer software. According to the copyright laws, for example, an idea might be expressed in a particular way in a computer program and, therefore, be subject to copyright protection. However, the idea underlying the program is not protected by copyright.   Thus, if one were to create a competing computer program which accomplished the same result and embodied the same idea as a previous work, but the resulting newer work is expressed through different code, the newly created work might not be considered to infringe upon the copyright in the work from which the idea was taken.

Although today, computer software poses particularly difficult questions regarding the distinction between the protectable expression of an idea versus an unprotectable idea, the problems encountered in making this distinction have pervaded copyright law since the landmark case of Baker v. Selden[16] decided over 100 years ago. In that case, the Supreme Court struggled with these very issues in considering plaintiff's attempt to enforce his copyright in a book of blank forms used for bookkeeping. The defendant published a competing form book embodying the same basic bookkeeping system and copied the ideas of plaintiff's form book, but did so through a different set of forms. The Supreme Court unanimously held that copyright protection did not extend to the ideas found in plaintiff's work but only to the specific expression of those ideas, and, thus, defendant did not infringe plaintiff's work.

Although courts still struggle with the issue of where to draw the line between an unprotectable idea and a copyrightable expression of an idea, the basic law enunciated in Baker v. Selden lives on and has been the subject of many cases involving copyrightability of computer programs, as well as other works. In one well–known case, the issue was whether a computer operating system (as opposed to an application program) was inherently uncopyrightable since there appeared to be no way to separate the expression of the idea from the idea itself. The Appeals Court, after considering Baker v. Selden, concluded that an operating system constituted an expression of a idea rather than an idea and thus constituted copyrightable subject matter.[17]

In other situations involving copyright protection for computer programs, case law had developed which attempted to protect the "look and feel" of computer programs, which was considered to constitute part of the copyrightable expression rather than the mere idea.[18] This concept of "look and feel" has waxed and waned in copyright jurisprudence over the last several years. Most recently, this concept has fallen out of favor with many courts and variations upon and substitutes for the "look and feel" test of copyrightability have taken hold.[19]

Cases involving computer games (and games generally) raise similar issues. While the rules or methods of playing games (including computer games) are not subject to copyright protection, the various elements which make up the games, such as game boards, audiovisual aspects or screen displays, and the expression of ideas in the game instructions are generally subject to copyright protection.

Government Works

A large body of works are never subject to copyright protection regardless of their creativity or originality. These are works of the U.S. government. Copyright protection is not available for any work of the U.S. government (although the U.S. government may hold copyrights transferred to it by assignment or otherwise). This results in a large class of works that are in the public domain, readily available for use by all. In fact, this body of works constitutes a significant portion of the material available on the Internet.

What Are The Copyright Rights?

Once it is determined that a particular work may be subject to copyright protection, just what does this mean? What rights are granted to a copyright owner? There are five basic rights which are extended to copyrightable works:

(1) the right to reproduce the copyrighted work and copies or phonorecords;

(2) the right to prepare derivative works based on the copyrighted work;

(3) the right to distribute copies or phonorecords of the copyrighted work to the public by sale or other transfer of ownership or by rental or lease or lending;

(4) in the case of literary, musical, dramatic or choreographic works, pantomimes and motion pictures and other audiovisual works, the right to perform the copyrighted work publicly; and

(5)   in the case of literary, musical, dramatic and choreographic works, pantomimes and pictorial, graphic or sculptural works, including the individual images of a motion picture or other audiovisual work, the right to display the copyrighted work publicly.[20]

These basic rights are subject to numerous and highly detailed exceptions.   For example, there are exceptions which relate to reproduction of works by libraries and archives,[21] as well as to the public performance of works by teachers and pupils;[22] there are detailed provisions for an exception to the exclusive right to publicly perform or display works relating to "secondary transmissions" via satellite and cable television,[23] and there are exceptions which allow for the making of one copy of a work by those who are otherwise permitted to transmit a performance or display of the work.[24]   There are also exceptions to the reproduction right which allow for advertising, commenting or news reporting relating to works reproduced in useful articles that are offered for sale or distribution to the public, e.g., someone can show a picture of a work in an advertisement to sell the product which embodies the work.[25]

Indeed, the above examples are just some of the exceptions to the exclusive rights granted to the copyright holder. Although it may seem that the exceptions may actually swallow the grant of rights, in practice, the copyright rights remain substantial and the exceptions are most often quite narrowly drawn. While it is beyond the scope of this book to discuss all or even many of the exceptions to the five basic copyright rights, certain of these basic rights and certain exceptions to these rights will be discussed in more detail below as their application is likely to arise in the context of the Internet.

The Right To Reproduce A Work

Perhaps the most fundamental copyright right is the right to reproduce one's copyrighted work.   Only the copyright owner is entitled to reproduce (make copies) of his or her own work.   In most cases, downloading a computer program from the Internet or downloading works of literature or art or music from the Internet would constitute the making of a copy of a work and thus potentially a copyright infringement. In fact, the Clinton Administration has recently proposed that on–line transmissions of works, such as books and magazines, as well as computer software, should be expressly classified as "copies" under the Copyright law.[26]

Obviously, certain works appearing on the Internet are put on the Internet specifically for the purpose of downloading, such as, in certain circumstances, shareware or freeware, and works which may be in the public domain.   However, great caution should be exercised in downloading works from the Internet, especially if the work will be used in any commercially significant way, as many works are subject to copyright protection and may be intended to be viewed, but not copied (downloaded).   While one would not expect the "copyright police" to come charging through the door of your home, one should be mindful of the exclusive rights possessed by copyright owners. Certainly, a World Wide Web site that downloads copyrighted material from one source and then posts that material, or a company that "borrows" works or portions of works from other sources for its World Wide Web home page, may be liable for copyright infringement. (Infringement matters are discussed in a subsequent section of this chapter.)

The Right To Make Derivative Works

A derivative work is a work which is based upon one or more pre-existing works and which adds copyrightable subject matter to the original work. Translations, musical arrangements, dramatizations, abridgments, condensations, adaptations or transformations of a work are examples of derivative works. Also, editorial revisions, annotations, elaborations and other modifications which represent original works of authorship constitute derivative works.[27]

The right to make derivative works is within the exclusive province of the copyright owner. Therefore, downloading a copyrighted work and incorporating it into another work or otherwise changing the work somewhat and then posting it on the Internet could very well be considered to constitute infringement of the basic exclusive right of the copyright holder to make derivative works. In the content of computer software, a translation from one computer language to another could be considered a "translation" and thus a derivative work.

Exception To The Exclusive Rights Of The Copyright Holder Regarding Computer Programs

One important exception to the exclusive rights to reproduce a work or to make a derivative work pertains directly to computer programs. The Copyright Act specifically provides that it is not an infringement on the exclusive rights of the copyright holder:

> for the owner of a copy of a computer program to make or authorize the making of another copy or adaptation of that computer program provided:
>
> (1) that such new copy or adaptation is created as an essential step in the utilization of the computer program in conjunction with a machine and that it is used in no other manner, or
>
> (2) that such new copy or adaptation is for archival purposes only and that all archival copies are destroyed in the event that

continued possession of the computer program should cease to be rightful.

Any exact copies prepared in accordance with the provisions of this section may be leased, sold, or otherwise transferred, along with the copy from which such copies were prepared, only as part of the lease, sale, or other transfer of all rights in the program. Adaptations so prepared may be transferred only with the authorization of the copyright owner."[28]

In plain English, this means that the owner of a copy of a computer program may make an archival copy or may adapt the work (i.e., make a derivative work) to make the program work according to its purpose in the environment of one's own computer. The exact copies which were made can be transferred with the original copy of the program. Adaptations, on the other hand, cannot be transferred except with the authorization of the copyright owner.

Compulsory Licensing For Phonorecords

Another important exception to the exclusive rights of copyright in a non–dramatic musical work concerns the right to make phonorecords (phonorecords are defined by the Copyright Act as any means by which sounds are fixed, e.g., compact disks, records, tapes, etc).[29] Here, the Copyright Act provides that if a non–dramatic musical work has been distributed to the public, anyone can reproduce, via a phonorecord, the same musical work, on payment of a specified royalty to the owner of the copyright in the musical work. This includes the right to make a musical arrangement (a derivative work) of the original music.

The method for implementing and the details of this compulsory license provision are quite complex. However, the basic notion of this exception to the exclusive rights of copyright in a musical work is to allow others to record their version of any musical work that has been publicly distributed. Upon public distribution of a phonorecord containing a musical work, the owner of the copyright in the musical work gives up the exclusive right to make copies or derivative works. Of course, however, the copyright owner is compensated for doing so by way of the compulsory royalties which must be paid to the copyright owner.

It is important to emphasize that this exception does <u>not</u> allow third parties to make copies of the particular sound recording of a musical work (as embodied in a phonorecord) as such would be an infringement of the copyright in that sound recording. What is permitted is for a third party to record the same <u>musical work</u> (or a variation thereof) which is embodied in the sound recording of it subject to payment of a royalty.

Fair Use

The most extensive potential exception to the exclusive rights of the copyright owner in the context of the Internet, concerns the concept of fair use. Generally, the concept of fair use means that under certain circumstances, the reproduction of a copyrighted work may be permissible if the amount taken is relatively small and/or if the reason for taking it is for purposes such as criticism, comment, news reporting, teaching, scholarship or research. In determining whether a particular use is considered fair use, four factors are generally considered:

(1) the purpose and character of the use, including whether such use is of a commercial nature or for nonprofit educational purposes;

(2) the nature of the copyrighted work;

(3) the amount and substantiality of the portion used in relation to the copyrighted work as a whole; and

(4)   the effect of the use upon the potential market for or value of the copyrighted work.[30]

The underlying purposes of the concept of fair use are to allow for the exercise of First Amendment rights and for the right to criticize and comment upon copyrighted works and to allow a small taking of copyrighted material which would not adversely affect the commercial value of the copyrighted material or bestow a commercial benefit to the taker. For example, taking a relatively small quote from a copyrighted work to comment upon the ideas expressed in that work will likely constitute fair use. At the other extreme, the wholesale reproduction of an entire work for sale or distribution by the taker will almost never be considered to be fair use, especially if such use usurps the market for the original work.

In between these two extremes, there are many permutations of use which may or may not constitute fair use. If one were considering whether copying all or part of a copyrighted work would be considered to constitute fair use, one should be guided by the following practical advice: the less taken from the original work the better. If the purposes of comment or criticism of a work can be served by taking less of the work as opposed to more of a work, take less. If the purpose of the taking is of a commercial nature, take _even_ less. And if, despite the amount taken, the newer work will usurp the commercial value of an earlier work, do not take at all. When in doubt, request and obtain permission of the copyright proprietor.

Additional Rights In Copyrighted Works

The Copyright Act was amended recently to supplement the rights which had previously been granted to copyright owners. Among the newer rights which have been bestowed upon copyright owners are those concerning the "Rights of Certain Authors to Attribution and Integrity."[31]

These "rights of attribution and integrity" otherwise known as "moral rights" or "droits morale" have been recognized for many years in many countries, but not in the United States. When the United States acceded to the Berne Convention (thereby joining a family of nations which agree that certain basic copyright rights should automatically, and without formality, be given to authors), the United States agreed to and did amend its copyright laws to include recognition of certain "moral rights" of the author. These provisions of the Copyright Act provide that independent of the five basic exclusive rights, the author of a work of visual art is given the right to (a) claim authorship of that work; and (b) prevent the use of his or her name as the author of any work of visual art which he or she did not create. In addition, an author has the right to prevent use of his or her name as the author of a work of visual art in the event of a distortion, mutilation or other modification of the work which would be prejudicial to the honor or reputation of the author.

In addition, subject to certain limitations, an author of a work of visual art has the right:

(1)   to prevent any intentional distortion, mutilation or other modification of that work which would be prejudicial to his or her honor or reputation, and any intentional distortion, mutilation, or modification of that work is a violation of that right; and

(2)   to prevent any destruction of a work of recognized stature, and any intentional or grossly negligent destruction of that work is a violation of that right.

The rights of certain authors to attribution or integrity would prevent, for example, any unflattering modifications of works which may be contained on the Internet. Although any such modification may be considered to be a violation of the exclusive right of the copyright holder to create derivative works, the provisions regarding rights of certain authors to attribution and integrity comprise yet another weapon in the arsenal of a copyright holder to prevent unflattering modifications of works and to prevent false attribution to a work which the author did not create.

While it is too early to know with any degree of certainty how these provisions will be interpreted by the courts, the reader should approach any contemplated distortion of a copyrighted work of visual art with caution. While manipulation of an image appearing on the Internet may seem to be a particularly inviting method of expressing comment or criticism, the reader is cautioned that conduct which might otherwise qualify as fair use might very well be considered to constitute a violation of the moral right of integrity of the author.

Copyright Notice

Until March 1, 1989, the United States was one of the only countries in the world where publication of a work without copyright notice could result in the complete loss of copyright protection. In fact, many otherwise copyrightable works have fallen into the public domain for the mere failure of the author or publisher to affix appropriate copyright notice. This situation was changed as of March 1, 1989 when amendments to the Copyright Act took effect which provided that copyright notice (while advisable and beneficial), is not required in order to secure copyright protection.

The proper form of copyright notice is specifically set out in the Copyright Act as consisting of the word "Copyright" or the abbreviation

"Copr." or the familiar "C" in the circle ("©") followed by the year in which the work was published, followed by the name of the copyright owner, e.g., "© 1995 XYZ Corp."[32]

Although failure to display the appropriate copyright notice for published works prior to March 1, 1989 could have resulted in works falling into the public domain, during the time period of 1978 through March 1, 1989, there were various provisions in the Copyright Act which tempered that harsh result, such as a showing:

(1)   that the omission of copyright notice was for a relatively few copies of the work; or

(2)   that the work was registered with the Copyright Office within five years from the date of publication without notice and a reasonable effort was made to add notice once the omission was discovered; or

(3)   the notice was omitted by a distributor of the work in violation of an express agreement that the work contain notice.[33]

However, for works published prior to 1978, even the accidental omission of copyright notice on a single or a few copies of a work could result in a complete loss of copyright protection. These older provisions regarding copyright notice remain quite important because the recent change in the law which no longer requires copyright notice is not retroactive.

Although copyright notice is not presently required, display of the copyright notice is recommended as copyright notice provides actual and clear notification to others that the work is a copyrighted work and sets out who the copyright owner is. In addition, use of the copyright notice can prevent a third party from later claiming that any taking of the copyrighted work was somehow innocent (innocent infringement can result in the mitigation of actual damages in an action for infringement). For these reasons, it is recommended that every published work in which a copyright owner intends to claim copyright protection be accompanied by the statutory notice mentioned above. Such notice should be placed in a prominent position *vis-à-vis* the work in which copyright is claimed.

It is noted that copyright notice was required (and is now optional) only for works which are (or were) "published." "Publication" under the copyright laws means "distribution of copies or phonorecords of a work to the public by sale or other transfer of ownership, or by rental, lease, lending. The offering to distributed copies or phonorecords to a group of persons for purposes of <u>further</u> distribution, public performance, or public display, constitutes publication."[34] However, mere public performance or display of a work does not itself constitute "publication."[35] A mere presentation of a work on–line on a computer screen may not be deemed to constitute "publication." However, the presentation of the work as shareware or freeware on the Internet changes the equation, as this type of display could be viewed as a distribution of the work or as offering of copies to the public for further distribution. Under those circumstances, display of a work on–line could constitute a publication of the work.

Notwithstanding the changes with respect to the requirement of notice, it is recommended that all copyrighted works made available on the Internet be accompanied by notice of copyright. This will avoid any confusion as to whether copyright is claimed in a particular work and who claimed such protection, and will warn the viewer that the work is not freely available for any and all purposes.

Restoration Of Copyright And Works That Have Fallen Into The Public Domain For Failure To Display Appropriate Notice

As discussed previously, the historical perspective of the notice requirement is still important as many works have fallen into the public domain for failure to display the appropriate copyright notice (and may, therefore, be available for copying by all who wish to do so). Also, as discussed previously, the United States was one of the only countries in the world which required copyright notice as a condition for obtaining and maintaining copyright in published works.

In order to comply with the Berne Convention, the United States needed to protect the works of authors of other member countries in the United States by at least the minimum standard of the author's home country. As a result, in 1994, the United States implemented legislation as part of the GATT agreements to restore copyrights in works of authors of Berne Convention and World Trade Organization member countries which had fallen into the public domain in the United States for the failure to display appropriate copyright notice, failure to timely renew the work, or failure to comply with certain other formalities.[36] Thus, the Copyright Act was amended to provide that certain works of foreign authors which had otherwise fallen into the public domain would be restored to copyright status for the remainder of the term which would have otherwise been granted to the work. These provisions are set to go into effect on January 1, 1996. Significantly, these provisions do not apply to works of U.S. authors.

Obviously, the restoration of copyright in various works will have consequences for those who have relied on the fact that such works were in the public domain. The amendments to the Copyright Act providing for restoration of a copyright contain detailed provisions that attempt to temper the effects of the restoration on so–called "reliance parties."[37]

In particular, parties who have relied on the fact that certain works were apparently previously in the public domain may have a grace period in order to "sell–off" the infringing works after the reliance party has been given notice (actual or constructive) of the owner's intent to enforce a restored copyright. In other circumstances (namely those who have created derivative works in reliance on the fact that the restored work was in the public domain) reliance parties can continue to exploit those works upon payment of "reasonable compensation" to the owner of the restored work.

The Copyright Act provisions regarding restoration of copyright may still undergo change and the full practical effect of these provisions may not be known for some time.

Copyright Registration

At the outset of this chapter, it was emphasized that copyright existed upon creation of a work and that copyright registration is not necessary in order to have a valid copyright. However, registration is a fairly straightforward procedure and is highly recommended for works of a commercial nature for several important reasons.

First, copyright registration is required for U.S. copyright claimants prior to the institution of a lawsuit for copyright infringement. (Foreign copyright claimants of Berne Convention countries are not required to register their works prior to instituting a suit for infringement.)[38]

Second, the copyright laws contain provisions for recovery of money awards in successful suits for copyright infringement. These provisions include an award of attorneys' fees and an award of statutory damages (i.e., an amount of money damages specifically set by statute). However, these statutory damages and attorneys' fees are generally only recoverable for acts of infringement which took place <u>after</u> registration of the work.[39]

Third, if registration of a work was made within five years of the date of publication of a work, the registration will give the copyright registrant significant evidentiary advantages in the event that the registrant later files suit for copyright infringement. These evidentiary advantages include a presumption of the validity of the copyright and of the facts stated in the copyright registration certificate.[40]

In view of the advantages which are accorded to works which are registered, it is highly recommended that copyright registration be secured as promptly as possible after creation of a copyrightable work which will be of any commercially significant value. Indeed, given the relative ease and low cost of obtaining copyright registration (discussed below), registration of copyright should be made for many other copyrightable works.

The copyright registration process involves filling out a form in which certain basic information concerning the copyrighted work is forwarded to the Copyright Office. Different forms are required for the different types of works, e.g., literary works (Form TX), sound recordings (Form SR), works which are primarily visual in nature (Form VA), among others. Samples of these forms are attached at Appendix 1. Actual forms can be obtained by calling or writing the Copyright Office. The address of the Copyright Office is:

> Register of Copyrights
> Copyright Office
> The Library of Congress
> Washington, D.C. 20559–6000
> (202) 707–3000

Obviously, a work may contain attributes of more than one type of work. The proper form to use is the form which relates to the predominant nature of the work. In other words, if the work is predominantly literary in nature, but has illustrations and other visual components, the work may be registered as a literary work.

The copyright registration form must be accompanied by the Government fee (currently $20.00) and submitted to the U.S. Copyright Office along with one or two copies of the work itself (the number of copies usually depends on the type of work and whether it is published or unpublished). The Copyright Office then examines the copyright application. If the Copyright Office has any questions regarding any of the information set forth in the application, the Copyright Office will send a written inquiry to the applicant in order to resolve any such questions. The applicant is then given a set period of time within which to reply.

As mentioned above, the copyright application form must be accompanied by a copy, or "deposit" of the work. The deposit represents the subject matter for which the applicant claims copyright. In the case of published works, two copies of the best available edition of the published work must usually accompany the copyright application form. For computer programs (as well as certain other works), the Copyright Office accepts representative samples of the work, for example, the first and last twenty–five pages of the source code. If the program contains trade secrets, the trade secret portions of the code may be blocked out.

A copyright application generally takes twelve weeks to be approved by the Copyright Office and thereby become a registration. However, the date of the registration is retroactive to the application date. If there is an urgent need to obtain a copyright registration (e.g., a copyright owner needs the registration to file an infringement suit), the copyright application process can be expedited and a registration obtained within days of filing. The expedited registration process requires payment of an additional government fee and an explanation as to why there is an urgent need to obtain the copyright registration (e.g., the existence of a potential infringement suit).

Duration Of Copyright

As mentioned at the outset of this book, copyright protection finds its basis in the U.S. Constitution which provides that Congress may protect of the writings of authors <u>for a limited time</u>.   Therefore, unlike trademark protection (which, as discussed in the succeeding chapter, could be for an unlimited duration), copyright protection is provided for a limited term. However, this "limited term" has varied over the years according to the law that was in place when a work was created.

For example, under the Copyright Act of 1909 (which was in force until 1978), copyrighted works were granted an initial term of 28 years and could be renewed for another term of 28 years. In the absence of a renewal, which required the filing of a renewal application with the Copyright Office, the copyrighted work would fall into the public domain. This version of the Copyright Act placed great importance on the registration and renewal processes, and copyright in many works secured under this Act was lost for the mere failure to timely file a renewal.

As of 1978, the copyright laws were relaxed with respect to copyright registration and ownership formalities, and Congress extended the length of the copyright term. Instead of two 28–year terms, Congress provided a basic term of copyright measured by the life of the author plus 50 years or, in the case of anonymous or pseudonymous works or works made for hire, 75 years from the date of publication of the work or 100 years from the date of creation of the work, whichever is shorter. These terms are still in force today.

Significantly, when the amendments to the copyright law were implemented in 1978, the term of copyright was extended for those works which were still subject to copyright as of the time of the new Act. Thus, the copyright term for certain works was extended for a term of total protection of approximately 75 years. The specific provisions of the Copyright Act regarding the term of copyright in works created prior to 1978 are fairly complex and will not be examined in depth here. However, as a very general guideline, the reader should assume that a work which is less than 75 years old (and if the work is unpublished, less than 100 years old) may still be under copyright.

Infringement And Liability Issues

The term "copyright infringement" has been mentioned frequently in previous sections, but just exactly what does it mean? Basically, an infringement occurs when someone undertakes to supplant one or more of the exclusive and non-excepted copyright rights granted by law to the copyright owner. That is, for example, when one copies, distributes, displays or creates a derivative work of a copyrighted work without permission from the author, such may constitute copyright infringement.

Different courts in different areas of the United States are divided as to just what types of activities constitute copyright infringement. The basic premise found universally in copyright cases, however, is that in order for there to be copyright infringement, there must be copying. The difficulty, of course, is in determining whether one work is a "copy" of another. This issue may be easily decided where the works are identical. In many cases of copyright infringement, however, the works do not have the same outward appearance or identity of language.

One common guideline used by courts in determining whether one work copies another work is whether the works are "substantially similar." Substantial similarity includes not only literal similarity, but since the copyright infringer may attempt to disguise the copying by making changes to the work or may otherwise engage in non–literal copying, substantial similarity may be shown by reference to the overall structure, look and feel of the work. If an ordinary observer would conclude that the second work is substantially similar to the original work, this could form the basis of a claim for copyright infringement.

In the context of computer software infringement, additional tests of substantial similarity have developed. In one well–known case, Computer Associates Int'l. v. Altai, Inc.,[41] the court adopted a three–step approach to determining substantial similarity. These steps involved abstraction of the plaintiff's program, filtering out non–protectable elements found in the program, and comparison of the remaining copyrightable elements with defendant's work. In another case, this type of analysis led a California court to find that a defendant's screen displays did not infringe plaintiff's computer program.[42] The recent case law has tended to move away from the earlier overall "look and feel" test for determining substantial similarity in computer software cases, and the abstraction/filtration approach and variations on that approach are now prevalent.

As discussed previously, copying is fundamental to a finding of copyright infringement. That is, copyright infringement will not be found where a newer work, even if identical to a prior existing work, was created without access to the original work. (Indeed, in such circumstances, the newer work could itself be entitled to copyright protection.) Copying can be proven by direct evidence (or by admission by the infringer) or by evidence of substantial similarity of the work along with evidence of access to the allegedly copied work. In many cases, courts have held that the stronger the evidence of substantial similarity, the less evidence of access will be required. Indeed, since as a legal matter, miracles are presumed not to have occurred, in cases where a work is identical or nearly identical to an earlier copyrighted work, little or no evidence of access may be required.

Proof of copyright infringement by direct evidence is often difficult to find. One method of setting the ground work for such proof which is sometimes employed in works which are particularly susceptible to copyright infringement (databases, directories, compilations, as well as other works), is for the author to "seed" the work with "trap" entries. That is, an author may include information in a work which has no real basis in fact (e.g., fictitious listings in directories) for the sole purpose of later showing (assuming that the same fictitious entry appears in an allegedly infringing work) that the work has been copied. While the advantages and utility of this practice have their limits (as an author would not want his or her work to be fraught with "errors"), where the inclusion of "trap" entries would not materially undermine the usefulness or value of a work, it is a practice which can be employed to help prove copying in certain types of works.

As mentioned in previous sections of this chapter, copyright does not protect ideas, it only protects expressions of ideas. If one merely copies the "idea" of another (and not the expression of the idea), this will not constitute copyright infringement. Therefore, while various computer programs may be created to accomplish the same result, unless they are structured in the same way, or have some identity of code, and unless actual copying has taken place, there will be no finding of copyright infringement.

Who Is Liable For Copyright Infringement?

Obviously, the party who copies the copyrighted work of another can be held liable for copyright infringement. However, other parties may also be held liable for an infringement which was actually committed by another. This concept, known as vicarious liability, means that a party that is in a position to supervise (and presumably prevent) an infringement from occurring and who would be in a position of benefiting from the infringement, should not be permitted to escape liability. This concept has been applied, for example, to owners of nightclubs and theaters in which performances took place which infringed upon the copyright in musical works or sound recordings.

A related concept which has also been employed as a means for finding liability against those who are not necessarily the primary party involved in an infringement, is known as contributory infringement. Under this concept, one who aided, abetted or otherwise acted to further an infringement, may be found to be liable for the infringement.[43]

In the context of the Internet, the concepts of contributory infringement and vicarious liability may have consequences for those who act as conduits for infringing activity, e.g., bulletin board services. In a case involving a Sega computer game, a California district court found a bulletin board service operator liable for contributory infringement based on the activities of its subscribers' uploading and downloading Sega's copyrighted video games. In that case, the court found that the bulletin board service had actively encouraged its subscribers to participate in the infringement.[44]

The concepts of vicarious liability and contributory infringement have been applied to bulletin board services even where the bulletin board service were not aware of the infringement. In a case involving Playboy photographs, a Florida district court held a bulletin board service liable for the acts of its subscribers in uploading and downloading copyrighted Playboy photographs, even though the bulletin board service did not have knowledge of the infringing activity.[45]

Remedies For Copyright Infringement

If copyright infringement is found, the consequences could be serious. Remedies for copyright infringement include an injunction (i.e., a court order preventing further dissemination of the copyrighted subject matter); destruction of any infringing subject matter; money damages which can be measured by actual damages or, at the option of the plaintiff, statutorily set damages which range from $5,000 to $20,000 for each act of copyright infringement (the amount of any statutory damages is determined by the court).[46] In fact, willful copyright infringement can result in increased statutory damages (up to $100,000) and can be a crime punishable by fines and imprisonment.[47]

Also, although the award (or more accurately the lack of an award) of attorneys' fees in United States jurisprudence is governed by the "America rule" which means that the prevailing party is not generally entitled to its attorneys' fees, in copyright cases, the prevailing party (plaintiff or defendant) may be entitled to recovery of its "reasonable" attorneys' fees.[48] That is, a plaintiff may be entitled to the attorneys' fees incurred in successfully prosecuting a copyright infringement case and a defendant may be entitled to recover attorneys' fees in successfully defending against a charge of copyright infringement. Given the high cost of litigation in the United States, the potential recovery of attorneys' fees can be both a valuable weapon in the hands of a plaintiff with a strong case of copyright infringement, and a powerful deterrent to willful infringement and frivolous lawsuits.

Recent Cases Involving On-line Services

Case law involving copyrights in the area of on–line services is still in its infancy. However, at least two recent cases have drawn great attention from the legal and on–line business communities.

In one such case (which has not yet been concluded on the merits, but which is already of considerable significance with respect to the law of copyright as it relates to on–line services), a California district court entered a temporary restraining order against a bulletin board service subscriber, preventing the subscriber from posting allegedly infringing copies of materials in which the Church of Scientology claims copyright and trade secret rights. Significantly, the court has not extended the restraining order to the bulletin board service or the Internet access provider.[49]

In another case, a court in Massachusetts found that a 21–year–old student was not liable under the federal criminal wire fraud statutes for urging users to upload copyrighted computer software which could then be downloaded by other users.[50] The defendant was alleged to have caused over $1 million in losses to computer software copyright holders. His activities, however, were found insufficient to meet the requirements of the criminal statutes related to copyright infringement because his actions were not for the purpose of, nor did he derive, any "commercial advantage or private financial gain." The court left it to the legislature to close the "commercial advantage/financial gain" loophole present in the criminal provisions of the Copyright Act.[51] Legislation has been introduced to close that loophole.[52]

Assignment And Licensing

As with other forms of intellectual property, copyrights may be assigned or licensed by the owner. Licensing and assignment of copyrights is discussed in detail in a succeeding chapter. Here, it will be merely noted that a copyright can be assigned, but in order for assignment to be valid, it must be in writing.

Also, it is noted that there are detailed provisions in the Copyright Act which provide for the possible termination of transfers of copyright which were executed by the author on or after January 1, 1978.[53] Under these provisions, a copyright owner (or the decedents of the copyright owner) may terminate an assignment or license of copyright between the 35th or 40th year after transfer. These provisions do not apply to authors of works by way of work made for hire.

Copyright Searching

The Copyright Office, located at the Library of Congress in Washington, D.C., is a good source for obtaining information regarding copyrighted works which have been registered. The records of the Copyright Office are also available on–line.

Copyright searches can be useful to determine whether a particular work may still be the subject of valid copyright and such searches can be conducted by searching the author, copyright claimant or owner or title of the work. However, there is no realistic way of conducting a search as to subject matter. Fortunately, unlike the situation under the patent laws where creators of new devices or methods should be concerned that their work does not infringe the subject matter of another's valid patent, under the copyright laws, the creator of a work need not be concerned that there may be a prior existing work covering the same or similar subject matter; since, as long as the author of a newly created work does not copy a prior existing work, there can be no copyright infringement.

In circumstances where someone may wish to find out whether a particular work is the subject of copyright and, if so, who owns the copyright, a copyright search is one means to attempt to obtain that information. Of course, as discussed in earlier sections, because copyright registration (and recordal of related assignments and licenses) is permissive rather than required, copyrights in many works are not registered or title is incomplete. Therefore, a copyright search cannot be considered to be a completely reliable means of locating information regarding the copyright status of a work.

International Considerations

Copyrights are automatically international in nature. That is, most countries of the world are members of one or more treaties regarding copyrights, including the Berne Convention or The Universal Copyright Convention, among others. The parties to such agreements provide for fairly equal protection under the various copyright laws of the member countries. Thus, many countries now provide for certain basic protections. For example, there is no need to register a claim to copyright in most countries of the world and the mere fact that a work was created in a country who is a member to one of the copyright treaties means that the work is protected in every other member country. Also, most countries around the world have extended copyright protection to computer software.

Many foreign countries have additional protections which are only now emerging in the United States. One such group of rights is known as the moral rights of the author which protects the author's integrity in and to a particular work *vis-à-vis* the character of the work. The United States has recently enacted certain moral rights legislation which (as discussed in a previous section of this chapter) provides that as to certain visual works, there is a separate right to maintain the integrity and character of that work. In many foreign countries, while all other rights can be assigned, the moral rights can never be assigned.

The existence of inalienable moral rights of authors in countries outside of the United States presents particular difficulties for those operating within the internationally boundryless context of the Internet. Conduct which might otherwise not be considered to constitute a derogation of the moral rights of an author in the U.S. may very well be considered to constitute a violation of those rights in foreign countries.

One must, therefore, be particularly careful in posting works on the Internet, the rights in which were acquired directly or indirectly from foreign authors. This is because even if an apparently otherwise valid copyright assignment has been obtained, the new "owner" of the copyright in the work could not have obtained an assignment of the moral rights of a foreign author (as such rights cannot be assigned). One should undertake modifications, and particularly potentially unflattering modifications, of works which were created by foreign authors only with extreme caution (or not at all).

Endnotes

1. Community for Creative Non-Violence v. Reid, 490 U.S. 730 (1989).

2. 17 U.S.C. § 101.

3. Id.

4. Id.

5. Id.

6. 17 U.S.C. § 102.

7. 17 U.S.C. § 101.

8. 17 U.S.C. §§ 108–120.

9. 17 U.S.C. § 102(a).

10. 37 C.F.R. § 202.1.

11. 17 U.S.C. § 102(b).

12. Lotus v. Borland, 49 F.3d 807 (1st Cir. 1995).

13. Mazer v. Stein, 347 U.S. 201 (1954).

14. Bleistein v. Donaldson Lithographing Co., 188 U.S. 239 (1903).

15. Feist Publications v. Rural Telephone Services Co., 499 U.S. 340 (1991).

16. 101 U.S. 99 (1879).

17. Apple Computer, Inc. v. Franklin Computer Corp., 714 F.2d 1240 (3d Cir. 1983) (reversing 545 F. Supp. 812 (E.D. Pa. 1983)), cert. dismissed, 464 U.S. 1033 (1984)

18. Whelan Associates, Inc. v. Jaslow Dental Laboratory, Inc., 797 F.2d 1222 (3d. Cir. 1986).

19. See, e.g., Computer Associates Int.'l v. Altai, Inc., 982 F.2d 693 (2d Cir. 1992).

20. 17 U.S.C. § 106.

21. 17 U.S.C. § 108.

22. 17 U.S.C. § 110.

23. 17 U.S.C. §§ 111, 119.

24. 17 U.S.C. § 112.

25. 17 U.S.C. § 113.

26. See, e.g., Cooper, Helene, "Task Force Proposes On–Line Copyrights," The Wall Street Journal, Sect. Technology, B6 (Sept. 6, 1995).

27. 17 U.S.C. § 101.

28. 17 U.S.C. § 117.

29. 17 U.S.C. § 101.

30. 17 U.S.C. § 107.

31. 17 U.S.C. § 106A.

32. 17 U.S.C. § 401.

33. 17 U.S.C. § 405

34. 17 U.S.C. § 101.

35. Id.

36.   17 U.S.C. § 104A.

37.   Id.

38.   17 U.S.C. § 411.

39.   17 U.S.C. § 412.

40.   17 U.S.C. § 410(c)

41.   Computer Associates Int'l. v. Altai, Inc., 982 F.2d 693 (2d Cir. 1992).

42.   Brown Bag Software v. Symantec Corp., 960 F.2d 1465 (9th Cir.), cert. denied, 113 S. Ct. 141 (1992).

43.   See Data General Corp. v. Grumman Data Systems Corp., 886 F. Supp. 927 (D. Mass. 1994).

44.   Sega Enters. v. Maphia, 857 F. Supp. 679 (N.D. Cal. 1994).

45.   839 F. Supp. 1552 (M.D. Fla. 1993).

46.   17 U.S.C. §§ 502–505.

47.   17 U.S.C. §§ 504(c)(2), 506.

48.   17 U.S.C. § 505.

49.   Bridge Publications, Inc. v. Vien, 827 F. Supp. 629 (S.D. Cal. 1993).

50.   United States v. LaMacchia, 871 F. Supp. 535 (D. Mass. 1994).

51.   Id.

52.   S. 1122.

53.   17 U.S.C. § 203.

Chapter 3

TRADEMARKS*

As discussed earlier in this book, a trademark should most appropriately be considered to be commercial property. In its simplest terms, a trademark is the brand name of one's goods or services. Actually, however, a trademark is much more than that. A trademark is a shorthand means of conveying commercial information.

For example, a trademark conveys information regarding the source of the goods or services identified by the trademark; the name "ACME" as applied to widgets, serves the function of identifying a particular brand of widgets and distinguishing those widgets from all other widgets. Similarly, whenever anyone encounters a name such as "Envi–Check" on the Internet, the Internet user will know that such is a reference to a particular (in this case, fictitious) interactive environmental compliance World Wide Web site. It is noted here that a trademark could also be a company name which is often referred to as a trade name. The difference between a trademark and a trade name will be discussed below.

In addition to performing the source identification function, a trademark may also function as an assurance of quality. That is, based on consumer's experiences with and use of goods or services which bear a trademark, opinions are formed as to the quality of goods or services made or rendered by the company whose products or services are represented by the trademark. For example, if the proprietors of the "ENVI–CHECK" World Wide Web site decided to expand from their Web site service into rendering consulting services under the name ENVI–CHECK, those encountering ENVI–CHECK consulting services who had been familiar with the high quality of the ENVI–CHECK World

---

*Chapter written by Raymond A. Kurz, Rothwell, Figg, Ernst & Kurz.

Wide Web site might be apt to utilize the ENVI–CHECK consulting services. This consumer behavior is influenced by the use of a single word, the trademark ENVI–CHECK, and relies on the association by the consumer of the name ENVI–CHECK with the high quality ENVI–CHECK World Wide Web site. Conversely, of course, if an individual had a very negative impression of the ENVI–CHECK World Wide Web site and then encountered a promotion for the ENVI–CHECK consulting services, that individual would associate a negative connotation with the ENVI–CHECK trademark and would be unlikely to utilize the ENVI–CHECK consulting services.

In addition to identifying the source of the goods or services and the quality of the goods or services, a trademark can also convey information about the nature of goods or services. For example, the trademarks BRODERBUND and LOTUS bring to mind different aspects or characteristics of the goods which they denote. One might associate BRODERBUND with educational computer software and one might associate LOTUS with financial or spreadsheet software. Thus, even before we examine a particular product designated by the trademark BRODERBUND or LOTUS, we have already formed a mental impression about not only the source and quality of the goods, but also as to the <u>qualities</u> of the goods represented by those marks.

The mere reference to a trademark brings to mind a significant amount of information concerning the source, quality and qualities of the goods or services designated by the trademark. Given the inherent communications power of the Internet, the functions served by trademarks are magnified, as are the problems encountered in failing to exercise sufficient care in selecting, protecting and respecting trademarks. This chapter is intended to provide the reader with basic information as to what trademarks are, how registration of trademarks is obtained and maintained and how to avoid losing or infringing trademark rights.[1]

Trademarks, Service Marks And Trade Names

Thus far, reference has primarily been made to the word "trademark," rather than "trade name" or "service mark." There are differences among trademarks, trade names and service marks. A trademark is what might commonly be referred to as a brand name and, as discussed in the previous section, it serves to distinguish one company's goods from the goods of another.

A service mark performs the very same function, but rather than referring to the goods of a company, it refers to a company's services. A particular term might be both a trademark and a service mark if a company sells goods and also renders services under the same designation. For example, a software company might sell software products under a particular trademark and may also offer support services, consulting services, on–line services or educational services under the same mark. The technical distinction between a service mark and a trademark is somewhat blurred in that the term "service mark" is frequently considered to be a subset of the more general term "trademark" and the term "trademark" is often used as a broader term to refer to service marks as well as trademarks. Throughout this book, for example, unless specified otherwise, the term "trademark" is also meant to include the term "service mark."

Within the general concepts of trademarks or service marks, are marks which relate to particular brands and marks which are intended to designate an entire line of products. A trademark which refers to a single product is often referred to as a brand trademark or brand name. A trademark which designates an entire line of products (each of them also designated by a particular brand trade name) is often referred to as a house mark. Marks such as MICROSOFT or INTEL would be considered to be house marks representing an entire range of goods sold under that particular mark. ENCARTA identifies a particular software product of the Microsoft Corporation and would be in the nature of a brand trademark rather than a "house" mark as it conveys information about a particular product.

A trade name is distinguished from a trademark or service mark in that a trade name is the company name, i.e., a name under which a company does business. As might be apparent, a trade name can also be a trademark or a service mark. MICROSOFT is a good example of a word which not only functions as a trade name when used to designate the company, Microsoft Corporation, but also serves the function of a trademark when referring to the goods of the Microsoft Corporation in that it distinguishes those goods from goods made by other companies. The same mark may also function as a service mark when used in connection with support services rendered by Microsoft Corporation.

A trade name, that is, a company's business name, is not necessarily a service mark unless that company renders services to others under that name. That is, the mere manufacture of goods by a company which are then sold under that company's trademark, is not considered to be a service, as the company is not selling its services, but rather its goods. However, if this company were to manufacture goods for and to the specifications of others for sale or use under another's mark, it may be providing "custom manufacturing" services.

The Value Of Trademarks

Trademarks are often overlooked as being the important corporate assets that they are. However, considering the amount and importance of the information which is conveyed by trademarks, it should be apparent that in many instances trademarks may be the most valuable assets of many corporations. Trademarks are protected by federal law, namely, the Lanham Act, 15 U.S.C. § 1051, et seq, as well as state common law and statutory law.

Trademarks are companies' primary vehicle to interface with the public and, indeed, may be viewed as a company's primary ambassador of goodwill to the outside world. This is particularly true in consumer-oriented businesses where use of a trademark results in instant consumer recognition of the products designated by the trademark and consumers consequently purchase a particular company's goods or services instead of those of another. Imagine the sales consequence to consumer-oriented companies such as Levi Strauss if that company no longer had exclusivity to use the term LEVI'S on jeans or if McDonald's Corporation no longer had the exclusive right to use the name McDONALD'S for its restaurants.

The ability of the Internet to instantaneously and continuously display trademarks to millions of people requires those who display their trademarks through the Internet or those who encounter the trademarks, to exercise particular care in presenting trademarks and in perceiving (and respecting) the significance of trademarks.

Considerations In Choosing A Trademark

Considerations in choosing a trademark involve commercial, business and marketing factors going to the type of image that a company wishes to project as well as legal considerations involving the relative strength and potential breadth of protection which would be afforded the mark which is selected.

The business, commercial and marketing considerations are beyond the scope of this book and are best left to the business decision-maker, marketing departments and outside marketing consultants (there are marketing companies that specialize in helping other companies choose trademarks). However, whoever is involved in the creative business aspect of choosing a trademark should take into account the legal aspects of trademark selection, not only with respect to deciding upon the legal availability of a mark, but also as to the inherent protectability and scope of protection which may be afforded the mark that is selected.

Terms and words which may be selected as trademarks generally fall into categories of potential protectability depending on the inherent characteristics of the word or term selected. The potential protectability ranges from terms which are completely unprotectable because they are in fact the generic name of the goods or services or completely descriptive of them to marks and terms which are entitled to the widest possible scope of protection because of their uniqueness. Also, a mark may or may not be available for use or registration in view of possible prior rights in the same or similar mark held by others. These considerations are discussed below.

Availability

Perhaps the most important aspect of the trademark selection process is to attempt to choose a mark which does not conflict with the established trademark rights of anyone else. This seemingly fundamental consideration is often overlooked by many businesses, and while the failure to take this fairly simple initial step in choosing a trademark has been a boon to the business of trademark litigators, it is of course detrimental, if not potentially devastating, to the businesses of those who adopt trademarks which conflict with the established rights of another.

The chances that a newly selected trademark will conflict with a prior existing trademark can be greatly minimized by conducting a trademark search at the initial stage of trademark selection. The search should be conducted as early as possible in the trademark selection process and before a company decision–maker becomes psychologically committed to a given trademark.

There are currently over a million federally registered trademarks and many more unregistered trademarks which can vest prior users with enforceable trademark rights (as will be discussed in succeeding sections, use of a trademark even without registration can vest a trademark user with significant enforceable trademark rights). Thus, several, if not many, initial choices for a trademark may be found to be unavailable. However, it is better to find out sooner rather than later that a given mark is unavailable. If a company adopts a trademark without ever searching to see whether there are conflicting marks, that company might invest great resources building name recognition by way of advertising, promotion and sales, only to find out, perhaps years down the road, that another company has superior rights which then may require the newcomer to cease using the trademark (and perhaps be liable to the prior owner for monetary damages). Obviously, the consequences are even more severe where the trademark selected and found to be confusingly similar to a prior existing trademark is also adopted as the newcomer's company name. In those cases, rather than merely having to give up the name of a particular product, a company might be faced with the prospect of giving up its entire identity.

Therefore, prior to adopting a new mark, it is wise to at least obtain a search of the records of the U.S. Patent and Trademark Office ("PTO") to make sure that there are no existing prior federal registrations or applications which would conflict with the proposed trademark. Sometimes the PTO search is all that is needed because it reveals an obviously conflicting prior mark. However, the search could be, and in many circumstances should be extended beyond the records of the PTO. This expanded search could include marks registered by the individual states of the United States as well as "common law" sources. Common law sources include sources which would reveal use (but not necessarily a federal or state registration) of trademarks owned and used by third parties, e.g., trade directories, telephone books and other data sources.

The importance of searching cannot be stressed enough and, even then, one should be aware that even a well–done search will not necessarily reveal all conflicting prior users or registrants and the unexpected sometimes arises. However, one can minimize the chances of something "unexpected" arising by simply conducting a thorough search prior to adopting a trademark.

Subject Matter Of Trademark Protection

When considering adoption of a trademark, companies should consider the various types of subject matter that may serve as trademarks. A trademark may consist of virtually any type of subject matter which distinguishes one party's goods or services from the goods or services of another. Thus, suitable trademarks may include words, terms, color and color combinations, symbols, slogans, numbers, letters or pictorial representations. Trademarks can also include distinctive and non–functional product package and wrapper designs, product configurations, sounds and even smells.

Fanciful aspects of computer screen displays and icons can serve as trademarks as could a distinctive sound which may, for example, be generated upon signing on to a computer program or on–line service. The potential subject matter of trademarks continues to grow and seems to be limited only by the imagination and creativity of those who may attempt to associate some unique aspect of promoting and selling their goods and services with those goods and services. If subject matter serves the function of identifying a particular source of goods or services, it has the potential of serving as a trademark. While one might consider it odd, for example, that mere sounds can be trademarks, one only needs to think of the NBC "chimes" sound to understand how sounds can be trademarks as, when we hear the familiar NBC "chimes," even if we don't see the NBC logo, we instantly think of NBC.

One type of subject matter which cannot serve as a trademark is something which is purely functional. Most often, this issue arises in the context of product configuration trademarks, as it is often difficult to conceptually separate out the completely utilitarian aspects of a product configuration from that which can serve the trademark function of source identification. Where this distinction cannot be made, i.e., where the utilitarian aspect of a product is co-extensive with the subject matter which is claimed as a trademark, and where those features are completely utilitarian such that competition in the product itself would be stifled if trademark protection were extended to the product design, trademark protection will be denied.

One reason trademark protection is denied in such circumstances is the policy consideration that trademark law should not supplant the patent laws. It is the patent laws which protect utilitarian aspects of products and provide the owner with exclusivity as to the patented subject matter. Indeed, since patents are only granted for a limited period of time, if trademark protection were extended to the same subject matter as patents, patent-like protection (and exclusivity as to the utilitarian object) may continue indefinitely. Thus, for example, trademark protection has been denied for such subject matter as the design of a loud speaker,[2] the spiral design on certain fishing rods (which was a requirement of a patented method for making the rods),[3] and the shape of a plastic screw anchor.[4] On the other hand, trademark protection has been extended for the design of a spray bottle,[5] the shape of a barbecue grill,[6] and the shape of a candy bar.[7]

While it may not be immediately apparent why in some cases trademark protection is granted to designs of utilitarian objects and in other cases it is not, a key factor in determining whether trademark protection will be granted to utilitarian designs is whether granting such protection will foreclose competition as to the utilitarian object itself, i.e., whether other companies could make a competitively effective design without appropriating the subject matter of the trademark. Also, the party attempting to establish that a particular product design is a trademark must show that the product design serves the trademark function of source identification in that consumers associate that product design/trademark with a single source.

Colors As Trademarks

In recent years, there has been increasing attention focused on the possibility that colors (as well as color combinations) could function as trademarks. A well–known instance of color per se being granted trademark protection involved Owens Corning's pink fiberglass. In that case, Owens Corning was successful in establishing the color pink as a trademark in that consumers had come to associate the color pink with fiberglass products that emanate from Owens Corning.[8] To accomplish this feat, Owens Corning engaged in an extensive advertising campaign which attempted to associate the color pink with their fiberglass insulation, for example, by employing a campaign featuring the Pink Panther and using advertising slogans which highlighted the fact that the color of their product was pink.

Following the Owens Corning case and Owens' success in establishing the color pink as a trademark for fiberglass insulation, several other companies were successful in establishing color as a trademark. However, over the years, there has been disagreement amongst the courts as to whether a single color could function as a trademark. While some courts held that color alone could function as a trademark, other courts denied such protection, citing the fact that there are only a limited number of colors in the rainbow and granting one company the sole right to use a particular color for a particular product will result in depleted color choices for other companies to use on their products (this is known as the "color depletion" theory). Recently, however, the U.S. Supreme

Court has seemingly put this issue to rest by holding that a single color can indeed function as a trademark.[9]

The recent Supreme Court case involved an off–color green for drycleaning press covers. In that case, the Court held that if the color served the trademark function of source identification, it could be protected as a trademark.[10] Thus, the present state of the law is that colors (as well as color combinations) are protectable as trademarks.

Scope Of Protection

When choosing a trademark, one should consider the potential scope of protection which will likely be afforded the proposed mark. Generally, potential trademarks fall into categories according to their protectability and enforceability against others.

Generic Terms

A first category of terms which are used in association with goods or services are generic terms. Generic terms do not identify a particular source and can never be trademarks. In fact, generic terms are considered to be the antithesis of trademarks because they signify a group or classification of products rather than a particular source of the product. The word "program" is a generic term for computer software. No one entity could ever obtain exclusive rights in the term "program" as used in connection with computer software as everyone should be free to use that generic term in connection with their computer software. Obviously, it would not be fair if one company could monopolize the use of a generic term for itself. Thus, generic terms are never protectable as trademarks.

Descriptive Terms

The next category of terms which may be used in connection with goods or services are descriptive terms. As the word suggests, descriptive terms describe the nature, quality or characteristics of goods. Surnames are considered to be analogous to descriptive terms, and are treated in much the same fashion. Examples of descriptive terms are terms such as "fast" for computers or "juicy" for hamburgers. Because terms such as these do not initially distinguish the goods of one company from those of another, descriptive terms are not initially entitled to trademark status or protection. The phrase "on–line, on–demand" has been found to be merely descriptive of computer lottery terminals.[11]

However, unlike generic terms which can never be considered to be trademarks, descriptive terms (and surnames), through use over time, can become protectable trademarks. This process is known in legal terms as achieving "acquired distinctiveness" or "secondary meaning." That is, these terms, while not initially protectable as trademarks, can gain new meaning as trademarks when they perform the trademark function of identifying a source of goods or services by becoming identified by consumers with a single source.

In order to acquire distinctiveness, a descriptive term must be used for a fairly substantial amount of time or the user must otherwise cause consumers to come to recognize the term as a trademark. Generally, there is a presumption that five years of continuous use of a descriptive term in a trademark sense, i.e., in a context in which it would appear to at least attempt to serve the function of a trademark, should be sufficient for the term to result in "acquired distinctiveness" or "secondary meaning."[12] Examples of descriptive terms which have become trademarks include PRINCETON PHARMACEUTICAL PRODUCTS for pharmaceutical products[13] and GENTLE DENTAL for dental care services.[14]

Suggestive Terms

Another category of terms which may serve as trademarks are suggestive terms. Suggestive terms do not describe the goods or services to which they are affixed or used and are not the generic name of the goods. Rather, suggestive terms merely suggest something about the goods or services without describing them. Examples of suggestive marks are COMSTOCK for telecommunications network which delivers "real time" stock information[15] and WEIGHT WATCHERS for diet food products.[16] A suggestive trademark sheds some light as to what the goods are, but thought or imagination is needed to connect the meaning of the mark with the goods. Often it is difficult to draw a fine line in determining whether a term is a suggestive trademark and therefore entitled to trademark protection or a descriptive term which is not entitled to trademark protection (unless and until it acquires distinctiveness).

Coined Or Arbitrary Terms

Further categories of terms used in connection with goods or services are coined terms and arbitrary terms. Coined terms are words that have no meaning in any language, but rather have been made up and used in connection with goods or services. Terms such as EXXON and KODAK are classic examples of coined terms.

Arbitrary marks are words which, while already existing in the English language, are completely arbitrary when used in connection with the goods. Classic examples of arbitrary marks are CAMEL for cigarettes and APPLE for computer products.

Why The Categories Of Trademarks Are Important

Trademarks and the protection afforded to trademarks do not exist in a vacuum. The protection which would be afforded any mark must be considered in connection with the goods or services for which the mark is used. In some circumstances, two different companies may own the exact same trademarks yet there will be no trademark conflict because although the marks are identical, the goods are so different that confusion is not likely to arise.

In other circumstances, marks may share certain common elements and may be used in connection with identical goods, but, overall, the marks may be sufficiently different such that while they are somewhat similar they are not sufficiently similar for confusion to arise.

These scenarios are greatly affected by the scope of protection that may be afforded the trademark in question. Coined and arbitrary terms are afforded the widest scope of protection against use by others. Such terms will be protected against use by others of the same or similar terms as applied to a broad spectrum of goods because they are so distinctive.

For example, whenever we see the marks APPLE, EXXON or KODAK, no matter what the goods are, we may likely associate the marks with their respective sources. Even a slight change to the mark by others may likely not avoid confusion.

On the other hand, highly suggestive terms and descriptive terms which may have become trademarks are often entitled to a narrower scope of protection. Others may come closer to these types of marks in terms of the goods which may be designated by the same or similar marks and, sometimes, a slight change to the mark will be sufficient to avoid confusion. For example, how many trademarks in the computer field begin with the term "Compu"? A recent search of the records of the PTO for goods involving computer products revealed more than 2,000 trademarks that begin with the term "Compu." Since there are so many "Compu" prefix marks used by so many companies, each one may only be entitled to a very narrow scope of protection.

Despite the fact that coined or arbitrary terms would be entitled to the broadest scope of protection, there appears to be a natural tendency for the creators of trademarks to want to tell the consumers something about the product when selecting the trademark. However, when one chooses a highly suggestive or descriptive term as a trademark, one necessarily limits the scope of protection which might be afforded that trademark.

One should, therefore, give careful thought when choosing a trademark. Certainly, selecting an arbitrary or coined term as a trademark will require the trademark owner to educate the consumers to associate the trademark with the trademark owner, as there is no suggestion in the term to aid the consumer in understanding what types of goods or services are denoted by the mark. However, there could be great rewards if one is successful in educating consumers to associate an arbitrary or coined mark with a company's goods or services, as the trademark would be entitled to a broad scope of protection.

Conversely, while it might take less investment initially to associate a highly suggestive trademark with a company's goods in consumer's minds, the eventual scope of protection that would be afforded that highly suggestive mark could be significantly less than that of an arbitrary or coined mark (absent the mark becoming a famous mark due to widespread consumer recognition in the marketplace).

How Trademark Rights Are Obtained

Use Is King

The trademark system in the United States, unlike that of most other countries around the world, is primarily based on rights acquired through use, rather than through registration. While federal registration can be extremely important and valuable, in the United States use is the fundamental basis of trademark rights. Both registered and unregistered trademarks are protected under the Lanham Act, 15 U.S.C. § 1051, <u>et seq</u>.

There are common misconceptions regarding the necessity for and consequences of federal registration. First, many people mistakenly believe that federal trademark registration is necessary to obtain trademark rights. Similarly, there is often a mistaken belief that once federal registration has been obtained, the registrant will have rights superior to all others. These beliefs regarding federal registration are simply wrong because in the United States trademark scheme, "use is king."

"Use" in the trademark sense can be divided into two conceptual aspects, "actual use" and "constructive use." "Actual use" of a trademark means what it appears to mean, namely, that rights arise merely from using a mark on or in association with goods or services. These rights are obtained with or without federal trademark registration. If such use is extensive, valuable and strong trademark rights can be acquired by the trademark user in the geographic area of use and notoriety <u>regardless of registration</u>. A basic underlying theme of United States trademark law is that the first to use a trademark in a particular geographic area is the owner of the trademark in that area, regardless of whether another party subsequently registers the trademark.

Another type of "use" which can give rise to valuable trademark rights is "constructive" use. Constructive use is a legislatively created concept which simply means that the filing of a trademark application with the PTO will be deemed to be the date that the mark is "used" in the United States even if at the time of filing the trademark application, the applicant had not yet made actual use of the mark. That is, when one files a trademark application with the PTO, whether or not the mark has been actually used, that trademark application filing date can establish priority of "trademark use" throughout the U.S. by what is known as "constructive" use. However, such date is contingent upon subsequent use and registration, i.e., in order for that constructive use date to become effective, one must obtain the trademark registration which has been applied for and, to do so, a U.S. applicant must eventually use the trademark. During the time in which a non–use based (intent–to–use) trademark application is pending, but before it is granted, the applicant has potential trademark rights which may be retroactive to the filing date of the application, but those potential rights will not become actual rights until the mark is used and the registration is granted.

An important distinction between trademark rights which arise from actual use versus constructive use (which may arise from the grant of a federal trademark registration), is that the rights which are derived from actual use are limited to those geographic areas in which the mark is actually used, while the rights which arise from the grant of a federal trademark registration, are nationwide. This highlights an important advantage accorded to federal trademark registrants and is an inducement to federally register trademarks.

Whether by actual use or constructive use, the first to use a trademark has superior rights (subject to possible geographic limits) and if a subsequent user happens to be the first to register a trademark, an earlier user may be able to cancel the second user's trademark registration and stop the second user's/registrant's use of the trademark in the first user's geographic trading areas.

The important caveat regarding trademark rights based solely on actual use, rather than federal registration, namely, that such rights can be geographically limited if the use of a trademark is geographically limited, would appear to be eliminated if one's trademark were used on the Internet because use of a mark on the Internet may not only nationwide, but international. However, in most foreign countries, unlike the United States where use is king, a trademark owner usually must register a trademark in order to have rights. Thus, mere use of a trademark on the Internet may not establish rights in foreign countries.

The Trademark Registration Process And Advantages Of Federal Registration

Although "use is king" under U.S. trademark laws, as is clear from the previous section of this chapter, federal trademark registration can be quite important.

First, as discussed in the preceding section, unless a trademark is registered, geographically restricted use of a trademark will result in geographically limited rights. Unlike rights based on limited geographic actual use, a trademark registration gives the registrant the right to prevent others from using a confusingly similar mark on a nationwide basis, i.e., in any geographic area where the registrant eventually uses a registered mark.

Even for those who use a mark nationwide (such as users on the Internet), trademark registration is still highly recommended for several reasons.

While there are two basic trademark registers of the United States, the Principal Register and the Supplemental Register, it is by far more advantageous to register marks on the Principal Register than on the Supplemental Register. The Principal Register is where trademarks which are protectable upon their adoption are registered. The Supplemental Register, in its simplest terms, is where marks which are potentially protectable are registered (e.g., descriptive terms which are not inherently protectable). However, trademark registration on either the Principal or Supplemental Registers is advantageous because it provides notice to others of one's actual (or, in the case of the Supplemental Register, potential) trademark rights. This could have beneficial practical implications, as third parties often search trademarks prior to adopting them and a prior existing registration may, therefore, discourage third parties from adopting confusingly similar marks.

Trademark registration on either the Principal or Supplemental Register can also serve as a basis for filing trademark applications in foreign countries.

Trademark registration on the Principal Register has several additional important advantages. First, it provides what is known as "constructive notice" of the registration. This means that the existence of the trademark registration is deemed to provide legally sufficient notice of its existence even to those who have no "actual" notice of the trademark registration. This "notice" prevents a third party from claiming to have innocently adopted a mark in a geographic location remote from the area of actual use of the trademark registrant, thus preventing the third party from establishing any valid use–based trademark rights subsequent to the date of the registration.

Perhaps most importantly, federal trademark registration on the Principal Register establishes other highly beneficial rights if there is ever litigation based on the mark of the trademark registration. These advantages include legal presumptions of validity and exclusive nationwide rights in the mark of the registration. Enforcement of trademark rights is thus greatly enhanced if one has a federal trademark registration on the Principal Register.

The Trademark Application Process

A person or entity who wants to register a trademark with the PTO does so by filing an application and, of course, paying a government fee. Whether the application will actually result in a registration depends on several factors, as explained below. The person or entity who files an application for federal registration is known as the "applicant," and the applicant must be the person or entity who actually uses or will use (or licenses others to use), the mark identified and described in the application.

A trademark application is a written form in which the applicant supplies certain required information regarding the mark for which the registration is sought. This information includes a list of the goods or services to which the mark is applied or used (or will be applied or used, if the mark has not yet been used), the official government classification of the goods or services (if the applicant knows), the legal identity of the applicant, a declaration by the applicant that the applicant is not aware of any confusingly similar marks used by others, a "drawing" of the mark (a depiction of the mark on a separate attached sheet of paper), and the government fee. The government fee for a trademark application is presently $245.00 (per class of goods).

A trademark application filed by a U.S. citizen (either an individual or company) can be based either on actual use or it can be based on an intent to use. If the application is based on actual use, the applicant must identify when the mark was first used anywhere and when the mark was first used in federally regulated commerce (that is, when the mark was used in connection with goods or services in commerce between the various states of the United States (interstate commerce) or between the United States and some specified foreign country). The applicant of a use–based application must also supply "specimens" with the application which show how the mark is used on the goods in commerce. (Floppy disk jackets bearing the mark, for instance, may be specimens for a trademark for a computer program.)

If an application is based on an intent to use, the applicant must have a bona fide intention to use the mark on the listed goods or services at the time of filing and, as discussed in previous sections, the applicant must eventually use the mark in order to obtain a trademark registration. A bona fide intention to use means that the applicant really expects to use the mark in the reasonably foreseeable future and is not filing the application for other reasons, such as to merely prevent others from using or obtaining registration. The suggested official PTO form which may be used is attached at Appendix 2. A listing of the international classification of goods and services (which has been adopted for use by the PTO) is attached at Appendix 3.

After the trademark application is filed, it is examined by the PTO as to form and substance. This examination includes such matters as assuring that the goods or services of the application are described in a certain precise manner which is in accord with the PTO's accepted descriptions and assuring that the goods/services are properly assigned to one or more various classes established by the PTO. The examination as to form would also include such matters as ascertaining whether the representation of the trademark appended to the application (the "drawing" of the mark) meets certain specifications and that the trademark set forth in the application satisfies other formal criteria.

In addition to examination as to form, the PTO will review the application to make sure that the trademark is not considered to be descriptive or generic. The PTO uses computer searching of various databases to assist it in determining whether the purported trademark is a descriptive or generic term. If the PTO initially refuses registration based on its belief that a registration is descriptive or generic, the applicant is allowed a period of time within which to argue against that refusal of registration.

The PTO will also check to see whether there are any conflicting (confusingly similar) registrations or applications which precede the application as filed. If there are, the PTO will refuse registration and it is then up to the applicant to set forth arguments as to why the applicant believes that confusion would not be likely if the prior mark and the mark of the applicant co–exist. In many cases, it is possible to eventually overcome an initial rejection of a trademark by the PTO through submission of legal argument, facts and/or amendment of the description of goods/services.

The application process usually takes about one year or sometimes longer if the PTO refused registration on the grounds that the mark is descriptive or generic or that it conflicts with a prior existing registration or application.

Assuming that a trademark is found to be registrable by the Trademark Office Examiner, it is then published in the Official Gazette of the PTO so third parties will have an opportunity to oppose registration. Many business (either themselves or through their trademark counsel) conduct routine reviews or watches of the weekly Official Gazette to check for publications of marks which conflict with their own or their client's trademarks.

If one does find a trademark which has been published in the Official Gazette and which is believed to conflict with one's prior rights, one may institute a trademark opposition. A trademark "opposition" is akin to a miniature lawsuit (although no live testimony is taken and the proceeding takes place in the PTO rather than in a court). An opposition may be based not only on an allegation of a likelihood of confusion with a prior existing mark, but may also be based on allegations by a competitor that the published mark is generic or descriptive and should, therefore, be available for use by the competitor.

If a trademark opposition is initiated, it usually takes several years until there is a decision rendered by the PTO (an opposition is heard and decided by administrative judges known as the Trademark Trial and Appeal Board, "TTAB"). A vast majority of oppositions are settled by some accommodation arranged between the opposer and the applicant.

Following either the successful resolution of an opposition or the mark successfully passing through the opposition period, the PTO will issue a registration or, in the case of an intent–to–use application, a notice of allowance indicating that the trademark is registrable.

In the case of an intent–to–use application, the issuance of a notice of allowance begins six, successive six–month time frames in which the applicant must make use of the trademark or obtain extensions of time to make use. After the first six–month extension is obtained and until the mark is used and proof of use is filed with the PTO, an applicant must continue to request extensions of time containing a description of the ongoing efforts to use the mark. Each successive extension requires the payment of a government fee for each class of goods contained in the application, and only five extensions of time are allowed. That is, the applicant has only 36 months from the date of allowance to begin and prove use in commerce.

Once use is made of the mark, the intent–to–use applicant must then supply the PTO with "specimens", i.e., evidence of actual use of the trademark on the goods or in connection with the services, and the dates of first use anywhere and first use in federally regulated commerce. Again, the filing of the proof of use requires a government fee for each class of goods or services in the application. (If the application was initially based on use, such specimens would have been provided to the PTO at the time of filing the trademark application, as mentioned above.) Following acceptance by the PTO of the applicant's proof of use, the intent–to–use application will then become registered in due course.

The trademark registration itself contains several important items of informational notice to the public such as, for example, a depiction of the trademark, the name of the owner, the goods/services covered, the dates of use, the filing date and any disclaimers or translations of foreign words in the registration. A disclaimer is a statement by the owner that no exclusive rights are claimed in certain unprotectable portions of the mark, e.g., a mark may contain portions that are descriptive or generic (such as in a mark ACME BRAND WIDGETS, the terms "Brand" and "Widgets" would be disclaimed apart from the whole mark).

Use Of The Trademark Symbol

After issuance of the trademark registration, the registrant may then begin to use the registration symbol consisting of the "®" symbol or a statement such as "Registered Trademark," or "Reg. U.S. Pat. TM. Office." The registration symbol or some other statutorily recognized notification that the mark is a registered trademark should be used whenever possible in connection with a federally registered mark to give notice of the registration. If a mark is not federally registered, use of the statutory notice of registration is not permitted.

Generally, if a proprietary warning notice is included on screen displays, such warning notice should include reference to the fact that a particular mark is registered. If the trademark is unregistered, the notice should include reference to the fact that a particular term is a trademark (even if unregistered). Also, for unregistered trademarks, the symbol "™" may be used next to a word to indicate that the user of the word considers the mark to be a trademark (this symbol is often used during the pendency of a trademark application). The use of a "™" symbol is of minor legal significance, but it can be helpful in providing notice to third parties that a company considers a certain term to be a trademark. This could be of some benefit if an unregistered mark were the subject of litigation.

Use of one of the official federal registration symbols or legends in connection with registered trademarks is important primarily in the context of enforcement of trademark rights. Most significantly, if one does not use the statutory notice of registration and one were successful in an infringement suit, damages for the infringement could only be obtained for the acts of infringement which occurred after the infringer had actual notice that the infringed mark was federally registered.

Maintaining A Trademark

Since "use is king," failure to use a trademark can result in a loss of rights. This is known as abandonment. Failure to use a trademark for two consecutive years (three years after January 1, 1996) results in a legal presumption of abandonment. If a trademark is abandoned, the corresponding trademark registration may be cancelled by a third party instituting a cancellation proceeding before the TTAB.

A federal trademark registration is issued for a term of ten years and can be renewed indefinitely for successive ten–year periods. At the time of renewal, the registrant must submit proof that the mark is still being used in commerce by way of specimens showing how the mark is it is actually used along with a declaration attesting to the fact that the mark is still in use and, of course, the applicable government fee must be paid.

If a trademark registration is not renewed, it will expire as a matter of law.

The fact that a trademark registration can continue to be renewed for successive ten–year periods for as long as the mark of the registration is used is an important difference between trademarks on the one hand and copyrights and patents on the other hand: a trademark registration and the trademark rights of the trademark owner can be maintained indefinitely as long as the mark is in use. Patents and copyrights, however, are granted for limited periods of time.

In order to help assure that the Trademark Register is not filled with "dead wood," there is also a requirement that a declaration of use be filed between the fifth and sixth year of the initial ten–year term of federal registration. The declaration of use attests to the fact that the mark of the registration is still being used in commerce and the declaration must be accompanied by a specimen showing how the mark is being used.

If a trademark owner fails to file the required declaration of use between the fifth and sixth year, the registration will automatically be cancelled by operation of law. However, if one merely failed to file the declaration of use (or failed to file a renewal) through neglect or inadvertence and the owner actually continued to use the mark on a nationwide basis, for example, via the Internet, the owner of that trademark may still have valuable trademark rights and can assert those trademark rights against others. The trademark owner would, of course, have lost the valuable procedural and litigation–oriented advantages of a federal registration.

Cancellation of a registration for failure to file the required declaration of use may be rectified somewhat by filing a new application for registration, subject to any intervening rights of a party who, in the meantime, filed for registration. The PTO expressly provides for examination out of turn for applications for re–register for inadvertent failure to file a declaration of use. However, the examination process and the five–year period for incontestability (see below) start all over.

Whenever a mark registered on the Principal Register has been used continuously for five consecutive years after registration and is not the subject of a challenge by a third party (and subject to certain other requirements), a declaration of "incontestability" can be filed. (Often, a declaration of incontestability is filed with the required declaration of use.) Once accepted, the "incontestability" status of a trademark means that the mark is conclusively presumed to be valid in the context of an infringement suit.

As mentioned in previous sections, even after a federal registration is obtained, one cannot necessarily rest easy, as the trademark is still challengeable by third parties with prior rights and a trademark registration can be cancelled by third parties who believe that they would be damaged by the continued existence of the registration. If a trademark registration has existed for five years, however, the registration can only be cancelled for certain specific reasons (e.g., abandonment, genericness, or fraud in obtaining or maintaining a registration). It could not, for example, be cancelled by someone who may claim prior rights or by a party who alleges that the mark is not a proper trademark because it is descriptive. (A party with prior use, may, however, continue to use the mark in the geographic area where they used the mark prior to the registrant.)

Within the first five years of the existence of a trademark registration, the registration may be cancelled for a number of reasons, including, for example, prior use by the party attempting to cancel the registration or proof that the mark in the registration has been abandoned or is merely descriptive or generic.

Significantly, aside from a failure to use a mark, a trademark registration can also be cancelled if the mark becomes a generic designation based on the public perception of the term. "Aspirin" and "escalator" were once valid trademarks owned by particular companies. However, because of the fact that the public repeatedly referred to these terms as indicators of a <u>class</u> of goods rather than goods emanating from a particular source, and because the owners of the marks failed to make sufficient efforts to stem the tide of changing public perceptions of the marks, both of these terms fell into the public domain as generic terms.

Trademark owners must, therefore, be vigilant in protecting against improper usage of terms and guard against uses of marks which tend to indicate that the reference to the mark is reference to a <u>class</u> of goods rather than to a particular brand. For example, a trademark should be used as an adjective to modify the generic name of the goods. It should never be used as a noun which indicates that it is the "thing" rather than a particular brand of the "thing." Where possible, use of a trademark should be followed by the generic name of the goods. When faced with the public's use of the term XEROX to mean the same thing as "photocopy" (and apparently fearful that the term XEROX might go the way of "aspirin" and "escalator" and fall into the public domain), Xerox Corp. undertook a campaign to counter consumer misperceptions and behavior. For example, Xerox Corp. has taken out advertisements in widely distributed publications indicating that there are two "R's" in XEROX, the reference to the second "R" being the "R" in the circle or "®" which is the federal registration symbol.

It is somewhat ironic that marks which are famous often tend to be the type of marks which are in the most danger of becoming generic terms because the public tends to improperly refer to all goods in a particular class of goods by the famous trademark (i.e., the public uses the mark as a generic name for similar goods rather than as a brand name for the goods of only one source). In the absence of efforts to halt the public misuse, even the most famous of trademarks can become a generic term.

One may notice that when Johnson & Johnson discusses its BAND–AID products, they refer to the product as BAND–AID brand "<u>adhesive bandages</u>" and when Kimberly Clark refers to its KLEENEX product it does so as KLEENEX brand "<u>tissue</u>." Companies such as Johnson & Johnson or Kimberly Clark use the generic name of the goods (adhesive bandages or tissues) in association with the brand name to highlight the fact that BAND–AID and KLEENEX are trademarks and <u>not</u> the generic name of the goods.

The ease with which trademarks are disseminated to millions of people on the Internet greatly increases the possibility that improper use of a trademark could result in a mark falling into the public domain. It is, therefore, of great importance for those who use their trademarks on the Internet to take extra care in making sure that the trademarks are properly used. As discussed above, care includes using the generic name of the goods or services following the trademark and refraining from using a trademark as a noun. Also, if the mark is registered, the registration symbol (®) should be used. If the term is unregistered but considered by the owner to be a trademark, the trademark owner should consider using the trademark symbol "™". Similarly, those who make reference to others' trademarks should respect the proprietary rights of others and assure proper trademark usage.

It is further recommended that those who make reference to a third–party trademark on the Internet should include a statement that the trademark is a trademark (or, if accurate, a <u>registered</u> trademark) of the company that owns the trademark. An example of an appropriate notice is as follows "ACME is a registered trademark of the XYZ Corporation."

Use And Registration Of Domain Names

The expanding use of the Internet by commercial entities has given rise to the desire of those entities to protect their Internet domain names as trademarks. Until recently, InterNIC, the entity which has responsibility for administrating the Internet domain name system in North America, merely assigned names as requested by companies on a first–come, first–serve basis without regarding to whether the Internet domain name infringed upon the trademark rights of another. This policy, however, is currently undergoing review and change. The latest Internet domain name registration policy can be obtained on the Internet at URL "ftp://rs.internic.net/policy/internic/internic–domain–1.txt." An application for an Internet domain name can also be obtained on–line at "ftp://rs.internic.net/templates" or by calling InterNIC at 703–742–4777.

As one might expect, since valuable rights such as trademarks are at stake, legal proceedings have ensued concerning third–party use of well–established trademarks as part of Internet domain names. One such case involved use of the mark "MTV" as part of a domain name, "mtv.com," by a former MTV veejay.[17] In another case, the MCDONALD'S trademark was registered as part of a domain name by an individual who had no connection with the McDonald's corporation. In both cases, the parties ultimately agreed to change their domain names.

The PTO has received numerous applications for registration of Internet domain names as trademarks. While the PTO itself does not determine whether a domain name may be appropriate for registration with InterNIC, the PTO does examine applications for registration of a particular domain name as a trademark as it would otherwise examine trademark applications. It should be kept in mind, however, that in order to be registerable, Internet domain names must be used as trademarks or service marks, i.e. as designations of goods of services. Therefore, if one applies for a domain name as a trademark, one must specifically set forth the goods or services which are designated by the domain name. Merely having an Internet address will not necessarily give rise to use of the domain name as a trademark. However, if the domain name is used on or in connection with goods or in the advertising and promotion of services in a prominent manner, such would tend to support registration of the domain name as a trademark.

Trademark Infringement

While it is beyond the scope of this book to attempt to explain the many intricacies of trademark litigation, at least a broad explanation of certain aspects of trademark litigation is appropriate.

If a trademark owner discovers that another party is using a mark that the trademark owner believes conflicts with the owner's rights in a registered or unregistered trademark, the trademark owner can assert those rights in order to prevent further conflicting use and possibly obtain damages.

Litigation can be lengthy and costly and attempts are often made to persuade the wrongdoer to stop (usually phrased as "cease and desist") without resort to litigation. However, if litigation is necessary, certain basic concepts should be considered.

An action based on conflicting use of a trademark by another party is referred to as trademark infringement. The basic standard as to whether a trademark is infringed, is likelihood of confusion, i.e., is the mark as used by another party likely to cause confusion to the relevant consuming public. While there are many factors which can be weighed to determine whether there will be likelihood of confusion, certain of these factors are commonly given greater significance.

First, it is not necessary that two trademarks be identical for there to be likelihood of confusion. A trademark can be deemed to be confusing if it is similar to another's in sight, sound or meaning. That is, if the trademarks are phonetically or visually similar to one another, they may be likely to be confused with one another. For example, the trade name and mark COMCET used by a corporation engaged in the sale of communications computers was found to be confusingly similar to the name and mark COMSAT used in connection with a worldwide satellite communications system.[18] In another case, the marks POWERDENT and POLIDENT, both for denture cleansers, were found to be confusingly similar.[19]

The mere meanings of trademarks could be sufficient to establish likelihood of confusion even if the words do not sound alike or look alike. For example, the marks TORNADO and CYCLONE for fences were held to be confusingly similar.[20] While, it might seem somewhat farfetched that marks as different in appearance and sound as "tornado" and "cyclone" could be found to be confusingly similar, if someone were to use the trademark RED DELICIOUS, for computers as opposed to MACINTOSH or APPLE for computers, it is understandable that the Apple Corp. would object, as RED DELICIOUS conjures up the image of an apple and, thus, those encountering the mark would likely believe that there is some association with the Apple Corp.

Cases involving trademark infringement and PTO proceedings abound in the field of computer–related goods and services. Indeed, hardly a month goes by without a court or PTO decision involving marks which are used in connection with computer–related goods and services. A few recent examples of decisions involving confusing similarity of marks in the computer field are illustrative. For example, the mark TSUNAMI for disk drives for computer work stations and personal computers was found to likely cause confusion with the identical mark for CD–ROM drives.[21] The mark in THE CENTER OF THE MACINTOSH

UNIVERSE for computer peripheral equipment and other computer related goods was denied registration and was found to be confusingly similar to the MACINTOSH mark for computers (and related computer equipment) owned by Apple Computer, Inc.[22]

In addition to the factors of sight, sound and meaning of the marks used in determining whether marks will likely be confused, other important considerations include the relationship between the goods of the trademark owner and the goods of the alleged infringer, the channels of trade in which the goods are used, the sophistication of the purchasers or those who would encounter the trademark, whether the goods or services are expensive (and whether the purchaser or user would thus take a long time in studying the goods or services thereby learning the true identity of the trademark owner), and significantly, the strength of the mark. As discussed in preceding sections, marks which are highly suggestive are entitled to a much more narrow scope of protection than are highly distinctive coined or arbitrary marks. More distinctive or famous marks will, therefore, be protected across a broader range of goods and will be found to be infringed by marks which are "not as close" in sound, appearance and meaning to the trademark, as compared to weaker suggestive marks. On the other hand, certain marks are so weak that the infringing mark would have to be practically identical and/or used in connection with nearly identical goods in order for there to be infringement.

An infringement action can be filed in Federal Court or state court and the relief sought may include an injunction (that is, a court order preventing the infringer from making any further use of the trademark), monetary damages and in certain instances, treble damages (i.e., three times the amount of actual damages), and attorneys' fees if the case involves blatant infringement warranting such relief (which is said to be an "exceptional" case).

Litigation should be entered into cautiously as such an endeavor is often much more expensive than the trademark owner might expect and it can be much more disruptive to one's business than one might expect. However, if a trademark owner becomes aware of the existence of infringing trademarks and does not enforce its trademark rights, the trademark owner may be deemed to have acquiesced or so lulled the infringer into a sense of well–being, that the trademark owner may later be prevented from ever enforcing those rights. Indeed, if a trademark owner completely fails to police its trademark and allows infringers to continue infringing, the trademark may be deemed weakened or the owner may be deemed to have abandoned the trademark.[23]

An important caveat regarding the policing of marks is that one should generally not approach a potential infringer with an accusation of infringement unless one is sure that he or she, and not the accused infringer, has the prior trademark rights. This is because the accusation may serve as an admission that the marks in question are confusingly similar, and if the accused had prior trademark rights, the accuser can become the accused and could then be considered to be the infringer.

Assignment And Licensing

Assignment and licensing of trademarks is the focus of a succeeding chapter. However, for purposes of this chapter, it should at least be mentioned that trademarks may be assigned and/or licensed. However, unlike patents or copyrights, trademarks do not exist apart from the goods or services which they designate and, therefore, the goodwill of the business symbolized by a trademark must also be assigned with the mark. Also, if a trademark is licensed, the owner of the mark must exercise quality control as to the goods or services which are the subject of the licensed mark in order to satisfy the "assurance of quality" function which trademarks perform. These concepts are discussed in more detail in a succeeding chapter.

International Aspects

Unlike copyrights, trademark rights are not automatically international in scope. In fact, trademark law is just the opposite. Namely, trademark rights are geographic in nature and in most circumstances do not extend beyond national boundaries. This, of course, may not be the case with respect to use of marks internationally on the Internet. The practical and legal effect of this instantaneous international use is not yet fully known. However, it is emphasized that in many countries of the world, registration, rather than use, is king. In these countries, the first to register, regardless of use, may have superior rights. Therefore, for companies that intend to do business internationally, it may be important to register their trademarks in the various foreign countries where they intend to do business. Since trademark laws vary considerably from country to country, if one intends to register a trademark in a particular foreign country, the specific law of that country should be investigated.

In most countries the existence of a U.S. registration (or an application which has been filed within six months of filing in the United States) can serve as a basis for filing a foreign trademark application. In fact, for purposes of establishing priority of rights, if the foreign application is filed within six months of filing the U.S. application, the U.S filing date will be deemed to be the filing date in the foreign country. Conversely, if a U.S. application is filed within six months of filing a foreign application, the U.S. application will be accorded the foreign application filing date for purposes of priority. Also, a foreign trademark registration can serve as a basis for filing a U.S. trademark application.

The international nature of marks appearing on the Internet poses difficult problems with respect to potential infringement. For example, use of one's trademark on the Internet may very well constitute infringement of the rights of another in a foreign country. The consequences of this scenario are yet to be resolved, as it would not appear to be practical to perform a trademark search in every country of the world in which one's Internet message may appear. For the time being, unfortunately, this issue must be considered to be an open one.

As a practical matter, it may be difficult for a foreign entity to obtain jurisdiction over (and, therefore, sue) a U.S. based company overseas, and the prospect of a solely foreign entity suing a U.S. corporation in U.S. courts for infringement presents daunting logistical difficulties for the foreign party. Nevertheless, in instances where substantial worldwide use will be made of an important mark, availability searches and registration for these important marks should be conducted and obtained in those countries of particular business interest to those utilizing the Internet for commercial activities.

Endnotes

1. Incidentally, INTERNET has been registered as a trademark by Internet, Inc. of Reston, Virginia, but the registration is being challenged by the Internet Society. The present policy of the PTO is to not allow the word Internet in the description of services recited in a pending application.

2. In re Bose Corp. 772 F.2d 866 (Fed. Cir. 1985).

3. In re Shakespeare Co. 289 F.2d 506 (C.C.P.A. 1961).

4. Mechanical Plastics Corp. v. Titan Technologies, 28 U.S.P.Q.2d 1522 (S.D. N.Y. 1993).

5. In re Morton-Norwich Products, Inc., 671 F.2d 1332 (C.C.P.A. 1982).

6. In re Weber-Stephen Products Co., 3 U.S.P.Q. 1659 (T.T.A.B. 1987).

7. In re Worlds Finest Chocolates, Inc., 474 F.2d 1012 (C.C.P.A. 1973).

8. In re Owens-Corning Fiberglas Corp., 774 F.2d 1116 (Fed. Cir. 1985).

9. Qualitex Co. v. Jacobson Products Co., _____ U.S. _____, 34 U.S.P.Q.2d 1161 (1995).

10. Id.

11. In re International Game Technology, Inc., 1 U.S.P.Q.2D 1587 (T.T.A.B. 1986).

12. 15 U.S.C. § 1052(f).

13. E.R. Squib & Sons, Inc. v. Princeton Pharmaceuticals, Inc., 17 U.S.P.Q.2d 1447 (S.D. Fla. 1990).

14. Tse, Saiget, Watanabe and McClure, Inc. v. Gentlecare Systems, Inc., 17 U.S.P.Q.2d 1571 (D. Or. 1990).

15. McGraw-Hill, Inc. v. Comstock Partners, Inc., 743 F. Supp. 1029 (S.D. N.Y. 1990).

16. Weight Watchers Int.'l Inc. v. Stouffer Corp., 744 F. Supp. 1259 (S.D. N.Y. 1990).

17. MTV Networks v. Curry, 867 F. Supp. 202 (S.D. N.Y. 1994).

18. Communications Satellite Corp. v. Comcet, Inc., 429 F.2d 1245 (4th Cir.), cert. denied, 400 U.S. 942 (1970).

19. Den–Mat Corp. v. Block Drug Co., Inc., 17 U.S.P.Q.2d 1318 (Fed. Cir. 1990).

20. Hancock v. American Steel & Wire Co., 203 F.2d 737 (C.C.P.A. 1953).

21. Norstrilla Software, Inc. v. Lacie Ltd., Opposition No. 84,913, Allen's Trademark Digest, Vol. IX, No. 1, F–10 at p. 7.

22. Allen's Trademark Digest, Vol. VIII, No. 3, F–105 at page 15.

23. See, e.g., E.I. duPont de Nemours v. Yoshida Int.'l, Inc., 393 F. Supp. 502 (C.D. N.Y. 1975).

Chapter 4

UNFAIR COMPETITION[*]

The law of unfair competition is wide–ranging and in many respects is as broad as the name suggests. Unfair competition laws attempt to redress wrongs inflicted through unfair and improper business practices.

The laws of unfair competition arise in three contexts. First, each state has its "common law" of unfair competition. The "common law" is law which is formed by way of judicial decisions (case law) rather than by way of legislative (statutory) law. Much of the law that we are most familiar with is based on the common law, e.g., breach of contract, trespassing, etc. Similarly, unfair competition law finds much of its basis in the common law of each state. However, in addition to state common law, each state may have certain legislatively created statutes which also make up the law of unfair competition. In many instances, these statutes codify the common law of unfair competition by specifically setting out the behavior that constitutes unfair competition. The state statutory law may also set out additional subject matter which may not exist under common law.

Apart from state statutory and common law, there is also a federal law of unfair competition, namely, the Lanham Act. There is a particular section of the Lanham Act, Section 43(a), which sets out the federal law of unfair competition. In many respects, state common law and statutory law tends to track the federal statutory law of unfair competition, and, therefore, for the purposes of this chapter, unfair competition will be referenced primarily to the Lanham Act.

---

[*]Chapter written by Raymond A. Kurz, Rothwell, Figg, Ernst & Kurz.

Wrongful Acts Proscribed By The Lanham Act

Section 43(a) of the Lanham Act is but a few paragraphs long. For reference, this entire section of the Lanham Act is set out below:

§ 1125   **False designations of origin and false descriptions forbidden**
[Section 43]

(a)(1) Any person who, on or in connection with any goods or services, or any container for goods, uses in commerce any word, term, name, symbol, or device, or any combination thereof, or any false designation of origin, false or misleading description of fact, or false or misleading representation of fact, which–

    (A) is likely to cause confusion, or to cause mistake, or to deceive as to the affiliation, connection, or association of such person with another person, or as to the origin, sponsorship, or approval of his or her goods, services, or commercial activities by another person, or

    (B) in commercial advertising or promotion, misrepresents the nature, characteristics, qualities, or geographic origin of his or her or another person's goods, services, or commercial activities,

shall be liable in a civil action by any person who believes that he or she is or is likely to be damaged by such act.

(2) As used in this subsection, the term "any person" includes any State, instrumentality of a State or employee of a State or instrumentality of a State acting in his or her official capacity. Any State, and any such instrumentality, officer, or employee, shall be subject to the provisions of this Act in the same manner and to the same extent as any nongovernmental entity.

Although the text of Section 43(a) of the Lanham Act is relatively short, the application of that section has been quite broad, and has been successfully asserted to prohibit many types of unfair and unscrupulous business practices. In general, the types of conduct prohibited by Section 43(a) of the Lanham Act include infringement of unregistered trademarks and other trade indicia, false advertising and false statements regarding the attributes of one's own products and the products of others. Each of these aspects of the Lanham Act is discussed separately below.

Protection Of Unregistered Trademarks

As discussed in the preceding chapter, trademark protection is available for registered as well as unregistered trademarks. Since, in the United States, "use is king" with respect to trademarks, the mere use of a trademark even without registration vests valuable trademark rights in the user. These trademark rights are often enforced through the unfair competition laws of Section 43(a) of the Lanham Act. The applicable portion of Section 43(a) provides that those who use any word, term, name, symbol or device which is likely to cause confusion, to cause mistake or to deceive as to source of origin or sponsorship may be liable to those who believe they will be damaged by such actions. In essence, this aspect of Section 43(a) of the Lanham Act provides much of the same type of protection provided for under the Lanham Act for registered trademarks. However, the protection provided under Section 43(a) of the Lanham Act for unregistered trademarks does not carry with it the benefits of registration described in the previous chapter. Nevertheless, Section 43(a) of the Lanham Act is the vehicle by which users of unregistered trademarks may sue infringers, in federal court, for acts of trademark infringement.

Section 43(a) of the Lanham Act also provides for protection akin to trademark protection for subject matter which would not otherwise technically qualify as a trademark. For example, this provision of the

Lanham Act provides relief for trade name infringement and trade dress infringement.

Trade name infringement occurs when one uses a word or words which are confusingly similar to another's trade name even if that trade name does not technically qualify as a trademark (i.e., a business name which might not be used as a trademark on or in connection with goods or services).

Trade dress infringement occurs when one party adopts the overall appearance of the packaging or other trade indicia of another in the advertising, promotion, sale or rendition of goods/services. For example, if one were to adopt a screen display which was confusingly similar to another's screen display, while the screen display itself might not qualify as a "trademark," the activity of simulating another's screen display might very well qualify as a violation of Section 43(a) of the Lanham Act.

Because the provisions of Section 43(a) of the Lanham Act broadly proscribe use of any word, term, name, symbol or device, or any combination of these, "which is likely to cause confusion," Section 43(a) has been recognized as being applicable to acts of trade name and trade dress infringement as well as infringement of unregistered trademarks.

False Or Misleading Advertising

The Lanham Act has been used extensively to prevent copying or imitating another's advertising and to prevent false or misleading statements in advertising about one's own goods or services or the goods or services of another. As with other aspects of Section 43(a) of the Lanham Act, the provisions which have been employed in connection with advertising injury have been quite broadly construed.

The portions of Section 43(a) of the Lanham Act which are most often relied on in connection with advertising injury, proscribe "false designation of origin, false or misleading description of fact, or false or misleading representation of fact, which . . . in commercial advertising or promotion, misrepresents the nature, characteristics, qualities, or geographic origin of his or her or another person's goods or services, or commercial activities."

Various types of false or misleading statements can trigger these provisions of the Lanham Act. For example, liability for false advertising under Section 43(a) of the Lanham Act has been found not only where a statement is actually false, but also where a statement misleads or confuses a purchaser, including misleading by omission of a material fact.[1] As long as there is an actual deception or at least a tendency to deceive which influences the purchasing decision of the consumer, and as long as a party can show that he or she will be injured by the accused statements, there can be a finding of false advertising under the Lanham Act.[2]

One court characterized the breadth of the Lanham Act as follows: "[w]hether or not the statements made in the advertisements are literally true, § 43(a) of the Lanham Act encompasses more than blatant falsehoods. It embraces 'innuendo, direct intimations, and ambiguous suggestions' evidenced by the consuming public's misapprehension of the hard facts underlying an advertisement."[3]

Remedies Under Section 43(a) Of The Lanham Act

The potential liability for false advertising can be great. Although damages are not awarded as a penalty (e.g., as punitive damages), actual damages, or defendant's profits attributed to the false advertising, may be awarded. In certain cases, remedial advertising may be ordered and/or the cost of advertising to respond to the false advertising could be awarded.[4]

Further, courts have discretion to increase damages up to three times the actual damages and, in exceptional cases (involving egregious or willful conduct), attorneys' fees can be awarded.[5] These remedies are similar to the remedies available in cases of willful trademark infringement discussed in the preceding chapter.

Infringement Of Rights Of Publicity

Section 43(a) of the Lanham Act has also been used to protect the names and likenesses of celebrities and characters.[6] Indeed, in some instances, where copyright protection may have ceased to exist because the subject matter has fallen into the public domain, the owner of the expired copyright might still retain rights under Section 43(a) of the Lanham Act, as the particular property in question might still be associated with a particular source. That is, Section 43(a) of the Lanham Act has been employed as a means for preventing use of confusingly similar renditions of characters, artwork, etc., which may not be protectable under the copyright laws.[7]

Other Causes Of Action

In addition to the types of wrongful conduct specifically discussed above, the reader should understand that Section 43(a) of the Lanham Act can be applied in virtually any other circumstance where a party attempts to deceive or confuse in the advertising, promotion, sale or rendition of goods and services.

Section 43(a) of the Lanham Act is a powerful adjunct and supplement to other forms of intellectual property protection. It can be relied upon to plug gaps in protections left open by failure to comply with certain formalities of the trademark or copyright laws. Recognizing that it is a means for promoting the public interest in preventing deception, the courts have given Section 43(a) of the Lanham Act particularly broad interpretation.

Dilution Of Trademarks

Another category of wrongful conduct which may generally be said to fall under the rubric of Unfair Competition concerns the dilution of the distinctiveness of trademarks. While this type of conduct is often considered as an adjunct to the law of trademark infringement, in actuality, the basis of the law of dilution is different from that of trademark infringement.

As discussed in the previous chapter, trademark infringement involves a finding of likelihood of confusion where the same or similar marks are used in connection with the same (or usually at least related) goods or services. In contrast, the law of dilution is not founded on the concept of likelihood of confusion. Rather, the wrong addressed is the dilution in value or distinctiveness of a well–known or famous trademark. The law of dilution is usually applied only to well–known or famous trademarks, and the activity most often addressed is the use of an identical or nearly identical trademark in connection with goods or services which are different than those generally identified by the well–known or famous trademark. In a sense, the law of dilution takes over where the law of trademark infringement leaves off. That is, where one uses a trademark which is identical or nearly identical to a well–known or famous trademark, but does so in connection with goods or services which are so different from those designated by the famous trademark such that the consuming public would not necessarily be confused, the law of dilution provides a remedy addressing the diminution in value or distinctiveness caused by such use.

The law of dilution is relatively new. However, the concept is growing and many states have enacted laws specifically providing for relief from conduct which causes dilution in value or distinctiveness of famous or well–known trademarks. Also, there has been consideration given to enacting federal anti–dilution legislation, but thus far, this legislation has not been enacted.

Endnotes

1. See, e.g., The Gale Group, Inc. v. King City Indus. Co. Ltd., 23 U.S.P.Q.2d 1208 (M.D. Fla. 1992); U–Haul Int.'l v. Jartran, Inc., 522 F. Supp. 1238, 1247 (D. Ariz. 1981).

2. See, e.g., Skil Corp. v. Rockwell Int.'l Corp., 375 F. Supp. 777, 782 (N.D. Ill. 1974).

3. Vidal Sassoon, Inc. v. Bristol–Myers Co., 661 F.2d 272 (2d Cir. 1981).

4. See, e.g., Alpo Petfoods, Inc. v. Ralston Purina Co., 997, F.2d 949 (D.C. Cir. 1993).

5. 15 U.S.C. § 1117.

6. See, e.g., Warner Bros. Inc. v. Gay Toys, Inc., 658 F.2d 76 (2d Cir. 1981); Estate cf Elvis Presley v. Russen, 513 F. Supp. 1339 (D. N. J. 1981).

7. See, e.g., Wyatt Earp Enterprises, Inc. v. Sackman, Inc., 157 F. Supp. 621 (S.D. N.Y. 1958).

Chapter 5

PATENTS·

Introduction

Patent protection offers what many consider the broadest protection for technological developments. While it is said that copyright protects the expression of ideas, but not ideas themselves, a patent can broadly protect against unauthorized use or sale of whatever is defined as the invention. When obtaining a patent, the inventor is free to define his or her invention as broadly as desired, limited only by what is already in the public domain (the "prior art") and the formalistic patent law requirements to distinctly and definitively define the invention.

It is now possible to define ("claim") computer software as a patentable invention, focusing on the idea behind the software's functionality and not merely the specific code that embodies the idea. The potential to patent broad software concepts, such as basic elements of a computer operating system, has been one of the most significant developments in the protection of computer–oriented technology. The patenting of software concepts that apply to conducting business on the Internet promises to stir much debate and will likely result in significant business advantages for those companies that avail themselves of a comprehensive legal protection strategy.

Although patent protection for broad categories of computer software is a very recent development, the value of patents has long been recognized by the computer and telecommunications industries. Computer hardware within the CPU and peripheral devices including input, output, memory and storage devices, for example, has been long regarded as patentable subject matter. Likewise, the processes and

---

·Chapter written by Bart G. Newland, Rothwell, Figg, Ernst & Kurz.

methods of enabling hardware devices to communicate amongst themselves so that the hardware will perform a desired function (such as the operation or monitoring of a chemical plant or a manufacturing facility) have long been patentable. Today, the prospect of patenting data encryption technology and formats for organizing multimedia data elements into a coherent presentation, for example, have heightened patent law awareness (and stirred much debate and controversy) among those doing business on the Internet.

The basic and fundamental concepts of patent law have been in place for decades. The governmental institutions that make the patent laws (Congress), that apply them to specific cases and controversies between parties (the Federal Courts), and that administer the patent laws by granting patents (the PTO – part of the Executive branch) thrive on the concept of legal precedent. The Courts and the PTO traditionally have not opted to make new law when new technologies become commercially important; rather, new questions of patentability (such as the patentability of computer software) have been decided under the existing laws and previous decisions of the courts. Congress, too, traditionally has been reluctant to enact changes to the patent laws to address the concerns of a single industry.

The PTO, starting in 1994, has been much more proactive concerning its stated goals of supporting U.S. businesses by providing strong legal protection for technological developments. Public hearings were held concerning the use of the patent system to protect software–related inventions, and the PTO has issued new guidelines to its Examiners that broaden the definition of patentable computer software inventions. Decisions of the Federal courts in 1994 and 1995 also have broadened the definition of patentable computer software inventions. In these recent decisions, the Court of Appeals for the Federal Circuit (the only U.S. Court of Appeals empowered to hear appeals in patent cases) moved away from several decades of precedent that limited the patentability of software. These recent changes make it imperative that patent law issues be considered for (1) protecting one's own technological innovations and (2) avoiding liability for infringing patent rights of others.

Patent Law Basics

An understanding of patent law issues pertaining to the Internet requires an understanding of patent law "basics."

What Is A Patent?

A patent is a legal grant, issued by the United States Government which permits the patent owner to prevent others from making, using or selling the claimed invention during the term of the patent. Patents contain various descriptions of the invention, both broad and detailed, but it is the language of the patent claims that defines the legal scope of the patent and what conduct can be stopped by the patent owner. The claims of a U.S. patent are the numbered paragraphs that appear at the end of the document. Unfortunately for the public at large, patent claim interpretation is not intuitive; claim interpretation has evolved over the years through case precedent. Specific words and phrases may have legal meanings that are not apparent. The legal interpretation of patent claims usually requires the assistance of a patent attorney well–versed in both the law and the technology.

The patent laws distill down into nine major requirements for a patent. Some of these are substantive, and define what can be patented. Others are procedural, and set forth the steps that must be taken to obtain a valid patent.

The substantive requirements are:

(1) Patentable subject matter – the patent must claim a process, machine, article of manufacture or a composition of matter.

(2) Originality – the named inventor(s) must have actually conceived of the invention, as opposed to deriving it from others.

(3) Novelty – the invention must be new and not already part of the public domain.

(4) Non–obviousness – the invention must exhibit some degree of 'inventiveness' and not merely be obvious to one of ordinary skill in the art of the invention in view of what is already in the public domain (the "prior art").

(5) Utility – the invention must exhibit a modicum of usefulness, and the stated utility must be credible.

The procedural requirements are:

(6) A patent application must be filed at the PTO in the name of the actual inventor(s).

(7) The application must be filed within one year of the first public use, sale or offer for sale of the invention. (However, using this "grace period" may eliminate the possibility of obtaining foreign patents.)

(8) The text of the application (its "specification") must contain a complete description of how to make and how to use the invention. The description must be complete enough so that a person of "ordinary skill in the art to which it pertains" may reproduce the invention.

(9) The patent application must conclude with one or more patent claims that define the invention with an appropriate degree of definitiveness and certainty, so that the public understands exactly what is and is not being claimed by the inventor.

Legal issues surrounding the ability to patent computer software inventions have concerned, almost entirely, point no. 1 above -- the patentable subject matter requirement. For many years the courts and the PTO refused to recognize most computer software as a "process." Likewise, hardware that differed from similar hardware only because it contained novel software was not recognized as a "machine" or an "article of manufacture." As discussed in greater detail below, as of 1995, the Federal Courts and the PTO have substantially modified this approach.

How Is A Patent Obtained?

A patent application is a hybrid legal and technical writing. Although inventors are entitled to prepare and file a patent application without the assistance of an attorney, all large corporations and virtually all small businesses engage the services of a registered patent attorney. Registered patent attorneys have an undergraduate degree in a discipline of engineering, the sciences, computer science or physics, as well as a law degree. Legal fees frequently can be kept to a minimum when the clients themselves do the majority of the technical writing, so that the attorney must focus primarily upon the legal requirements of the document.

The costs of preparing a patent application vary widely depending upon the billing rate of the person preparing the application, the complexity of the subject matter and the degree to which good written materials have been prepared and provided by the inventor. In most major cities it is difficult to have a patent application prepared and filed by a registered patent attorney, for even a very simple invention, for less than $2000.00. The cost of preparing an extremely complex application can rise well above $8,000.00.

Presently, all applications filed in the PTO must be submitted in writing. Electronic filing of patent applications has been experimented with but has not yet been fully implemented. Applications in complex fields of technology, including high–tech electronics, computer software and telecommunications can be quite lengthy (25 pages or more) and will also include one or more drawings, circuit diagrams, flow charts and the like.

The PTO's rules regarding the format of the application are very specific. An application that contains all of the required elements, but is not in the proper format, may be accepted and awarded a filing date, subject to later correction. An application that is missing one of the required elements may not receive a filing date. The rules regarding drawings are equally rigid, and a commercial patent draftsman often is used to prepare drawings for the application.

When the inventor(s) is satisfied that the application accurately describes the invention, the application is mailed or hand–delivered to the PTO, along with a signed Inventor's Declaration and the government filing fee. As of September 1995, the government filing fee was $365.00 for individual inventors, non–profit organizations and small businesses of five hundred or fewer employees and $730.00 for other entities.[1] After the application is filed, the PTO makes a preliminary review of the application to ensure that it is complete, and then forwards it to the examining group which has a number of examiners that are knowledgeable in the particular subject matter of the invention.

The application will be assigned to an individual patent examiner who examines applications in the specific subject matter that is claimed. The examiner's role is to review what is described and claimed and then conduct a prior art search, through the available literature sources (including prior U.S. patents, some foreign patents and trade literature), so that the novelty and non–obviousness (inventiveness) of the claims can be assessed. The examiner reviews the specification to ensure that it provides an adequate explanation of how to make and use the invention, and reviews the claims to ensure that they meet formal requirements. Applications are examined by the individual examiners in the order in which they are received (unless a petition to make the application special is filed and granted, e.g., if there were a need to obtain the patent on an expedited basis). It is not uncommon for an application to remain unexamined for many months in technically complex fields.

The results of this initial examination are communicated in writing to the patent attorney if one has been designated, otherwise directly to the inventor. The examination results are presented in a paper called an "Office Action" and may include rejections of the claims as being unpatentable for lack of novelty and/or for being obvious in view of the prior art. The examiner may also enter rejections based upon a failure of the specification and/or claims to comply with the formal requirements regarding completeness and clarity. The vast majority of initial Office Actions present at least one rejection, although the acceptance ("allowance") of the application in that first Office Action can occur.

Office Actions typically require the applicant's written response to be submitted within three months, with up to an additional three months being available retroactively upon the payment of increasingly expensive one–month extensions of time. The preparation of a response to the Office Action usually requires the assistance of a patent attorney, as both the technical and legal bases of any rejections often must be argued. In addition to arguing against the rejection(s), it is common to present amendments to the claims in order to avoid the rejection(s).

Meetings ("interviews") with the patent examiner, either in person or over the telephone, can facilitate the allowance of the application. Interviews are held in only a small percentage of all applications, and can be particularly helpful when it is apparent from the Office Action that the examiner has not fully understood or appreciated an important aspect of the invention or the prior art. Some examiners welcome the opportunity to discuss the technology with the inventor, while other examiners view the interview process as time–consuming and unnecessary. Even those examiners who fall into the latter category often are willing to lend extra assistance to inventors who are representing themselves without the assistance of an attorney.

The Examiner issues a "Notice of Allowance" once all of the rejections are overcome. A three–month deadline is provided for paying the final government fees ($605.00 as of September 1995 for individuals, non–profit organizations and small business concerns; $1,210.00 for other concerns). The patent usually is granted two to three months after the final fees are paid.

Several possibilities exist for continuing to pursue the application if the examiner maintains the rejections, rather than issuing a Notice of Allowance. The application can be re–filed, affording additional opportunities to present arguments, additional evidence of patentability and to amend the claims. Alternatively, the rejections can be appealed to the PTO's Board of Patent Appeals and Interferences, where the rejections will be considered by a three–judge panel of Administrative Patent Judges. Appeals from an adverse decision of the Board may be taken to the Federal Courts, but such appeals are quite expensive to maintain and difficult to win.

Patent rights — the rights to stop others from making, using or selling the invention (and, after January 1, 1996, also including the right to prevent others from importing the invention) — attach only upon the issuance of a patent. Inventions can and should be marked as patented (by use of the word "patented" and the U.S. patent number) after patent issuance. Inventions can be marked "patent pending" while an application is pending in the PTO, but no substantive rights will have yet arisen. Nevertheless, the "patent pending" designation serves to warn others that a patent is "in the works," and may discourage others from copying the invention. The intentional false marking of a product as "patented" or "patent pending" is illegal and punishable by payment of a fine.

Recent changes to the patent laws have affected the manner in which the term of patents is determined. For patent applications filed after June 7, 1995, the patent term runs twenty years from the filing date of the patent application, even though substantive rights do not arise until patent issuance. For patents filed prior to June 7, 1995, including patents already issued and in force on that date, the patent term is the longer of (1) seventeen years from the issue date or (2) twenty years from the filing date. The payment of government fees is required in order to maintain a patent in force for its full term. Increasingly expensive "maintenance fees" are due 3-1/2, 7-1/2 and 11-1/2 years after issuance. Failure to pay these fees results in the patent rights being lost and the subject matter of the patent being dedicated to the public.

How Is A Patent Enforced?

The right to stop others from making, using or selling the claimed invention is a private right of the patent owner. As such, patent rights are enforced via civil litigation. Typically, patent suits are brought in Federal court in the name of the patent owner. Patent infringement litigation is one of the most complex forms of civil litigation, and it is extremely expensive to maintain. Nevertheless, obtaining a favorable judgment in a patent litigation can entitle the patent owner to a permanent injunction order prohibiting the infringer from continuing to practice the invention, plus monetary damages in the form of lost profits or a reasonable royalty on the infringing sales (which can be increased by three fold in cases involving willful infringement), as well as the costs for bringing the litigation (but typically not the attorneys' fees unless it is an "exceptional" case). An "exceptional" case for which the patent owner's attorneys' fees may be recovered, is usually a case where the court finds that the infringer acted willfully, in knowing disregard of the patent rights and/or was guilty of other egregious conduct.

How Can Patent Rights Of Others Be Investigated?

The planned introduction of a new product into the marketplace should always be accompanied by at least consideration of the question, "Will this product infringe another's patent?" There is no affirmative legal duty to investigate the answer to this question, but the early avoidance of patent infringement problems may make it more efficient to consider the issue before the product is introduced and market share is gained.

Searching for pertinent patents is as much an art as it is a science. Professional firms that conduct patent searches typically use a combination of on–line computer database searching and manual searching through the files of the PTO. To date, the full text of U.S. patents dating back to the 1970's, 1980's and 1990's are available on–line on the PTO's own database, and on commercial databases (Lexis/Nexis and Dialog) that charge for access. The PTO's database is accessible to members of the public at public libraries in major U.S. cities.

Although there is no affirmative duty to conduct a search, there is a duty to exercise reasonable care not to knowingly infringe patent rights of others. (It is generally considered prudent to seek the advice of competent counsel upon becoming aware of another's patent rights.)

Breach of this duty through the "willful infringement" of another's patent rights can entitle the patent owner to recover its own attorneys' fees and up to triple the monetary damage award if a patent infringement litigation is brought and won.

Searching for patents of others often is useful prior to filing one's own patent application. Again, there is no affirmative duty to investigate the state of the prior art or to conduct such a search. Good knowledge of the prior art, however, makes it possible to prepare a better patent application focusing on the truly novel and inventive aspects of the invention. These "preliminary patentability searches" often can be conducted at modest cost compared to the cost of preparing, filing and pursuing a patent application.

Patent Protection For Computer Software

A series of independent but important events in the mid–1990's have thrust the patent protection of computer software inventions into the limelight and, importantly, into the corporate consciousness of every company whose business concerns the development of computer–related technology. These events are highlighted by the legal developments which point up the growing importance of patent protection for basic technological developments embodied in computer software. The following examples are illustrative:

(1) In July of 1994, the United States Court of Appeals for the Federal Circuit, in In re Alappat, 33 F.3d 1526 (1994), held that claims to "a rasterizer for converting vector list data . . . into anti–aliases pixel illumination intensity data to be displayed on a display means" encompassed patentable subject matter even though each of the elements responsible for the conversion were mathematical algorithms carried out by software in a digital computer. Although the Board of Appeals at the PTO had held

that the claims recited unpatentable subject matter, the court took a plain–language approach to the claim. The claim was drawn to a "machine" (rasterizer) and machines are per se patentable subject matter. Because of the software elements, the rasterizer was different from previous rasterizers (i.e., novel) and was not obvious in view of the prior art. Given that the claimed invention "as a whole" was a machine, and not merely a disembodied software algorithm for carrying out a calculation, the court held that the claimed invention squarely falls under the "machine" category of patentable subject matter.

(2) On June 1, 1995, following a series of cases in which the Court of Appeals for the Federal Circuit overturned PTO Boards of Appeal decisions rejecting computer software inventions, the PTO published a draft set of new "Guidelines" for use by patent examiners for "their review of patent applications on computer–implemented inventions." The full text of the draft guidelines appear in Appendix 9. Published public comments and the PTO's final Guidelines will be published before the end of 1995 and will be available on the PTO's World Wide Web site (http://www.uspto.gov) and anonymous ftp site (ftp://ftp.uspto.gov).

The PTO's proposed guidelines, if adopted, could remove many of the legal fictions (e.g., the unpatentability of "mathematical algorithms" per se) previously used to reject claims to inventions embodied in computer software. The PTO proposes to adopt the "claim as a whole" approach taken by the Federal Circuit in In re Alappat. Moreover, the PTO has identified a specific methodology for classifying computer–related inventions into the pre–existing categories of patentable subject matter:

Considering each claim as a whole, classify the invention defined by each claim as to its statutory category (i.e., process, machine, manufacture or composition of matter). Rely on the following presumptions in making this classification:

(a)   A computer or other programmable apparatus whose actions are directed by a computer program or other form of "software" is a statutory "machine."

(b)   A computer–readable memory that can be used to direct a computer to function in a particular manner when used by the computer [1] is a statutory "article of manufacture".

(c)   A series of specific operational steps to be performed on or with the aid of a computer is a statutory "process".[2]

The note embedded in the text of paragraph (ii) offers much practical guidance as to the breadth of subject matter the PTO proposes to consider as patentable:

(1)   Articles of manufacture encompassed by this definition consist of two elements: (1) a computer–readable storage medium, such as a memory device, a compact disc or a floppy disk, and (2) the specific physical configuration of the substrate of the computer–readable storage medium that represents data (e.g., a computer program), where the storage medium so configured causes a computer to operate in a specific and predefined manner. The composite of the two elements is a storage medium with a particular physical structure and function (e.g., one that will impart the functionality represented by the data onto a computer).

(2)   For example, a claim that is cast as "a computer program" but which then recites specific steps to be implemented on or using a computer should be classified as a "process." A claim to

simply a "computer program" that does not define the invention in terms of specific steps to be performed on or using a computer should not be classified as a statutory process.

The proposed Guidelines also offer guidance as to classes of inventions that remain unpatentable:

A claim that defines an invention as any of the following subject matter should be classified as non–statutory:

– a compilation or arrangement of data, independent of any physical element;

– a known machine–readable storage medium that is encoded with data representing creative or artistic expression (e.g., a work of music, art or literature); [3],[4]

– a "data structure" independent of any physical element (i.e., not as implemented on a physical component of a computer such as a computer–readable memory to render that component capable of causing a computer to operate in a particular manner); or

– a process that does nothing more than manipulate abstract ideas or concepts (e.g., a process consisting solely of the steps one would follow in solving a mathematical problem).

Claims in this form are indistinguishable from abstract ideas, laws of nature and natural phenomena and may not be patented.

Again, the imbedded notes provide practical guidance:

(3) The specific words or symbols that constitute a computer program represent the expression of the computer program and as such are a literary creation.

(4) A claim in this format should also be rejected under §103, as being obvious over the known machine–readable storage medium standing alone.

(5) A claim to a method consisting solely of the steps necessary to converting one set of numbers to another set of numbers without reciting any computer–implemented steps would be a non–statutory claim under this definition.

The provisions of the PTO's proposed guidelines, coupled with the expansive definition of patentable subject matter provided by the Federal courts, present enormous new opportunities for the protection of computer–software related inventions. A hard disk containing software for operating a computer in a novel and non–obvious manner will be considered patentable. While debate as to the practical effect of such "software patents" will continue, it is clear that (1) the courts and the PTO have embraced the notion of "software patenting," (2) technology companies are rapidly filing applications for software protection; and (3) industry devoted to the development of this technology will increasingly rely upon software patents to protect their research and development investments.

Avoiding Patent Problems On The 'Net

A patent attorney's professional life is split between helping his or her clients (1) secure and enforce patent protection for technological developments and (2) avoid running afoul of patent rights of others. The simple statement "If you want to avoid patent infringement problems, don't copy technology of others" is neither practical nor within the underlying policies of the patent system. Inasmuch as patents are awarded only for novel and inventive discoveries or inventions, the converse of this policy is that unpatentable technology may be freely used by all (so long as it is not illegally obtained).

Although another's patent rights may be used to prevent you from making, using or selling their patented invention, it is a principle of patent law that the patent owner, by selling or giving away their patented product (or a product that embodies their patented process) conveys an implied license to the purchaser to practice the patented invention during the ordinary use of the product for the ordinary life of the product. Thus, for example, each purchaser of Compton's multimedia encyclopedia automatically received a license under Compton's (controversial) patent, even absent any formal patent license in the packaging. Thus, absent any express contractual obligation to the contrary imposed by the patent owner (such as an obligation to pay a shareware fee beyond an initial evaluation period), the authorized downloading of patented software for its intended use would not create liability for patent infringement.

Use of patented software outside of the scope of terms imposed by the patent owner may lead to patent infringement liability and thus must be avoided. Although financial liability may be minimal, the use of patented shareware without payment of the shareware license fee could constitute patent infringement (if the shareware was patented) as well as copyright infringement. Substantially increased liability would arise, however, if the patented technology is copied and incorporated into a commercial product. Thus, it is prudent to inquire as to the possible patent status of any technology that one desires to incorporate into a commercial product without the permission of the technology owner.

Endnotes

1. The governmental filing fees are expected to increase in October of 1995, and typically increase every October.

Chapter 6

TRADE SECRETS[*]

Introduction

Trade secrets are sometimes last in line in the consideration of intellectual property assets. However, trade secrets are important intellectual property with potentially broad applicability to a variety of subject matter that can range from microprocessors in the telecommunications field to methods of sorting mail. Trade secret rights are perhaps often most valuable because they are separate from traditional copyright or patent rights, and, in fact, may be available when copyright or patent rights are not.

This chapter provides an overview of basic principles of trade secret protection with a focus on the application of such principles to doing business on the Internet.

The Requirements Of A Trade Secret

Trade secret protection is governed by state common law and statutory law. Although there is no single federal statute governing trade secret protection and there is currently no real means of registering trade secrets as one would register a copyright or obtain a patent, many states have adopted the Uniform Trade Secrets Act ("UTSA") which encourages the application of uniform principles of trade secret protection.

---

[*]Chapter written by Celine M. Jimenez, Rothwell, Figg, Ernst & Kurz.

Under the UTSA, a trade secret is commonly defined as:

Information, including a formula, pattern, compilation, program, device, method, technique or process, that:

(a)   derives independent economic value, actual or potential, from not being generally known to, and not being readily ascertainable by proper means by, other persons who can obtain economic value from its disclosure or use; and

(b)   is the subject of efforts that are reasonable under the circumstances to maintain its secrecy.[1]

As can be seen from the above often quoted definition, there is broad variety in the types of information and know–how that can be considered to be trade secrets. For example, methods of manufacturing computer hardware, algorithms for processing data, formulas for chemical compounds, ingredients in beverages, methods of operation of a machine, methods of medical or agricultural treatments, designs for computer software systems, computer source code, and other technological know–how can be trade secrets.

Although trade secrets often involve or relate to technological know–how, subject matter such as customer lists, pricing methods, accounting or bookkeeping procedures, and other methods of doing business may, in certain circumstances, also be trade secrets. In fact, in a recently filed case, the Church of Scientology has argued that certain of its religious texts are trade secrets.[2]

Subject matter does not need to be patentable or copyrightable in order to be a trade secret. For example, a product formula may not be copyrightable for lack of the creative expression necessary to support a claim of copyright, but may be protected by trade secret principles. However, trade secrets often accompany or relate to subject matter which is patented or protected by copyright. For example, certain instructions for manufacturing a patented machine, although perhaps not protectable by patent (e.g., they may not constitute a legally novel or nonobvious process), may be protectable under trade secret principles.

There is an additional important relationship between patent protection and trade secret protection. This relationship concerns both the requirement of disclosing the "best mode" of an invention in a patent application, and the fact that the information contained in a patent cannot be a trade secret (as patents are public documents). More specifically, the description portion of a patent application (the specification) is required to contain, not only a written description of the invention and the manner and the process of making and using it, but also a description of "the best mode contemplated by the inventor of carrying out his invention."[3] Therefore, although in many circumstances trade secret protection might be available, for example, for a particular design of a machine which allows the machine to perform its function most effectively, if such design were kept confidential and not disclosed in a patent application for the machine (in order to keep that particular design a trade secret), that could result in the patent being found invalid for failure to disclose the best mode.

As is seen, from the above definition, the applicability of trade secret protection generally depends on the nature of the information or material sought to be protected and the treatment of the information or material. It is noted that a variety of factors are sometimes considered in determining whether particular information or material is a trade secret and, therefore, protectable. Some of these factors are:

(1) the extent to which the information is known outside of the relevant business;

(2) the extent to which it is known by employees and others involved in the relevant business;

(3) the measures taken to guard the secrecy of the information;

(4) the value of the information to the owner's business and to the business of competitors;

(5) the amount of effort or money expended in developing the information; and

(6) the ease or difficulty with which the information could be properly acquired or duplicated by others.[4]

Despite the variety of factors sometimes considered in determining whether trade secret protection is available, the requirements for a trade secret often come down to two basic concepts:

(1) A trade secret must not be commonly known or readily ascertainable by others; and

(2) A trade secret must be kept secret.

These two requirements are discussed in more detail below.

A Trade Secret Must Not Be Commonly Known

In order to be protectable as a trade secret, the information or material must generally not be commonly known in the relevant market or business. However, the information or material does not necessarily have to rise to the level of "novelty" required to obtain a patent in order to be protectable, and, of course, a trade secret need not be patentable. (See earlier chapter on patents for a discussion of "novelty" requirement in patents.) Rather, it has been said that trade secrets arise from some "discovery" which has economic and competitive value, but do not need to approach the level of "invention" required to obtain a patent.[5]

Further, if others can independently create or arrive at the information or material sought to be protected, trade secret protection is of no value. This is also true if the purported trade secrets are easily observable from the very goods or services themselves. For example, if the means by which a lever operates with a jack is readily observable by simply viewing the jack and lever apparatus, the lever/jack means of operation would not be protectable as a trade secret. The same principle would apply, for example, to <u>unrestricted</u> distribution of software source code to third parties. One could not likely claim later that such publicly accessible source code contained trade secrets.

A Trade Secret Must Be Kept Secret

The second requirement of a trade secret (which is the aspect of trade secret analysis that often receives the most attention) is that a trade secret must, in fact, be a secret. This aspect of trade secret protection is particularly relevant in the context of the Internet and on–line services. Trade secrets must be kept private within a company or group and not be disclosed or accessible to third parties or the public at large. Loss of secrecy, by disclosure to the public or otherwise, forfeits the trade secret.

Companies generally do not risk losing trade secret protection by, for example, communicating their trade secrets to lower level employees or communicating proprietary information to customers or other individuals in the context of licensing arrangements which include confidentiality agreements. However, disclosing trade secrets to others through on–line e–mail systems or in public newsgroups could very well result in loss of protection.

Also, for example, disclosing source code to the public by making it available on–line, or by submitting it to the Copyright Office as a deposit copy for a copyright application (without taking the necessary precautions for protection of trade secrets provided in the Copyright Rules)[6] can result in loss of protection. In short, it cannot be emphasized enough that in order for trade secrets to be protected, one needs to take steps to keep the trade secret information confidential and within the company.

A variety of techniques can be used within one's business to protect trade secrets. Some common techniques which may or may not be applicable in particular circumstances are listed below:

(1) Marking proprietary documents and materials with legends such as "CONFIDENTIAL" or "PROPRIETARY" and taking reasonable measures to ensure that such documents and materials are not disclosed or accessible, physically or over a computer network, to individuals outside of the company;

(2) Restricting visitors and otherwise limiting access to laboratories, plants, computer systems and any physical structures where proprietary materials are contained or where proprietary processes are practiced, e.g., employing computer network security systems, locking rooms and file cabinets, logging–in

visitors, use of video monitors, use of visitor and employee identification tags, and other security measures;

(3) Posting warning signs advising of restricted access or of the requirement to keep proprietary information confidential;

(4) Educating employees as to what the company's trade secrets are and the procedures for maintaining such trade secrets;

(5) Using secret, unnamed ingredients;

(6) Entering into appropriate written non–disclosure agreements with employees to whom trade secrets have been disclosed (as a protection in the event the employees leave the company);

(7) Limiting access to secret information only to employees whose jobs require that they have access to the secret information, for example, by electronic passwords; and

(8) Ensuring that trade secrets are disclosed to those outside the business only when and to the extent necessary <u>and</u> in conjunction with written agreements that limit use and disclosure of the information and that compel secrecy.

Businesses that employ these techniques are more likely to avoid significant challenges to their trade secret rights.

Interesting issues of trade secret protection have arisen with the advent of Internet e–mail and internal e–mail systems. These issues concern whether and to what extent employers may monitor or view their employees' e–mail transmissions in order to determine, for example, whether the employees are improperly disclosing company trade secrets. The analysis of these questions, which primarily focuses on privacy issues, involves inquiry into such facts as whether the e–mail messages were sent over a system not provided by the employer, whether employees have been specifically informed that the employer would be monitoring their e–mail messages, and whether clear policies and guidelines regarding e–mail monitoring were established by the company. Commentators have stated that an employer's suspicion that an employee is using an e–mail system to transmit trade secret information to a competitor might constitute sufficient cause for an employer to monitor that employee's e–mail.[7]

Enforcement Of Trade Secret Rights

Trade secret owners have the right to prevent others from taking their trade secrets without authorization (often called "misappropriation"). Accordingly, those who believe their trade secrets have been wrongfully appropriated can bring court actions requesting relief in the form of injunctions and damages. As trade secret protection is governed by state law, the scope and nature of protection can differ from state to state. (This can be important when entering into contracts concerning the use and disclosure of trade secrets if there is a "choice of law" provision in the contract.) However, as mentioned earlier, a number of states have adopted the UTSA.

The elements of a trade secret misappropriation claim under the UTSA are generally:

(1) The acquisition of a trade secret of another by a person who knows or has reason to know that the trade secret was acquired by improper means; or

(2) Disclosure or use of a trade secret of another, without express or implied consent, by a person who:

(a)   Used improper means to acquire knowledge of the trade secret; or

(b)   At the time of disclosure or use, knew or had reason to know that his or her knowledge of the trade secret was:

  (i)   derived from or through a person who utilized improper means to acquire it;

  (ii)   acquired under circumstances which gave rise to a duty to maintain its secrecy or limit its use; or

  (iii)   derived from or through a person who owed a duty to the person seeking relief to maintain its secrecy or limit its use; or

(c)   Before a material change of his or her position, knew or had reason to know that it was a trade secret and that knowledge of it was acquired by accident or mistake.[8]

Practitioners in the trade secret law field often say that trade secret cases are hard to prove. This can be true for several reasons. First, at the outset of an inquiry into trade secret misappropriation, it is generally necessary to precisely identify what trade secrets are at issue. In the case of stolen source code, this could be fairly simple. However, more often, especially where trade secret protection is serving as a substitute for patent protection, one may need to separate out the secret technological features from any non-secret features and then proceed to show that the secret features have been taken without authorization. This parcelling out of secret from non-secret information can be difficult. The second common challenge in bringing trade secret misappropriation cases is fending off allegations that insufficient measures were taken to keep the information or material secret.

Careful handling of trade secrets from the start can alleviate these common problems that often arise in the context of attempting to enforce a trade secret. Some techniques for protecting trade secrets internally have been described above. The techniques for protecting a company's trade secrets when they are used outside of the company are discussed below.

Protecting Trade Secrets By Contract

A trade secret owner who desires to disclose the trade secrets to another for a limited purpose may enter into an agreement providing that the owner will disclose the trade secrets subject only to the recipient's agreeing to:

(1) Keep the trade secrets confidential (i.e., not disclose the trade secrets to another); and

(2) Not to use the trade secrets outside the limited scope of the agreement.

Such agreements are often referred to as "Confidentiality," "Non-Disclosure," or in some cases, "Submission" agreements.

Generally speaking, disclosure of trade secrets to others with restrictions, should be by way of a written contract or agreement. In certain circumstances, contractual agreements can be implied, either by an oral contract or by an implied confidential relationship, such as between an employee and employer or between two parties conducting licensing negotiations. A trade secret disclosed by way of an implied agreement of confidentiality or in the context of an implied confidential relationship may receive protection on grounds of fairness if the implied contract to keep information and material confidential or the confidential relationship can be proven. However, often the best means of attempting to clearly express the intent of the parties to an agreement to maintain the confidentiality of trade secrets is to have an express agreement in writing or have such included in any agreement to do business. It is much easier to prove the existence of a confidential relationship if it is written into an agreement.

Written confidentiality agreements frequently include provisions regarding, among other things, the following:

(1) The purpose and nature of the parties' relationship;

(2) A definition and/or description of the trade secrets or confidential information to be disclosed and the fact that such is proprietary to the owner;

(3) Explicit restrictions on this use of the trade secrets for the limited purpose expressly set forth in the agreement and not otherwise for use in the recipient's business;

(4) Prohibition on disclosure to third parties;

(5) Time period for which the agreement is in effect; and

(6) Choice of law provisions.

A sample form Confidentiality Agreement is included at Appendix 8.

Reverse Engineering

Absent contractual provisions, the principles of trade secret law, in and of themselves, generally do not protect against reverse engineering by a party who is not in a confidential relationship (or other relationship from which a duty of confidentiality can be implied) with the owner of the trade secrets. Accordingly, the most effective means of preventing another from reverse engineering, for example, proprietary software, is often by way of contract or license.

In fact, software licenses frequently include, in addition to confidentiality provisions, a provision requiring the licensee to refrain from reverse engineering software code provided pursuant to the license. Such provisions are generally upheld if the software is truly a trade secret and the license is otherwise valid. However, a contractual provision may not be effective in preventing reverse engineering where the software code has been widely distributed (and thus may not be secret) or where the reverse engineering of the software is easy to accomplish (thereby making it more difficult to prove reverse engineering in violation of the agreement).

Some software licenses go even further than prohibiting reverse engineering and include "no–compete" provisions which provide that the licensee will refrain from competing with the software owner with respect to software of similar function for a particular time period. The enforceability of these types of provisions often depends on the purpose of the no–compete clause (e.g., whether it was legitimately designed to protect trade secrets). It is noted, however, that no–compete clauses which do not include a specific time limitation, or which are otherwise overly broad (e.g., in that they are not directed to the subject matter of the agreement), may be considered unenforceable.[9]

Protecting Trade Secrets On The Internet

Trade secret disclosures to others are made in a variety of contexts which can include employer/employee relationships, licensor/licensee relationships, buyer/seller relationships, and publisher/developer or author relationships. Increasingly, parties enter into such relationships over the Internet and on–line services and this type of activity brings the issue of trade secret protection in the context of the Internet to the fore.

The entry into and conducting of business relationships on–line is especially prevalent in international business or in other long–distance business relationships where parties often find it more economical and efficient to communicate or transmit letters, licenses, technical data and other information via an on–line network instead of by mail, facsimile or telephone. However, on–line communications are often conducted quickly and without the intermediary step of generating hard copies of the information or material being communicated (the time it takes to generate and review hard paper copies often affords time for reflection and planning). Accordingly, one should take extra care that confidential information or material is not disclosed to the public or made easily accessible to the public via transmission on–line.

The following are suggestions for protecting one's trade secrets when conducting business over the Internet.

First, take care that proprietary information not be communicated to others on–line absent appropriate restrictions on use and disclosure. Transmitting proprietary information to another without any agreement with respect to confidentiality would likely forfeit trade secret protection. Similarly, allowing an Internet user unrestricted access to proprietary information via a home page or other site would likely forfeit trade secret protection.

Secondly, to the extent that trade secret material is transmitted on–line to those authorized to receive and use it under restrictions, take care to maintain the privacy of the trade secrets. For example, transmissions of a trade secret between two parties via private e–mail pursuant to a confidentiality agreement, or in the context of license negotiations (where a confidential relationship could be implied), would very likely not be considered a public disclosure of the trade secret.

On the other hand, placing proprietary or trade secret material in a public forum/bulletin board context would very likely be considered a public disclosure of such material or information that could deprive the material or information of trade secret protection. This would likely be so even if the number of participants in the forum was small, as the material would generally be accessible to the public in an unrestricted manner.

Much of this section has focused on techniques for protecting one's own trade secrets when conducting business over the Internet and otherwise. However, one should also be aware when doing business on the Internet that disclosing the proprietary or trade secret information of others (assuming such information is, in fact, a trade secret and there is some duty of confidentiality), could subject one to allegations of trade secret misappropriation.

A recent example of this potential problem in the context of on–line communications is illustrated in the cases involving The Church of Scientology against former members of the church who have allegedly posted church documents in public discussion groups on the Internet. In certain of these cases, The Church of Scientology has alleged that the individuals who have posted such information and material have violated Scientology's trade secret rights by distributing secret church scriptures over the Internet. (The Church of Scientology has contended that it keeps the scriptures in guarded rooms in a limited number of places and that the scriptures are shown only to members of Scientology at high levels.) In some instances, The Church of Scientology has successfully obtained court orders allowing them to seize the computer and accompanying disks of the individuals accused of improperly disclosing the protected information on–line.[10]

A Sample Form Confidentiality Agreement

The basic sample form Confidentiality Agreement provided at Appendix 8 contains examples of provisions that could be included in an agreement to protect trade secrets. However, because it is intended merely as a basic form, one should consult competent counsel prior to entering into any agreement regarding trade secrets.

It is also noted that, as with agreements generally, Confidentiality/Non–Disclosure Agreements are sometimes drafted from a particular point of view, i.e., either that of the owner of the trade secrets who seeks to disclose the trade secrets under certain restrictions or from the point of view of the entity receiving the trade secrets. The precise language of confidentiality agreements can differ significantly depending on the point of view of the drafter. For example, the discloser of trade secret information may want an attorneys' fee provision (providing for recovery of attorneys' fees to the prevailing party in any litigation regarding the agreement) or a provision that a running list be kept of the individuals to whom the trade secret information is disclosed pursuant to the agreement; the receiver of trade secret information may want provisions delineating broad categories of information which do not constitute trade secrets.

Confidentiality agreements can be as restrictive or particular as the situation warrants. The following specific issues are also sometimes addressed in such agreements.

(1) Liability of the party to whom the information is disclosed if there is an inadvertent disclosure of Confidential Information.

(2) Protection of Confidential Information only if it is disclosed in written or other fixed form and clearly marked "Confidential."

(3) Protection of Confidential Information that is specifically set out in an attachment to or otherwise specifically identified in the Agreement.

(4) Any limits on the right to develop or release materials similar to the Confidential Information.

(5) Restrictions on decompilation, disassembling, tracing or any other actions whatsoever to reverse engineer, in whole or in part, any aspect of the Confidential Information.

(6) Warranties such as that the Confidential Information being submitted represents the original material of the discloser and does not infringe on any copyright rights, trademark rights, patent rights or any other property rights of any party, and that the discloser has full title to the Confidential Information.

(7) The applicability of binding arbitration to actions arising out of or relating to the Agreement.

(8) Consequences for breach of the Agreement such as payment of the prevailing party's attorneys' fees, expenses and costs.

In sum, trade secret protection can be one of the more flexible and potentially broadly applicable forms of intellectual property protection. It can conceivably cover subject matter that ranges from sophisticated electronics systems to business customer lists. However, the requirements for trade secret protection are strict, especially, as they concern secrecy, and care needs to be taken when doing business on-line (and otherwise) that valuable trade secret protection is not inadvertently forfeited.

Endnotes

1. Uniform Trade Secrets Act § 1(1).

2. See, e.g., Abbott, Karen, "Scientology Critic Wins Round In Battle Over Computer Files," Rocky Mountain News, Denver Publishing Co., Sect. Local at 8A (August 26, 1995); Beckett, Jamie, "Scientology Lawsuit Goes to Judge In San Jose – Church Claims Trade Secrets Revealed Online," The San Francisco Chronicle, The Chronicle Publishing Co., Sect. News at C2 (June 24, 1995).

3. 35 U.S.C. § 112, first paragraph.

4. See Restatements of Torts, § 757 comment b (1939).

5. See, e.g., Milgrim, Roger M. Milgrim on Trade Secrets, § 1.08[2] (1995).

6. 37 C.F.R. Ch. II, § 202.20(c)(2)(vii).

7. See, e.g., Pallasch, Abdon M., "Company Policies to Monitor E-Mail Licking Edge of Electronic Envelope," Chicago Lawyer, Law Bulletin Publishing Co. at 4 (August 1995).

8. Uniform Trade Secrets Act § 1(2).

9. For a more in depth discussion of reverse engineering and intellectual property law, see The Committee on Computer Law, "Reverse Engineering and Intellectual Property Law," 44 Rec. of the Ass'n of the Bar of the City of N.Y. 132 (1989).

10. See Abbott; Beckett; and Laine, George, "Niwot Raided by U.S. Marshalls." The Denver Post, The Denver Post Corporation, Sect. A at A-01 (August 23, 1995).

Chapter 7

ASSIGNMENT AND LICENSING·

Introduction

Assignments and licenses are the key instruments for conducting business in connection with intellectual property rights, and, therefore, play a part in the Internet in a variety of contexts. Consider the following hypothetical circumstances:

(1) While "listening" in on your favorite software developers forum, you become aware of a new, little–known, but easy–to–use computer program for preparing tax returns; you decide to look into distributing the program on–line, perhaps initially to test it before selling it commercially.

(2) You see a photograph of your favorite scenic view from Yosemite National Park in an on–line version of a travel magazine and you want to use that photograph in your home page on the World Wide Web.

(3) You decide to call your new architectural business SKY'S THE LIMIT, but discover, while browsing various newsgroups and home pages, that SKY'S THE LIMIT is the name of an apparently small architectural business in Canada.

(4) You want to give others permission to distribute a digital signature encryption software program you have patented.

(5) You want to give others permission to distribute a digital signature encryption program you have patented and you want to set the price for resale of the program and limit distributors

---

·Chapter written by Celine M. Jimenez, Rothwell, Figg, Ernst & Kurz.

to certain territories, but you are unsure how to structure the deal.

Having read earlier chapters in this book, you are aware that the above scenarios could pose potential problems with respect to copyright, trademark and patent rights (and perhaps other property rights). You decide, therefore, that rather than risk allegations of infringement or other legal pitfalls, you will consider licensing or obtaining the rights to the products, works, names and know–how you want to use.

Many licensing and transfer of ownership issues involved in conducting business on the Internet begin with basic aspects of intellectual property licensing. This chapter focuses on such aspects in order to provide an understanding that will be useful in more specific situations. This chapter also highlights selected issues common to licensing and transfers of ownership (assignments) in the context of computer software, multimedia products and on–line services generally.

It is emphasized that the subject of negotiating and drafting license agreements and assignments, and the various aspects of contract law surrounding the interpretation of such agreements are often complicated and involve detailed areas of the law. Considerations in negotiating and drafting agreements can often be particular to the subject matter of the agreement (whether that subject be music, motion pictures, software, business know–how, multimedia works, etc.) and the nature of the business involved. This chapter does not attempt to discuss in detail the licensing or transfer of any particular type of content or subject matter. Rather, it is intended to highlight some common intellectual property issues which should be considered when negotiating and/or drafting assignments and license agreements in the context of doing business on–line.

Definitional Aspects Of Assignments And Licenses

There are generally two types of agreements or contracts which come into play in the context of ownership and use of intellectual property rights. These two types of contracts are assignments and licenses, and they generally have characteristics which are different from one another. There are, of course, numerous ways to name and structure agreements involving intellectual property. For example, there are "Development Agreements," "Publishing Agreements," "Video Clip Licenses," "Sync Licenses," "Artist Agreements," "Distribution Agreements," etc. However, regardless of the name of the agreement, most, if not, all agreements concerning subject matter protectable by copyright, trademark, patent or trade secret rights contain assignment or licensing provisions which address the ownership and use of the rights at issue.

Assignments are <u>transfers of ownership</u> of the underlying rights, whether those rights are copyright, trademark, patent, or trade secret rights. A basic sample form assignment of rights in a work, including copyrights appears at Appendix 4 and a basic sample form trademark assignment appears at Appendix 5.

An important point to remember about assignments of copyright, trademark and patent rights is that they <u>must</u> be in writing and should specifically mention the particular rights being transferred – for example, "all copyright rights" or "the right to sell the product." In certain instances, a later writing or "memorandum" can serve as a confirmation of an earlier oral agreement to assign rights. However, in order for an assignment to be effective, the assignment must at some point be reduced to writing.

Licenses, on the other hand, permit a third party to use the tangible or intangible property which is the subject of the license under particular conditions and/or for a specific purpose(s), but licenses do not, in and of themselves, involve a transfer of any ownership of rights. A basic form trademark license appears at Appendix 6. Contrary to assignments, licenses can be effected orally or implied from conduct. However, it is, of course, often much more difficult to prove, after–the–fact, the existence of an oral or implied license (much less interpret the provisions of such a license) that is not reduced to writing.

Recordation

Because assignments are transfers of ownership, statutory regulations encourages owners to record assignments of patents, trademarks and copyrights with the PTO and the Copyright Office so that the public is on notice of such transfers.[1] Other documents which affect the title to patents, trademarks and copyrights, such as corporate name changes and merger documents, are also often recorded in the respective Offices.

Recordation of an assignment is generally accomplished (at the PTO or Copyright Office) by forwarding a copy of the signed document to the appropriate Office along with the required fee and a cover sheet which contains identifying information and which requests recordation. To be effectively recorded, an assignment should properly identify the patent, trademark or copyright being transferred by listing any relevant titles, registration or application numbers, filing or issue dates, and the inventor or registrant's name. The parties to the assignment should also be clearly identified in the document. In short, it should be readily apparent who is transferring what property to whom and when. Once the Office receives the document to be recorded, it numbers the document and keeps it in the Office's file records pertaining to the particular registrations or applications identified.

In certain instances, the recipient's failure to record an assignment of patent, trademark and copyright properties can essentially nullify the assignment. Take the following example:

> Tom, an owner of trademark rights in a mark for computer software, assigns the rights in the mark to software developer Dewey. Dewey does not record the assignment. Four months later Tom (for some unknown reason) sells the same trademark rights to software developer Joe, who buys the rights without knowledge of the prior assignment to Dewey. Dewey, attempting to enforce his assignment and claim ownership of the trademark rights, notifies Joe that he believes he is the rightful owner of the trademark rights. However, Dewey will likely be unsuccessful in enforcing his previously acquired ownership rights against Joe because Dewey did not record his assignment. That is, Dewey's assignment is void with respect to Joe and, as between the two, Joe would be considered the owner of the trademark rights.[2]

With respect to licenses, except for computer shareware (discussed below), licenses are often not recorded in the PTO or the Copyright Office (and are not required to be). However, the copyright statute specifically provides that <u>any</u> document relating to a copyright may be recorded with the Copyright Office. Such recordation serves as notice to the public of the facts contained in the recorded document (so long as the document identifies the subject copyright registration and registration was in fact made).[3]

Licensing Of Copyrights

Once you have prudently (and appropriately) decided that rather than simply copying your favorite photograph or computer program and using it as you choose, you want to consider a license for the right to use the work or maybe even acquire ownership of all rights in the work, one of the first questions that should be asked is what types of rights will be involved in such a license or assignment. In this section, we consider the various issues involved in the transfer and licensing of copyright rights.

Are Copyright Rights Involved?

In determining whether copyright rights are involved in a contemplated agreement, one simply asks at the outset, is the subject matter of the agreement protectable by copyright. As discussed in an earlier chapter, copyright protection is available to original works of authorship which are "fixed" in some "tangible medium," and that works such as textbooks, photographs, drawings, motion pictures, other audiovisual works such as computer games, and computer software are often protectable by copyright. Accordingly, when considering assignments or licenses of such works, the assignments or licenses almost always concern the transfer or use of copyright rights.

Of course, subject matter which is protectable by copyright may also involve material or information which is protectable by patent and/or trademark rights. Although this chapter discusses transfer and licensing of copyright, trademark and patent rights under separate headings, this is for clarity, as it is quite common that agreements combine various aspects of copyright, trademark and patent principles, see, e.g., the form assignment at Appendix 4.

Identifying The Rights-Holders

The next consideration with respect to the assignment or licensing of copyright rights concerns how many and what types of copyright rights are involved in the transfer or license of the work and who owns them. For example, are all of the copyright rights in a work owned by a single author? Were any portions of the work commissioned or otherwise created by various authors? Questions such as these highlight one of the most important and difficult areas in copyright assignments and licenses, namely:

(1) identifying all of the rights–holders (that is, authors of copyrightable subject matter or their assignees) who may have a claim to the work being licensed or assigned; and

(2) acquiring the necessary rights from those individuals or entities.

Accomplishing these tasks is critical to ensure that all necessary rights are acquired or licensed for use.

As is easily seen, failing to acquire or obtain permission to use all of the desired rights in a work (e.g., because one fails to obtain transfers or licenses from all rights–holders) can be a real obstacle to doing business with respect to that work. For example, an assignment of copyright rights from an author of a computer program to a publisher to enable the publisher to distribute and sell the program, may not fully authorize the publisher to conduct this business if there is a another distinct author who owns rights in the program by virtue of his or her design of key screen displays. In the context of a license, these authors might either have agreements which limit each others' rights to license a work, or the work might not qualify as a work of joint authorship thereby limiting the right of each author to exploit the other's contribution to the work. Such circumstances can seriously hamper a potential licensee's ability to use the work in the manner desired if the authorization of all rights–holders is not obtained.

In short, when considering obtaining an assignment or entering into a license regarding copyrightable subject matter, one should ensure that the purported grantor of rights is the owner of <u>all</u> copyright rights in the subject matter to be acquired or licensed, and if they are not, that all rights–holders are located and the necessary rights acquired. This task, however, can be difficult for a number of reasons.

As stated in the earlier chapter on copyright law, a copyright comprises five separate rights: the right to reproduce, to distribute, to create works derived from the original (called derivative works), to display and to perform. Also, legislation has been proposed to add a performance right in the digital transmission of musical recordings and there has also been consideration of a separate "digital right" which conceivably would consist of rights in the digital image of a work separate and apart from other embodiments of the work. Each of these separate rights could be owned by different individuals or entities. For example, a composer might retain his right to create derivative works, but transfer his right to distribute recordings of his music to a publisher. Accordingly, more than one rights–holder can be involved even with respect to a single copyright.

Also, a single work can contain multiple copyright rights. For example, a book that includes illustrations by one author, photographs of another and text written by two other authors, or a motion picture which includes music, an underlying story, cinematography and other aspects of production all from different creators, in and of themselves, could contain a number of different copyrights owned by different individuals or companies.

As is discussed later in this chapter, this issue of identifying rights–holders and acquiring the necessary rights from them is perhaps made most complex with multimedia works. These works often include combinations of graphics, text, music, software, film or video and other content, thereby bringing even more creators and rights–holders into the picture.

The above scenario no doubt seems complicated; however, one can come away from this with an understanding which can help to avoid pitfalls with respect to unidentified rights–holders in assignment or licensing situations. Namely, one should be aware of the fact that individuals and companies seeking to license or transfer ownership of works sometimes do not consider the fact (or are not aware) that there may be other entities involved who own rights in the works. It is therefore often prudent to inquire, even in the context of apparently simple works, whether there are any others, not initially disclosed, that contributed to the creation of the work, such as illustrators, individuals who wrote any portions of text, translators, editors, etc.

Also, many agreements (for example, software agreements), commonly include a warranty provision in which the entity transferring rights ("transferor") warrants that it owns all rights in the subject matter being transferred. Such a warranty places contractual responsibility on the transferor to ensure it owns or will otherwise acquire the necessary rights prior to effecting transfer.

This situation of potentially "hidden" co–authors very often arises where an individual has commissioned another (and paid them) to create a work, such as the design of a corporate logo, a book cover or other illustrations, or a computer program (or portions thereof). In such circumstances, it is the author (creator) of the work who is initially considered to be the owner of the copyright in the work, regardless of whether another paid him or her to create the work or came up with the idea for the work. The only exceptions to this rule are when the work was created in the context of a "work made for hire" relationship (in which case the employer or contractor owns the work), or when there is an express <u>written</u> assignment of the copyright rights in the work.

As discussed in the earlier chapter on copyright law, a "work made for hire" only arises in the context of either an employer/employee relationship or, for particular types of works, where there is an independent contractor relationship <u>and</u> a <u>written</u> agreement that the work is a work made for hire. However, the concept of a work made for hire, especially in the context of an independent contractor relationship, is generally <u>not</u> broadly applied. For example, recent cases have held that a written agreement executed after the creation of the work has begun cannot create a work made for hire relationship. Accordingly, a common means of ensuring that a contractor obtains ownership of all copyright rights in a work created for them is for the contractor and author of the work to enter into an express written assignment of the copyright rights, in addition to an agreement that the work to being created will be a work made for hire. A sample clause to effect this appears at Appendix 7.

In sum, one must take care in assignment and licensing situations to assure that the grantor of copyright rights in a work is the <u>owner</u> of such rights and not simply one who commissioned a designer or developer to create the work for them (and who may believe they own copyright rights in the work, but, in actuality, do not).

Common Provisions In Licenses Involving Copyrights

Although there are countless strategies for structuring copyright licenses depending, among other things, on the subject matter of the license and the purpose of the license, this section provides a short list, which is by no means exhaustive, of issues commonly addressed in licenses involving copyrights.

(1) The license should adequately identify the work or works which are the subject of the license. This can be done by attaching, as appendices to the license, copies of the subject works or other identifying material (such information as titles of works, authors and any applicable copyright registration numbers should be included).

(2)   If not all copyright rights contained in a work are the subject of the license, the license should specify which of the copyright rights (e.g., only the reproduction or distribution rights) are involved.

(3)   The specific use of the work permitted or the purposes for which the work can be used should be specified.

(4)   The license should indicate whether any modifications to the work are permitted and, if so, who owns the rights, including the copyright rights, in the modified versions (called "derivative works" in copyright parlance). This issue is particularly applicable and important in software licenses.

(5)   If a license pertains to distribution or reproduction of a work, the particular medium (or media) in which the work can be reproduced should be specified; and similarly, it should be specifically stated in the license whether the license applies to technologies not yet known or only those known at the time of the license.

(6)   For licenses (and assignments) involving works of art such as pictures, film, sculpture, etc., consideration should be given as to whether a waiver of the artist's so-called "moral rights" is desirable or necessary. "Moral rights" refer, among other things, to the rights of an artist not to have his or her work changed in such a fashion so as to destroy its original artistic expression or integrity. For example, it has been urged that colorization of old films is a violation of the author's moral rights. It should be recognized that these rights are not easily waived absent an express written agreement to that effect, and in a number of foreign countries, moral rights <u>cannot</u> be waived even by written agreement.

Copyright licenses also often contain provisions regarding any term or time period for the license; whether the license is exclusive or non–exclusive; the details for termination of the license agreement (e.g., when and whether material disclosed or provided under the license is to be returned); who has rights or obligations to sue for infringement; escrow of the subject matter of the license; any applicable confidentiality precautions; and the particular language for or instructions for use of appropriate copyright notices for the work(s) involved.

Shareware

"Shareware" is a term used by those in the computer software field to refer to software which is permitted to be disseminated and typically used under fewer restrictions than commonly associated with commercial software. The conditions of use of shareware are often spelled out in a simple agreement or license between the author and user. Shareware often arises in the context of distribution of software for testing, where individuals desiring to use the software notify the author and pay a minimal licensing fee.

A related term used in the context of computer software is "freeware" which generally refers to software that is permitted to be used without any payment from the user (although some restrictions on use, such as restrictions against modification, may be imposed). Although both shareware and freeware are generally much more freely distributed and available for use than typical commercial software, the authors of shareware and freeware retain their copyrights (and other intellectual property rights in the software). This is not true of software in the public domain which is freely available to be disseminated and used without restriction or payment.

As indicated in the earlier chapter on copyrights, given that authors of shareware and freeware generally retain their intellectual property rights in the software, one who incorporates shareware or freeware into a program or modifies shareware or freeware owned by another without authorization may be subject to allegations of infringement. With respect to public domain software, one who modifies or incorporates such software into a new program does not gain copyright ownership of the public domain software, but does own rights in the modifications or additions.

A significant amount of software which can be obtained via the Internet ("FTP'ed") is shareware, freeware and public domain software. For example, older and/or not-full-featured versions of applications software, computer operating systems (e.g. Macintosh Systems 6.X), games, and much of the software enabling use of the Internet, such as NetScape and Mosaic, have been available as shareware, freeware and/or public domain software on the Internet.

There is fairly recent legislation and much discussion regarding the concept and treatment of shareware under the copyright laws (there has been less specific discussion of the treatment of freeware). In fact, the copyright statute now explicitly provides for the recordation of documents, such as licensing agreements, pertaining to the use of shareware, with the Copyright Office.[4] The Copyright Office maintains the shareware-related documents in its records and publishes them to provide notice to users. At present, the Copyright Office undertakes no inquiry to determine whether documents received regarding shareware do, in fact, meet any particular definition of shareware.

The Copyright Office policy toward shareware is intended to encourage the distribution of software with fewer restrictions as software developers will be able to put users on notice of their copyright rights by filing documents pertaining to the shareware with the Copyright Office.

Licensing Of Multimedia Works

"Multimedia" is a term used to refer to the multitude of literary, audiovisual, musical, graphical and computer software content contained in such works as CD–ROM computer games and digital interactive products. Many multimedia works are contained on CD–ROM. However, multimedia works will increasingly be transmitted over on–line services which operate on a subscription basis.

The licensing of multimedia works is rooted in basic tenets and guidelines of copyright (and other intellectual property law) and licensing principles. However, multimedia works put a new twist on and complicate the application of certain of these guidelines and principles. The application of legal principles in licensing and intellectual property is now required to look to the future to address issues raised by the new media formats and technologies that are developing in this area.

One of the more complicated and time–consuming areas of licensing multimedia works concerns the sheer number of property rights that are conceivably embodied in such works. Multimedia works can involve not only federal intellectual property rights of copyright, trademark and patent, but also can involve such rights as rights of publicity, character rights and rights of privacy. Consequently there can be an extraordinary number of rights–holders involved in a transaction and possibly assignments and licenses to be obtained from such rights–holders.

Consider the following example. A hypothetical multimedia work includes a music track, instructional text, direct quotes from a fiction novel, a video clip, photographs, the appearance of a well–known actor (in the video clip), the trademarks of a large company and proprietary computer software. If one looks only at the musical aspect of the work, the following questions, among others, could be asked.

(1) Have all the copyright owner(s) in the work been identified and have the rights from these owner(s) been obtained? Copyright owners could include the composer, the musicians, the singer and the music publisher.

(2) If the music consists of a sound recording, have the appropriate licenses been obtained to permit use of the recording (e.g., a master recording license, a mechanical license, a sync license), and has consent been obtained from the musicians and singers?

(3) Are there any guild or union agreements that might affect use of the work?

(4) Are there any moral rights of the authors that might interfere with modifications or adaptations of the work?

The same types of questions, and others, could be asked with regard to the literary and audiovisual material mentioned above. The above example also involves clearance of trademark rights, rights of publicity (for the appearance of the actor), and rights embodied in the software (which could be patented). As can be seen, a significant amount of time, effort and resources is often required to clear the way for a publisher's use of a multimedia work. Accordingly, the cost of clearing the rights in a multimedia work is often a primary consideration in the pricing of a multimedia development or distribution deal.

The increase in the transmission of multimedia works (and other content) over on-line services also raises new issues as to how rights-holders, especially publishers, can track the various reproductions and distributions of their works and how they can collect royalties (often on behalf of authors) for such reproductions and distributions. This particular issue is the subject of current lobbying and legislative efforts in connection with on–line services.[5]

Further, in the age of digital transmissions and multimedia, the issue of an artist's moral rights has become increasingly important as works reproduced digitally can often be easily manipulated. In fact, for interactive entertainment products, the very intent of such products may be to modify aspects of the content. However, many authors or other rights–owners, for example, those owning rights to characters (the depictions of which are often protected by copyright), are adamantly opposed to even the slightest changes to their works.

Lastly, given that the Internet is international (and many CD–ROM products are sold internationally), multimedia licensing frequently involves issues of international law. International copyright laws can differ from U.S. copyright law (e.g., there may be more copyright rights–holders involved due to inapplicability of work made for hire principles). Also, as mentioned previously, in a number of foreign countries, authors cannot waive their moral rights or rights of integrity. Accordingly, one should be aware of and consider the laws of applicable foreign countries when entering into licenses which include international works or which concern works to be sold internationally.

Shrinkwrap-Type Licensing

A "shrinkwrap" license is a term common in the software field used to refer to the type of form license that often appears inside or on product packaging. Such a license agreement is supposedly "accepted" by one who has already purchased a copy of the product, not by a signature, but upon the purchaser's opening of the package (or by loading the product onto a computer or proceeding to run a program). In the context of on–line services and the Internet, an analogous situation might arise where acceptance of a license to use particular software is premised on the downloading or running of the software or "clicking" on a particular button after having paid, for example, a subscriber's fee.

Software developers use shrinkwrap licenses, as opposed to outright sales of products, for a variety of reasons. One reason may be to attempt to avoid the "first sale" doctrine of copyright law, where once a copy of a work is sold, the owner of the copy may be free to resell that copy. Another reason is to attempt to avoid liability by including warranty and liability disclaimers in the license.

A number of cases have seriously questioned whether shrinkwrap-type licenses are enforceable contracts. Cases in the late 1980's found such licenses to be unenforceable as "contracts of adhesion" (form contracts often prepared by a seller/manufacturer where the purchaser was said to have no real choice but to sign the contract in order to make the purchase).[6] More recent cases, namely, Step–Saver and Arizona Retail Systems, analyze shrinkwrap licenses under the rubric of the Uniform Commercial Code (UCC).[7]

In both the Step–Saver and Arizona Retail System cases, the courts found the shrinkwrap licenses to be ineffective. This was essentially because the shrinkwrap license was considered to be a modification to the initial purchase contract and the purchaser had not specifically assented to the modification. However, neither court found shrinkwrap licenses to be per se unenforceable. Accordingly, commentators have suggested that shrinkwrap licenses might be effective in situations where a customer is specifically advised prior to purchase that the product is subject to a license which accompanies the purchase, where the licensing terms can be viewed prior to purchase, and where the seller expressly states that it will not license the product unless the purchaser/licensee agrees to the license.[8]

Some of the same principles would conceivably, apply to the execution or acceptance of unsigned shrinkwrap–type license agreements on–line. For example, clicking on a button to indicate acceptance of a "license" to download an interactive game, where the licensing terms become apparent only after the downloading occurred, may not be enforceable. However, such a license might be enforceable where the terms of the license were made available prior to downloading and the software "vendor" clearly expressed its intention not to authorize use of software unless the license was read and agreed to.

Despite questions as to the enforceability of shrinkwrap licenses, the licenses are quite common and are now being used not only, for example, on packaging to prevent distribution of single copies of software to other users, but also to provide for use of software on a network where the purchaser/licensee pays a license fee for each network user. Shrinkwrap type licenses designed to contend with use of software on a network can include clauses that provide, for example, that after set–up, the program cannot be copied to a hard drive or other permanent storage device, and if the program is used in connection with a network, that the program be installed on a network server in such a way that the total number of users can be monitored in order to pay the appropriate license fee.

In sum, it seems clear that shrinkwrap licenses are here to stay despite questions as to their effectiveness.

Licensing Of Trademarks

In the hypothetical example at the beginning of this chapter, an Internet user is in the process of choosing a slogan or name for its business only to learn that the favored slogan or name is apparently being used by another in connection with a very similar business. Not willing to risk charges of infringement, the user considers buying (which can be accomplished with an assignment) or licensing the potentially conflicting slogan and/or name, and approaches the owner of the subject mark with a proposal. Both the owner of the mark and the potential purchaser/licensee have a number of issues to consider in their possible transfer of ownership or licensing arrangement for the trademark property (or properties) at issue.

Common Provisions In Trademark Licenses

Certain of the considerations discussed above in connection with drafting copyright assignments and licenses are also applicable in drafting trademark assignments and licenses. For example, the subject matter of a trademark assignment or license should be precisely identified by listing the marks at issue (including any registration or application numbers, and issue or filing dates) along with the products or services in connection which with the marks are used. However, trademark assignments and licenses differ from those involving other types of intellectual property because trademarks are inextricably linked to the goods or services with which they are used and the goodwill that comes from such use (i.e., the association of the product with the source of the product).

Trademarks cannot be transferred or assigned without also transferring the goodwill of the business with which the mark is used or the goodwill of the business connected with the use of and symbolized by the mark.[9] Assignments which do not include transfer of the goodwill associated with the mark are invalid and could lead to loss of trademark rights. Accordingly, trademark assignments must include a provision which specifically provides for this transfer of the goodwill of the business associated with the mark.

Similarly, trademarks cannot be licensed separately from the goods or services on which they are used. Since one of the key functions of a trademark is to assure consistent quality vis–à–vis the owner of the mark, trademark licenses should include a specific provision that the trademark <u>owner</u> will maintain control over the nature and quality of the goods or services being provided under the licensed mark (even if those goods and services are made or provided by the licensee). To this end, trademark licenses generally include provisions whereby the licensee will either submit samples of the goods to be sold under the mark to the trademark owner for inspection, or will permit the trademark owner to inspect the goods or the services being provided under the mark at a specified time (or upon the trademark owner's request). It is emphasized that trademark licenses which appear to lack a "quality control" provision (often called "naked" licenses) can result in the owner's loss of trademark rights.

Also, trademark licenses often contain clauses which provide that the goodwill accrued by the licensee's use of the trademark inures to the benefit of the trademark <u>owner</u> and that the licensee has no rights in the mark by virtue of its use (aside from the right to use granted by the license).

Further, trademark licenses of registered marks or pending applications may provide that either the licensee or the trademark owner is responsible for prosecuting the marks in the PTO by filing any necessary documents to keep the registrations alive. However, documents filed in the PTO with respect to a particular registration or application almost always need to be signed by the <u>owner</u> of the mark and not the licensee. Therefore, while trademark licenses may require that the licensee agree to cooperate with the trademark owner/licensor with respect to required PTO filings, it is ultimately the owner who should be responsible for maintaining the registrations at the PTO.

Trademark licenses also usually contain provisions describing how the mark will be used, i.e., the format of the mark as it is used on the goods or in connection with the services, for example, on advertising or promotional material. This can be accomplished by attaching a drawing of the mark or product packaging that shows how the mark should appear in connection with the goods or services, and is considered part of the requisite control.

However, a provision describing or providing for control over how the mark is used in advertising or promotions is <u>not</u> a substitute for a specific provision requiring that the trademark owner control the nature and quality of the goods or services provided under the mark. It is this latter "quality control" provision with respect to the goods/services which is required in trademark licenses to avoid abandonment of trademark rights. See the sample trademark license appearing at Appendix 6.

Licensing Of Patents

More so than other intellectual property licenses, patent licenses frequently concern technically or technologically complex products and processes and are, therefore, frequently more complicated and lengthy than licenses involving copyrights and trademarks.

Patent licenses generally include (as do certain more complicated copyright–based licenses involving multimedia works and computer software) detailed provisions that address, merely by way of example, such matters as:

(1) the description of the subject matter to be licensed;

(2) what particular patent rights or portions of patent rights are to be licensed;

(3) territorial use or customer restrictions on distribution of licensed products or processes;

(4)   details of royalty calculations, payment schedules, and delivery schedules;

(5)   the duration of the license agreement;

(6)   accounting methods and taxes;

(7)   what constitutes breach, grounds for termination and choice of law;

(8)   responsibilities for enforcing the patent rights, including who will pay for litigation expenses;

(9)   international sales and manufacturing issues; and

(10) indemnities and warranties.

Patent licenses sometimes include or are accompanied by licenses to use related proprietary technical or business know–how and information (trade secret licenses) which are not necessarily the subject of patent protection.

Further details of negotiating and drafting patent licenses are not addressed in this overview.[10]   Rather, what is discussed here is a patent licensing issue which has been the subject of recent concern in connection with on–line services and software licensing, namely, the issue of antitrust problems in patent licensing (and intellectual property licensing generally).

The acquisition of patent rights frequently presents antitrust concerns more often than the acquisition of other types of intellectual property rights. This seems to be primarily because the owner of a patent has the right to exclude others from making, using or selling the patented subject matter for a significant period of time, e.g., seventeen (17) years from the date of issue or twenty (20) years from the date of filing (sometimes incorrectly viewed as a seventeen or twenty year "monopoly"). Also, in all practicality, the subject matter of patents may represent significant technological developments (such as pharmaceuticals and sophisticated electronics), the availability of which can significantly affect the welfare of the public. In short, patent rights can be very powerful and some fear they can be misused.

There is, therefore, a potential conflict between, on the one hand, wanting to reward inventors for their efforts, and, on the other hand, making important innovations available to the public. Accordingly, although the patent laws are intended to promote innovation by granting inventors the right to exclude others from making, using and selling the patented subject matter for a limited time period, concerns over anti-competitive effects can arise when a large, dominant company begins to accumulate patent rights or when patentees attempt to extend the scope of their patent rights beyond the patented subject matter or to otherwise extend the term or scope of their patent(s). The antitrust laws can thus be viewed as a check on the powerful incentives of the patent system.

The following patent licensing practices which have raised antitrust issues:

(1) Tying the sale of unpatented products to the sale of patented products (often simply referred to as "tying");

(2) Resale price restrictions;

(3) Cross–licensing arrangements, patent pools or grant–backs between competitors;

(4) Territorial, field of use, and customer restrictions on resale or distribution;

(5)   Mandatory package licensing;

(6)   Unreasonable royalty payments not related to the licensee's sales of products covered by the patent; and

(7)   Restrictions on developing or dealing in competing goods.

Tying arrangements (defined as agreements to sell one product, but only on the condition that the buyer also purchase a different product), and price restrictions on the resale of products in particular have often raised serious questions of antitrust violations.

On the other hand, territorial restrictions in patent licenses, in and of themselves, have often been found to be lawful, as have field of use restrictions limiting a licensee's use of the patented subject matter to a specific field or application, and customer restrictions which, for example, limit a licensee's sale of patented subject matter to particular customers.

Cross–licensing agreements and patent pooling generally refer to situations where competitors cross–license to one another or otherwise pool together their significant patents. Such arrangements have been found to violate antitrust laws where they have acted to create a monopoly for the two entities. In fact, a recent antitrust action was filed by Distrionics Texas, Inc. and others against Sony Corp., Philips Electronics and Pioneer Electronics. Distrionics alleged that defendants violated antitrust laws where Sony and Philips cross–licensed their patents applicable to compact discs and agreed not to compete with one another in areas related to the design of formats for compact discs and disc players, and Pioneer allegedly attempted to extract unreasonable royalties from licensees of the cross–licensed patents.[11]

Generally, the analysis of licensing practices under antitrust principles has followed what is known as the "rule of reason" approach which involves such inquiries as whether and where competition is restricted, what types of vertical or horizontal restraints are involved, and whether there are any pro–competitive effects of the practice at issue. See, e.g., the Justice Department 1988 Antitrust Enforcement Guidelines for International Operations (also applicable to domestic transactions).[12]

The Justice Department and Federal Trade Commission have recently issued antitrust guidelines for the licensing of intellectual property which particularly address issues of patent licensing.[13] Although these guidelines broadly state that intellectual property licenses should be no more suspect than other types of transactions when it comes to antitrust concerns, it is generally accepted that the current administration has been more active than administrations in recent years in scrutinizing possible anti–competitive effects of technology licensing practices.

An example of the application of the current administration's antitrust policies is a frequently reported case involving Microsoft. One licensing practice scrutinized by the government in that case was Microsoft's use of licenses which require a royalty payment for each computer sold by the licensee regardless of whether the computer uses the Microsoft DOS operating system. Microsoft and the government reached a settlement which precluded Microsoft from certain of its licensing practices, such as entering into licenses which limited the licensee's ability to use other operating systems. However, a district court initially refused to accept the settlement, essentially finding that the settlement was not in the public interest (presumably because it was too lenient on Microsoft). Both Microsoft and the government appealed the district court's ruling. The Court of Appeals reversed and sent the case back to district court which approved the settlement.[14]

In all practicality, significant antitrust concerns usually arise in the context of the licensing practices of large, dominant companies. However, a basic understanding of some of the problems in this area can aid all in the drafting of enforceable patent licenses and other intellectual property licenses.

Digital Signatures

The feasibility and advisability of conducting business over the Internet will depend on available methods for conducting secure communications. Electronic funds transfers, in–home shopping or banking, accessing private databases, electronic contracts and tax returns, and other transmissions of proprietary and private information are examples of on–line business transactions that require the secure transmission of data and information.

There are various technological means which have been and are being developed to protect data and information transmitted on the Internet. One concept for securing communications involves the use of "digital signatures." Digital signatures are digital codes used to authenticate the source and content of material and information transmitted electronically. One analogy is to that of a digital PIN number.

Most digital signature techniques use "public–key" encryption. In this type of encryption, a sender uses a secret "key" to generate a signature line for the specific material to be transmitted. The signature can be verified on the receiving end by using the sender's public "key." Essentially "envelopes" are created that can only be opened by the addressee; the contents of the envelope include the digital signature to verify their authenticity. A digital signature algorithm (DSA) has been developed to serve as the standard for verifying a sender's identity and the authenticity of the message. Also, states are beginning to enact legislation which specifically authorizes the use of digital signatures in electronic communication.[15]

Additionally, encryption methods for securing transmissions from central network servers have been and are being developed. A number of companies are developing data encryption programs for the transmission of sensitive information, such as credit card information, over the Internet. One contemplated system for securing credit card purchases on the Internet would allow purchasers to encrypt credit card information, send it to a server at the "home" of the designer of the encryption program and then on to another network to process credit approval. Another encryption system, called the Clipper Chip, has been developed for encoding telephone calls and e–mail to protect against tapping by everyone but the government.[16]

In sum, the field of cryptography and encryption is one of the more technologically sophisticated areas of the Internet. Such systems are clearly essential to conducting any significant business on–line, and are part of the emerging technologies brought on by the Internet which have and will raise new questions as to how to apply existing laws.

Endnotes

1. <u>See</u> 35 U.S.C. § 261; 15 U.S.C. §1060; and 17 U.S.C. § 205.

2. 15 U.S.C. § 1060 provides that an assignment of registered trademarks is not effective against a subsequent bona–fide purchaser who purchases the mark without notice of a prior assignment unless the prior assignment is recorded in the PTO within three months after the date of the assignment or prior to the subsequent purchase. The patent and copyright statutes contain analogous provisions, 35 U.S.C. § 261 and 17 U.S.C. § 205, respectively.

3. <u>See</u> 17 U.S.C. § 205(c).

4. <u>See</u> Judicial Improvements Act of 1990 Title VIII (Computer Software Rental Act) Sec. 805; Copyright Office Shareware Regulations, §201.26.

5. A Commerce Dept. white paper is expected to be released on this issue on September 5, 1995.

6. <u>See, e.g.</u>, <u>Vault Corp. v. Quaid Software, Ltd.</u>, 655 F. Supp. 750 (E.D. La. 1987), <u>aff'd.</u>, 847 F.2d 255 (5th Cir. 1988).

7. <u>See</u> <u>Step–Saver Data Systems, Inc. v. Wyse Technology</u>, 939 F.2d 91 (3d. Cir. 1991); <u>Arizona Retail Systems, Inc. v. The Software Link, Inc.</u>, 831 F. Supp. 759 (D. Ariz. 1993).

8. <u>See, e.g.</u>, Hayes, David L. "Shrinkwrap License Agreements: New Light On A Vexing Problem," 9 <u>The Computer Lawyer</u>, No. 9, Sept., 1992.

9. 15 U.S.C. § 1060.

10. A legal reference which discusses details of patent licensing is Einhorn, <u>Patent Licensing Transactions</u>, Mathew Bender & Co., Inc. (1995).

11. <u>See</u> <u>Distrionics Texas, Inc. et al. v. Sony Corp., et al</u>, 4–95CV–300Y (N.D. Texas. May 1, 1995).

12.   See Einhorn, § 7.02[1] at 7–13 – 7–14.

13.   The April 6, 1995 version of these guidelines is located, for example, in "Antitrust Guidelines for the Licensing of Intellectual Property," FTC Today, Washington Regulatory Reporting, April 7, 1995.

14.   See United States of America v. Microsoft, 56 F.3d 1448 (D.C. Cir. 1995).

15.   The first state to approve digital signature legislation is Utah. See Utah Code §§ 46–3–101 through 504.

16.   Two articles which discuss issues such as privacy and free speech in the context of encryption/cryptography are: Marks, Richard D., "Security, Privacy and Free Expression in the New World of Broadband Networks," 32 Hous. L. Rev. 501, 513 n. 93 (Spring, 1995); see also Froomkin, A. Michael, "The Metaphor Is the Key: Cryptography, the Clipper Chip, and the Constitution," 143 U. Pa. L. Rev. 709 (January, 1995).

Chapter 8

DEFAMATION[*]

Scenario:

Computer, Inc. owns an on–line service, is involved directly or indirectly with an electronic bulletin board, or operates a World Wide Web site. One day, a subscriber to the bulletin board (or an Internet user who gains access to the Web site) posts a message on the bulletin board accusing ACME Widget Corp. of having dumped toxic wastes into the source of drinking water of an elementary school, and thereby, causing the death of half of the kindergarten class.

Does Computer, Inc. have any obligation to screen this message for truthfulness before it is posted? If the ACME Widget Corp. subsequently complains to Computer, Inc. that the message is untrue, is it required to delete the message? Is it required to investigate the facts and, if appropriate, print a correction? If the ACME Widget Corp. sues Computer, Inc. for defamation, can Computer, Inc. be held liable?

What if the ACME Widget Corp., which has its principal place of business in Tupelo, Mississippi sues Computer, Inc. and the subscriber in a Mississippi state court, even though Computer, Inc. has no property or employees in Mississippi, has no business in Mississippi, and derives only very limited revenue from the State of Mississippi and the subscriber has always lived and worked in New York? What if subscriber's message is downloaded by a second subscriber in Singapore, and then ACME Widget Corp. sues in Singapore, a jurisdiction in which a defamation plaintiff has many procedural and substantive advantages not available to such plaintiffs in the United States?

---

[*]Chapter written by Steven Lieberman, Rothwell, Figg, Ernst & Kurz.

What if the statute of limitation for a libel action has expired and then a second subscriber reads the initial message and re–posts it on another bulletin board?

The scenarios described above are not farfetched. In recent years, both the authors of on–line messages and the owners or operators of on–line services (and related companies) have been sued for defamation arising from on–line messages. Lawsuits involving Internet communications have been brought in jurisdictions having virtually no connection to the entities posting the messages, and have been adjudicated under laws very different from those that apply in the jurisdiction where the posters reside.

This chapter outlines some of the more significant legal principles that relate to defamation on–line and applies those principles, wherever possible, to factual events that have actually been adjudicated or their closest analogies. This chapter also provides some practical advice on how to minimize or limit potential liability for defamatory statements. Any advice contained in this chapter must be viewed through the cautionary prism that while the law of defamation is extremely well–developed (having been formed in thousands of cases over many centuries), the application of that law to on–line and Internet communications is still rather sparse. There have been only a few decisions directly addressing allegedly defamatory statements on–line and those decisions are all from lower courts. New cases involving defamation on–line are being filed on a regular basis and it is likely that as they are decided (and as these cases percolate up through the appeal process), they will provide more concrete guidance.

An Overview Of General Defamation Principles[1]

Defamation consists of two legal wrongs or torts: libel and slander. In general, a claim for libel arises from a written statement; slander arises from an oral statement. On–line publications have been viewed in the defamation context as written communications. Therefore, the tort at issue here is the tort of libel.[2]

A defamatory (or in the case of a written statement, libelous) communication has been defined as one which tends to hold the plaintiff up to hatred, contempt, or ridicule, and to cause him to be shunned or avoided. Defamation is:

> that which tends to injure "reputation" in the popular sense; to diminish the esteem, respect, good will or confidence in which the plaintiff is held, or to excite adverse, derogatory, or unpleasant feelings or opinions against him. It necessarily, however, involves the idea of disgrace. . . .[3]

In order for a libel plaintiff to prevail, the allegedly defamatory statement at issue must be false. In layman's parlance, "truth is an absolute defense," although under current constitutional doctrine, at least in libel suits brought by plaintiffs who are public figures or which concern a subject involving issues of public concern (discussed below), it is the plaintiff's burden to prove that the allegedly defamatory statement is false. (This is not the case in many countries outside the United States — particularly, England — and that fact accounts for many libel suits being brought in those jurisdictions wherever possible.)

For a statement to be actionable, it must be "of or concerning" the plaintiff. That is, would a part of an audience reasonably think that a particular person (or persons) is the subject of the allegedly defamatory statement? In general — and this is an area of the law where there is an enormous amount of complexity — in order to be defamatory, a statement must be one of fact rather than opinion. This is true because as discussed above, only false statements are actionable, and the Supreme Court has held that:

> under the First Amendment, there is no such thing as a false idea. However pernicious an opinion may seem, we depend for its correction not on the conscience of judges and juries, but on the competition of other ideas.[4]

This does not mean, however, that one may cloak one's statements in the mantle of opinion, and thereby avoid liability. It is not sufficient, for example, to say "I think Joe killed Mary." Moreover, under recent Supreme Court precedent,[5] this protection (which is no longer denominated as the "opinion privilege") applies only so long as the statement at issue is not verifiably true or false. For example, "Joe killed Mary" is a statement subject to verification; "the food in this restaurant is terrible," is not.

At common law, defamation was viewed in many jurisdictions as a "strict liability" offense. That is, if you got it wrong and it was defamatory, you lost. It did not matter whether you had been careful or had published inaccurate information through no fault of your own. Under current law, when a libel suit is brought by either a public figure or a public official, in order to prevail, the plaintiff must prove either that the defendant knew that the allegedly defamatory statement was false or had serious doubts as to its truth. "Public figures" are broadly defined as those who "have assumed roles of special prominence in the affairs of society" and have thereby "voluntarily exposed themselves to increased risk of injury from defamatory falsehood."[6] In cases where a libel plaintiff is neither a public official nor a public figure, a lower standard applies; generally (although not always) requiring at least that the person who made the libelous statement was negligent in doing so.

Any living person and most nongovernmental entities (such as corporations, labor unions, etc.) may bring an action for libel. In most states, if a person who was defamed while he was alive dies during the pendency of a lawsuit, the cause of action dies with him.

The general rule is that one who repeats or "republishes" a defamatory statement may be liable in an action for defamation. For example, if "A" were to post a message on a computer bulletin board that "B" had told him that ACME Widget Corporation killed kindergarten students by polluting their drinking water, A is subject to an action for libel, even though he fully and accurately attributed the allegedly defamatory statement to B. (A may have other defenses.) Under the same principle, if "C" reads A's message on a bulletin board and decides to re-post it on another bulletin board or to retransmit it to a particular individual or a group of individuals, C may be liable.

As discussed in considerably more detail below, there is a vigorous and unresolved dispute wending its way through the courts as to whether the owner or operator of an on-line service may be liable under the republication doctrine for allegedly defamatory statements uploaded by subscribers. Traditionally, "distributors" (such as libraries, newsstands, or book stores), and common carriers (such as, telephone and telegraph operators) were not subject to defamation liability absent extraordinary circumstances. On the other hand, "publishers" such as newspapers and publishing houses were responsible under the republication doctrine for the material they printed. There is still an open question as to whether owners and operators of an on-line service will be treated by the courts as publishers, distributors, common carriers, or some hybrid.

Liability Of Owners And Operators Of On-line Services For Statements Uploaded By Subscribers

In recent years, speech on electronic bulletin boards has given rise to a number of defamation suits against the owners and operators of the on–line services, as well as against the authors of the allegedly defamatory material. Such lawsuits raise a variety of novel legal issues concerning the potential liability of owners and operators of on–line services for defamatory statements. These include the issue of whether there is an obligation to police the content of the on–line services for defamatory material, and the consequences of choosing either to police or not to police the services. These issues, and some strategies that on–line services owners and operators may use to protect themselves, are discussed below.

Protecting oneself from on–line liability for allegedly defamatory statements "uploaded"[7] onto those on–line services by subscribers, readers or others is no longer of interest only to owners and operators of multi–million subscriber services such as CompuServe or Prodigy. During the last few years a wide variety of traditional media entities, such as the publishers of newspapers and news magazines, have begun to make news or news–related products available on–line. And, on a number of the electronic systems now being utilized by traditional publishers, users/readers/subscribers can now provide their own input in the form of letters to the editor, comments to publishers, or responses in electronic discussion groups or on–line seminars.

Current Case Law On The Publisher/Distributor/Common Carrier Issue

One of the threshold issues in evaluating potential liability is whether the owner or operator of an on–line service will be considered a "publisher," "distributor," or "common carrier" of the allegedly defamatory material. This distinction is crucial since distributors of written material (such as news vendors, bookstores, and libraries) are generally not liable for allegedly defamatory statements contained in publications they distribute, unless they know or have reason to know of the allegedly defamatory statements.[8] Thus, if the owner or operator of an on–line service can convince a court that it should be considered a "distributor" rather than a "publisher," it has a good chance of prevailing in a lawsuit without ever going to trial by way of a summary judgment motion (a motion which asserts that the matter can be resolved by the court as a matter of law) early on in the case (or perhaps, as in Cubby, before the parties engage in the costly deposition process).

Any entity that is sued for defamation as a result of a message placed on an on–line service by a user or subscriber should consider arguing that it should be judged by an even more lenient standard –– that applicable to a common carrier. There are many useful parallels between the operator of an on–line service on the one hand, and the telephone company or an express mail service on the other. With the right set of facts –– and that point is emphasized –– this argument can be made persuasively. In view of the unformed state of the law, however, an attempt to push this theory on a bad factual record could result in a very dangerous precedent.

There are only two published decisions directly addressing the issue of which standard applies to an on–line service.[9] The first is Judge Leisure's thoughtful opinion in Cubby, Inc. v. CompuServe, Inc.[10] Cubby involved allegedly defamatory statements made available to the subscribers of CompuServe Information Service ("CIS"), an on–line service which its subscribers could access from their own personal computers or terminals. Subscribers to CIS could gain access to more than 150 special interest forums containing different electronic bulletin boards, interactive on–line conferences, and the like. The allegedly defamatory material appeared in an electronic publication available through one of the forums relating to the journalism industry. This journalism forum was operated by Cameron Communications Inc. ("CCI"), which was independent of CompuServe, and had entered into a contract with CompuServe to manage, edit and otherwise control the contents of the journalism forum. The particular publication involved, Rumorville, was published and managed by Don Fitzpatrick Associates ("DFA"), which provided Rumorville to the journalism forum under a contract with CCI. DFA had no contract with CompuServe. The plaintiff sued CompuServe and DFA. It did not sue CCI.

In granting CompuServe's summary judgment motion (DFA did not move for summary judgment), Judge Leisure recognized the complete absence of any law directly on point and drew from analogous areas to determine the applicable legal principles. He reasoned that CompuServe performed precisely the same function as news vendors or libraries, and cited several cases applying New York law on this point. He also looked to the Supreme Court's ruling in Smith v. California,[11] striking down an ordinance that imposed liability on a bookseller for possession of an obscene book regardless of whether the bookseller had knowledge of the book's contents. Invoking both New York law and the First Amendment, Judge Leisure held that CompuServe was entitled to the application "of a lower standard of liability applicable to a public library, bookstore, and newsstand," and that therefore, CompuServe could not be liable unless "it knew or had reason to know of the allegedly defamatory Rumorville statements."[12] After finding that the plaintiff had failed to raise any genuine issue concerning CompuServe's knowledge, Judge Leisure dismissed the libel claim. He also dismissed the plaintiff's related claims for business disparagement and unfair competition on similar grounds.

In a discussion of some significance to managers of on-line sites, Judge Leisure also rejected the plaintiff's argument that CompuServe could be held "vicariously liable," concluding that neither CCI nor DFA "should be considered an agent of CompuServe."[13] Judge Leisure reached this conclusion because CCI, pursuant to the terms of its contract with CompuServe, had agreed to "manage, review, create, delete, edit, and otherwise control the contents" of the journalism forum and thus CompuServe had "delegated control over assembly of the contents" of the journalism forum to CCI.[14] Judge Leisure held that this "level of control is insufficient to rise to the level of an agency relationship."[15] Because the plaintiff did not sue CCI, there was no discussion of its potential liability.

The second decision addressing the issue is <u>Stratton Oakmont, Inc. v. Prodigy Services Co.</u>[16] In <u>Stratton Oakmont</u>, an unidentified individual uploaded certain statements onto the "Money Talk" computer bulletin board. Prodigy was the owner and operator of the computer network on which that bulletin board was located. The statements at issue accused plaintiffs of having committed criminal and fraudulent acts in connection with the initial public offering, referred to the individual plaintiff as a "soon to be proved criminal," and referred to the corporate plaintiff as a "cult of brokers who either lie for a living or get fired." Plaintiffs thereafter filed a libel action against Prodigy.

After a brief period in which the parties exchanged information through the litigation mechanism of discovery, plaintiffs moved for partial summary judgment arguing that: (a) Prodigy was the "publisher" of certain allegedly defamatory statements uploaded by an unknown user onto Prodigy's "Money Talk" bulletin board, and therefore is subject to the same standards of responsibility and liability as a newspaper; and (b) the "board editor" or "board leader" (depending upon which party's definition you choose) of "Money Talk" acted as Prodigy's agent with respect to the statements at issue.

In support of the motion on the publisher issue, plaintiffs offered a wide variety of public statements by Prodigy personnel characterizing Prodigy as a "publisher" and describing Prodigy's role in "editing" and certain types of speech that Prodigy deemed offensive or otherwise inappropriate. Plaintiffs also cited several law review articles which pointed out that by taking on the additional responsibility of editing for content, Prodigy was also inviting additional liability thereby creating a "Prodigy" exception to the holding of the Cubby case. In addition, plaintiffs offered deposition testimony concerning the extent to which Prodigy uses both screening software and live "editors" to block the publication of certain messages.

In opposition, Prodigy did not dispute earlier admissions that the service was a "publisher," but rather, argued that it had changed its editorial control policy since the admissions were made because it is no longer feasible for the service to use human editors to edit for content. On the issue of agency, Prodigy argued that the "board leader" should be treated as an independent contractor and that liability for his acts or omissions should not fall upon the service.

On May 24, 1995, Justice Ain granted the plaintiff's motion for partial summary judgment holding that Prodigy is a publisher of statements uploaded onto the "Money Talk" computer bulletin board for purposes of the libel law. The Court also found that the "Money Talk" board leader had acted as Prodigy's agent for purposes of libel law. Justice Ain reached this conclusion because of his determination that Prodigy had exercised editorial control over the content of the computer bulletin board. Specifically, the Court found: (i) that Prodigy had held itself out to the public and to its members as controlling the contents of its computer bulletin boards; and (ii) that Prodigy had:

implemented this control through its automatic software screening program, and the Guidelines which board leaders are required to enforce. By actively utilizing technology and manpower to delete notes from its computer bulletin board on the basis of offensiveness and "bad taste" . . . Prodigy has uniquely arrogated to itself the role of determining what is proper for its members to post and read on its bulletin boards. Based on the foregoing, this Court is compelled to conclude that for the purposes of plaintiffs' claims in this action, Prodigy is a publisher rather than a distributor.[17]

Following Justice Ain's ruling, Prodigy retained new counsel to represent it in the case.

That counsel has filed a motion for reargument which motion is being supported by amicus briefs from various on–line service entities. Although such motions are rarely successful, Prodigy has assembled some forceful arguments in support of its motion. At the time of this writing, the motion for reargument is still pending. Prodigy has made quite clear that if its motion is denied, it will appeal Justice Ain's summary judgment ruling.

The Cubby and Stratton Oakmont decisions, taken together, are a stern warning to owners and operators of on–line services that the exercise of editorial discretion from material uploaded by subscribers or others carries a significant risk that such entity will be treated as a publisher rather than as a distributor. Practical steps to avoid such a result are discussed below.

Analogous Case Law

While Cubby and Stratton Oakmont are interesting cases, they by no means address all of the publisher/distributor issues of interest to owners and operators of on–line services. Indeed, in many ways, they raise more questions than they answer.

To obtain some of these answers, courts are likely to look to analogous areas of the law. One such related area is defamation suits arising from live republication by a broadcaster of listener comments on call–in radio shows. The central question in these cases (when they involve public figures) is whether a radio station has published listener comments with knowledge of their falsity or awareness of their probable falsity, if it fails to use an electronic delay system to screen callers' statements for allegedly defamatory material, and thereby broadcasts a defamatory statement which the broadcaster knows or believes to be false. The courts have apparently split on this issue: a Louisiana court holding that the broadcaster is liable; the courts of Utah and Wyoming holding that it is not.[18]

A related area involves the potential liability of television network affiliates for allegedly defamatory material prepared elsewhere and then broadcast by the affiliates without any editorial review.[19] In Auvil v. CBS *60 Minutes*,[20] the court granted a motion to dismiss filed on behalf of three Washington State CBS affiliates who had been joined in a defamation suit arising from a *60 Minutes* broadcast concerning the use of Alar in the apple industry. The facts before the district court were that (i) the affiliates had exercised no editorial control over the broadcast, although they had the power to do so under the terms of their contracts with CBS; (ii) the affiliates had in the past occasionally censored programming; and (iii) the affiliates were in possession of the broadcast (and a memorandum setting forth in general terms the subject matter of the broadcast) three hours prior to air time. The court assumed for the purposes of its analysis that the affiliates had "published" the *60 Minutes* program. It then held that under Washington law there is no liability for defamation absent fault. The court concluded that because there was no evidence that the affiliates knew or had reason to know of the allegedly defamatory character of the broadcast, there was no fault and thus no liability. In reaching this conclusion, the Court relied on decisions addressing the liability of other "conduits" of information (including the Cubby case) and touched on both First Amendment and policy concerns. In a particularly well–reasoned passage, the court rejected plaintiffs' argument that the affiliates were at fault because they had the power to censor the broadcast but chose not to do so:

> plaintiffs' construction would force the creation of full time editorial boards at local stations throughout the country which possess sufficient knowledge, legal acumen, and access to experts to continually monitor incoming transmissions and exercise on–the–spot discretionary calls or face $75 million dollars lawsuits at every turn. That is not realistic.[21]

This reasoning would appear to apply with considerable force to the operators of on–line services — although, based on the sparse factual record before it, the Court in Stratton Oakmont specifically distinguished Auvil, holding that Prodigy had "virtually created an editorial staff."

Practical Advice To Owners And Operators Of On-line Services

In the absence of clear guidance from the courts, what steps can traditional media entities take to protect themselves against liability for allegedly defamatory statements uploaded onto an electronic bulletin board or other electronic media?

First, if the on–line service is owned, but not operated by the media entity itself, care should be taken to ensure that the contractual agreement between the media entity and the service operator contains appropriate provisions protecting the media entity. Based on the Cubby decision, it is important that the contract provide that the operator be solely responsible for the content of the publication. You may wish to consider including in the contract a further provision requiring the on–line service operator to review the contents of the bulletin board (or other on–line site) on a regular basis to delete material known or believed by the operator to be false and defamatory. While this is likely to give the traditional media entity additional protection, it is, for obvious reasons, likely to be resisted by on–line service operators. For reasons discussed below, it is also inconsistent with an argument that the on–line service owner or operator should be treated as a distributor or a common carrier.

Indemnification provisions (which should include the obligation to reimburse the costs of litigation) are, of course, always useful. You should also consider whose libel insurance, if any, is applicable, and how indemnification provisions can be used to reduce your insurance costs. If the indemnitor does not have sufficient assets to cover potential claims, consider a contractual provision requiring the indemnitor to obtain and maintain appropriate insurance, naming you as an additional insured.

Second, if the media entity does itself operate the on–line service or Web site, it needs to decide what, if any, content control should be exercised over information uploaded onto it. (This question also applies to the increasingly common scenarios of an entity operating a portion of a commercial on–line service (e.g., "@Times," The New York Times area of America On–line). Stratton–Oakmont is likely to be cited by libel plaintiffs for the proposition that any content control should result in an on–line services owner or operator being treated as a publisher for libel purposes. This is too expansive an interpretation of the case. Moreover, given the law in analogous areas and the nature of the technology, it cannot be correct. It is, therefore, reasonable to predict that as the law develops, new cases will make clear that considerably more than "some" control over content is necessary to convert the owner or operator of an on–line service into a publisher.

This is so because on–line service owners and operators have a wide variety of legitimate — and often compelling — reasons to exercise some content control over their bulletin boards. At the most basic level, for example, an on–line service owner or Web site operator will wish to ensure that an on–line site contains only messages relating to the designated topic. For example, a bulletin board concerning the O.J. Simpson trial should, to be attractive to potential users, not contain messages regarding Newt Gingrich, the war in Bosnia, or pedophilia. The moderator of such a bulletin board will therefore (depending upon how the site operates) either prevent such messages from being posted or remove them shortly after they are posted. Although this sort of "editing" is content–based, it is highly likely that as the case law develops, courts will conclude that such behavior does not transform an owner or operator into a publisher. Such behavior is in no way similar to the type of content control exercised by a newspaper, a television network, or a book publisher. It is far closer to the decision of a library to order for its children's section books by Dr. Seuss, but not books by James Joyce.

Similarly, owners and operators of on–line services will wish moderators to take steps to ensure that conversation on the site flows freely and smoothly. Such control, which may involve deleting or blocking certain messages, is widely viewed as necessary for the commercial success of an on–line site. Operators may also wish, as Prodigy did, to screen for obscenity and certain types of personally harassing messages.

Indeed, there are currently under consideration legislative proposals which would require owners and operators of on–line services to ensure that "obscene" material is not posted in areas where minors will have access to such material. (Some of the legislative proposals also purport to ban "indecent" communications. These proposals, should they be enacted into law, will have series of constitutional infirmities and will likely be challenged.) It may, therefore, be that federal criminal statutes will <u>require</u> owners and operators of on–line services to exercise a certain degree of content control.

The best way to minimize the likelihood of being held a publisher, is to exercise no control of any kind over the content of the site. Since very few commercial entities wish to follow this practice, the question becomes how one can exercise some degree of content control while at the same time minimizing the likelihood of publisher liability. Several suggestions are offered:

1. In the message that appears when a subscriber logs onto a bulletin board or other on–line site, there should be a very clear statement outlining precisely what content control the on–line service exercises and what control it does not exercise. For example, the notice could state that the bulletin board does not permit obscene material, profanity, or certain racial and personal epithets. It could state that control will be exercised in order to keep the flow of on–line service conversation moving. It should also state what control is not being exercised. Specifically, the notice should make clear that there is no substantive review of the posted material for truth or accuracy. The notice should make clear that the owner or operator of the on–line service is not endorsing in any way the accuracy or correctness of any statements made, and that the posting of those statements should not be interpreted as an endorsement of them. Indeed, an owner or operator may wish to require a user to provide a "electronic signature" acknowledging his or her understanding of these points, and agreeing to treat subscriber comments <u>as if they came directly from the subscriber, rather than from the bulletin board</u>. While this approach is by no means bullet–proof, it may provide the best possible factual scenario for a favorable court decision on the publisher/distributor issue.

2. On–line service owners and operators must resist the very strong temptation to vet material for truth. Once the owner or operator engages in such an evaluation process, the genie is out of the bottle. It does not matter how many disclaimers the owner or operator includes, if the owner or operator in fact edits out

allegedly false and defamatory information, it will thereafter be very difficult for that entity to resist being classified as a publisher. This means that even if a subscriber (or other person) complains that a statement is inaccurate, the position taken by the owner or operator should be that "more speech" —- not deletion or correction —- is the remedy. The owner or operator should allow the person allegedly defamed to post a response (if he or she wishes) free of charge. Moreover, the owner or operator should both: (a) electronically link the response to the original message so that the original message cannot be viewed without the response; and (b) repeat the owner/operator's disclaimer. The owner or operator should, however, try to avoid any foray into investigating or determining truth or falsity.

As experienced media lawyers will recognize, this is a strategy that entails considerable legal risk. It is dangerous because in libel cases brought against the owner or operator of an on-line service, the plaintiff will be required to prove some degree of fault (discussed above). Absent a complaint from the person allegedly defamed about the truth of a particular message and a subsequent refusal to correct, it will typically be very difficult for a libel plaintiff to prove negligence of the owner or operator and, likely virtually impossible for a libel plaintiff who is a public figure or public official to prove that the owner or operator of the on-line service acted with knowledge of falsity or substantial doubts as to the truth. When a target of a message complains that a statement is false and defamatory, and the owner or operator then refuses to delete that statement, it will be far more difficult for the defendant to prevail on the fault issue. It is also dangerous because even under the oft-quoted standard applicable to distributors, one may be liable if he either knows or has reason to know of the defamation.[22] Thus, the on-line service must make quite clear that it is not equipped to review messages for truth and does not review messages for truth.[23]

The greatest risk of not editing is, of course, presented when the on–line services owner or operator in fact believes (or even knows) that an uploaded message is false. Putting aside the business reasons for wishing to edit or delete such a message,[24] leaving such messages on–line requires a great deal of intestinal fortitude. And, a decision to adopt such a policy should be made only after the most rigorous analysis of the specific facts applicable to that entity since the risk/reward ratio may be very different depending upon such factors as the nature of the on–line service, the degree of involvement of the operator, the number of messages uploaded on a daily basis, and the commercial realities of the service.

This is not an easy decision. Both the business and the legal aspects of the choice must be weighed. On the one hand, an across–the–board decision not to edit or delete potentially defamatory statements on the basis of falsity will most likely weaken substantially the fault defenses that the owner or operator could otherwise have asserted. Of course, content–based editing for anything but truth –– e.g., obscenity –– should not weaken the entity's fault–based defenses. On the other hand, once the owner or operator of an on–line service uses the route of editing for truth, there are downsides far beyond the legal risk of being classified as a publisher rather than as a distributor or common carrier. These include: (a) the "veto" power that will be given to targets of critical statements; and (b) the institutional and legal pressure that will follow to increase the level of screening and review of posted messages. In light of the increasing use in recent years of libel suits as a technique of high profile individuals or entities to prevent critical comment (e.g., the Church of Scientology, the tobacco industry, the political leaders in Singapore, Robert Maxwell), once it becomes known that owners and operators of on–line services are following this practice, it is reasonable to expect that complaints about posted messages will rise dramatically –– perhaps eventually leading to certain issues which, as a practical matter, simply cannot be discussed on bulletin boards. (It has been reported that at the time of his death, Maxwell had more than 100 pending defamation suits. Maxwell's litigiousness no doubt contributed to the media's lack of interest in Maxwell's financial affairs during his lifetime.)

Another factor to keep in mind is that this is not a "one way street." That is, if an owner or operator chooses to edit or delete statements known or believed to be defamatory and then determines a year or two down the road (for the reasons discussed above or for any other reasons) that this was not a wise choice, it may not be possible for the owner or operator to undo the damage that has been caused. It will likely be in the next few years that the courts will render decisions on the publisher/distributor/common carrier issue. It is likely that those decisions will rest heavily on whether the courts believe that it is practical or even possible to perform such editing or screening functions. If owners and operators of on–line services perform those editing functions during the formative stages of this case law, the chances of the correct result being reached will have been substantially diminished.

Where A Suit Based On An Internet Message May Be Maintained

Libel plaintiffs are, by and large, rational actors who bring their lawsuits in jurisdictions where they believe it is most likely that they can win. For this reason, libel plaintiffs, wherever possible, have instituted such suits either in (a) foreign countries (such as England or Singapore) in which the libel laws are much more favorable to plaintiffs than in the United States; or (b) states where the defendants will be particularly disadvantaged.

For the first reason, England has in the last few years become the "forum of choice" for libel plaintiffs, hosting suits by celebrities such as Sylvester Stallone, Bianca Jagger, the Sheik of Dubai, and the Greek Prime Minister.[25] Commentators have stated, "British libel law is so notoriously favorable to plaintiffs that an increasing number of forum–shopping foreigners are taking action in London against newspapers and books that are printed, and mostly circulated abroad."[26] The well–known commentator, Professor Smolla has observed, "London has become an international libel capital. Plaintiffs with the wherewithal to do so now often choose to file suit in Britain in order to exploit Britain's strict libel laws, even when the plaintiffs and the publication have little connection to that country." The well–known commentator on defamation, Professor Smolla has described some of these cases as follows:

> An American journalist, Dusko Doder, the former <u>Washington Post</u> Moscow bureau chief, for example, sued <u>Time</u> magazine in London. <u>Time</u> distributes most of its 5,510,000 weekly copies in the United States, and Doder was an American citizen living in Belgrade. Similarly, the famous American industrialist Armand Hammer sued in London for statements contained in an unauthorized biography, even though the book was distributed predominantly in the United States, and Robert Maxwell sued the <u>New Republic</u> in London for a story distributed to over 98,000 American subscribers, and 135 subscribers in England.[27]

Within the United States, libel suits are often instituted in the forum that the plaintiff believes will be most favorable to him, even though the connection between the libel defendant and the chosen jurisdiction is quite tenuous –– such as the sale of a relatively small number copies of the publication at issue or telephone calls by the defendant journalist to sources in the jurisdiction. Perhaps the best (and best known) illustration of such geographically–chosen libel suits is the series of defamation actions in the early 1960's by southern law enforcement officers against civil rights leaders and northern newspapers. These suits, typically instituted in state courts in Mississippi and Alabama, resulted in enormous damage awards against civil rights leaders such as the Reverend Ralph Abernathy and publications such as The New York Times. (In 1964, there were eleven libel suits brought by local or state officials pending in Alabama alone against The New York Times and five more against CBS.)[28] The most famous of these suits resulted in the landmark Supreme Court decision of New York Times Co. v. Sullivan.[29] In that case, L.B. Sullivan, a Montgomery Alabama City Commissioner, filed a libel suit against The New York Times and four Alabama clergymen (and supporters of Martin Luther King, Jr.) concerning an advertisement relating to the actions of southern law enforcement personnel during a recent civil rights rally. A Montgomery County jury awarded damages of $500,000 against all five defendants, which award was affirmed by the Alabama Supreme Court. The Supreme Court reversed that judgment.[30]

The problem of libel suits brought in jurisdictions in which the defendant has only a very limited connection is likely to arise frequently from on–line and Internet communications. Imagine, for example, the scenario in which an individual who lives and works in Manchester, New Hampshire, posts politically–sensitive messages (e.g., messages criticizing (i) groups that picket abortion clinics or (ii) the human rights policies of the government of Jamaica) on–line or on the Internet, which messages (depending upon the particular on–line service) are then accessible to subscribers in all 50 states (and, indeed, around the world). Imagine further that those messages have the effect of generating considerable on–line discussion. It is not unreasonable to predict that that person will soon find himself a defendant in lawsuits in states (or even countries) with which he has no connection other than that his messages were read there.

Similarly, the owners and operators of on–line services — who are generally perceived as the "deep pocket" in such libel cases — will likewise find themselves named in lawsuits filed in jurisdictions from which they derive little or no revenue, and where they would quite decidedly prefer not to be defendants. In some instances, the lawsuits will be genuine actions filed in good faith by a plaintiff who feels himself to have a cause of action; in others, the lawsuit will have been instituted solely for its in terrorem effect on the plaintiff and other potential critics. In all such cases, the mere filing of the lawsuit in a distant and inhospitable jurisdiction will cause considerable pain to the defendant. How are such suits to be dealt with?

With respect to the individual defendant who has no greater connection with a jurisdiction than that a posted message has been down–loaded there, under established law, it seems fairly clear that the court in that jurisdiction will have no power to adjudicate a dispute against that defendant. The Supreme Court has held that the United States Constitution requires a state's assertion of personal jurisdiction over a non–resident defendant to be predicated on certain "minimum contacts" between the defendant and the state.[31] This minimum contacts test is unlikely to be satisfied merely because the defendants' messages were downloaded by a service subscriber in that state. The individual defendant would thus have the option of: (i) entering an appearance for the sole purpose of moving to dismiss the action for lack of jurisdiction; or (ii) defaulting (i.e., ignoring the lawsuit by not answering the complaint) and then challenging the resulting default judgment when it is sought to be enforced in a state in which the defendant has assets. While the second tactic would typically be less expensive since one would not have to hire an out–of–state lawyer (and since the libel plaintiff may never seek to enforce his judgment in a state in which the defendant has assets), it is also riskier. If a default judgment is entered in the first jurisdiction and the court in the defendant's home jurisdiction later determines that the initial court did have jurisdiction, the libel defendant may be unable to challenge the judgment on substantive grounds. While each case must be considered on its facts, a defendant should not merely ignore the lawsuit, unless that course is the result of careful analysis and consideration.

Individual defendants sued in a place with which they have little or no connection should also consider the possibility of seeking sanctions against the libel plaintiff under a variety of theories (including the sanctions provisions in the Federal Rules of Civil Procedure, state malicious prosecution laws, or state Anti–SLAPP suit statutes[32]).

The jurisdiction issue is considerably more complicated with respect to on–line services owner or operator that is sued in a state in which it has few subscribers and from which it derives little revenue. (Of course, large media companies will often have many jurisdictional contacts throughout the United States.) The Supreme Court has held that the First Amendment provides no special protection to media defendants on the issue of jurisdiction.[33] In those cases and others, the courts have held that newspapers or magazines that deliberately exploit a market by "continuously and deliberately" selling their publications into a state, "must reasonably anticipate being haled into court there in a libel action based on the contents" of that publication.[34] Although the precise question of "how many sales is enough" has not been addressed by the Supreme Court, a substantial number of lower court decisions have found that insubstantial or de minimis circulation (which in most cases has meant considerably less than 1% of the total circulation) is not sufficient to satisfy the statutory and constitutional requirements for jurisdiction.[35] This same principle is likely to be applied with respect to on–line services owners or operators. Thus, if the number of subscribers in a particular state is considerably less than 1% of that entity's total subscribers, a strong argument can be made that there is no jurisdiction.

Several cautions are necessary, however. Intentional solicitation of subscribers in the forum state (i.e., advertising, telephone solicitations, direct mailing) will affect the analyses. The more of such activity there is, the less the chances for a dismissal based on jurisdictional grounds. In addition, if the nature of the on–line service or site is directly related to the jurisdiction, there is a considerably greater chance that even a <u>de minimis</u> number of subscribers in a jurisdiction will be deemed sufficient. For example, if a bulletin board is devoted to the Susan Smith murders, the likelihood of a suit being successfully maintained in South Carolina, even though there are only a small number of subscribers there, is heightened.

With respect to lawsuits brought outside the United States in particularly pro–libel plaintiff jurisdictions such as England or Singapore, recent case law provides some good news for Internet speakers. Because of the very substantial differences between the law of defamation in the U.S. and England (such as the fault requirement and burden of proving falsity), several U.S. courts have recently refused to enforce British judgments in defamation actions. Just last month, for example, the United States District Court for the District of Columbia dismissed an action seeking enforcement of a British libel judgment in the well–known case of <u>Matusevitch v. Telnikoff</u>.[36] The Court analyzed the libel law of both jurisdictions and concluded that the differences between British libel law and U.S. libel law were so substantial, and so closely related to fundamental constitutional concerns regarding free speech, that the judgment could not be enforced.[37]

Thus, for a libel defendant sued in a foreign country as a result of an Internet communication who has assets only in the United States, one option that may be available is to ignore the foreign lawsuit and then challenge its enforceability when the prevailing plaintiff seeks to enforce the resulting default judgment in the United States. However, as noted above, with respect to lawsuits brought in other states within the United States, a decision not to appear and defend in the foreign lawsuit should be made only after careful consideration and analysis.

This course of action will not be available to corporate (or individual) defendants who do have substantial assets in the foreign jurisdiction in which the lawsuit is brought. Because a judgment in that jurisdiction can be enforced against the foreign assets without resort to the United States courts the lawsuit may not simply be left undefended. This applies with particular force to owners and operators of on–line services, and to media defendants whose content is available on worldwide databases.

The threat of libel suits in foreign countries as a result of on–line or Internet communications is a substantial one. Political leaders in Singapore have recently filed at least two libel suits against the International Herald Tribune for articles allegedly critical of certain Singapore government officials. One of those suits resulted in a ruling in August 1995 imposing a fine of $678,000 against the International Herald Tribune. The evident purpose of these lawsuits was to curtail criticism by the international press of Singapore's political leaders.

With virtually all major U.S. newspapers and magazines now available on–line through services which provide worldwide access or World Wide Web sites, we can expect an increasing number of foreign libel suits against U.S. publications that provoke the ire of foreign political leaders. It is not also unreasonable to predict that such libel suits will be brought against the owners and operators of bulletin boards through which, for example, the citizens of both the U.S. and Singapore may criticize the Singapore government. While such suits can, as discussed above, be ignored if the defendant does not have assets outside the U.S., if the entity does have assets outside the U.S., the suits present serious difficulties. Both publications and on–line services owners and operators, for obvious commercial reasons, may be reluctant to curtail the worldwide distribution or accessibility of their information — even if such a limitation could be accomplished technologically. It is likely, therefore, that such suits will need to be defended, at least in the first instance,[38] in the jurisdictions in which they are brought.

When Must A Libel Action Arising From An Electronic Publication Be Brought?

The availability of civil causes of action is limited in all fifty states by "statutes of limitations" which require (with certain exceptions) that lawsuits be brought, if at all, within a specified time from when the plaintiff's cause of action "arose" or "accrued." In New York, and many other states, the statute of limitations for libel is one year, although in some states it is three years or more. Although the law varies from state to state, typically a cause of action for libel "accrues" or "arises" upon publication of the allegedly defamatory statement.

In the context of on–line or Internet communications, the question arises whether the "publication" occurs when the message is first posted, or whether a new publication occurs whenever a subscriber accesses and reads the message (which could be several years later). This issue has not yet been the subject of a reported decision, but it is fairly clear from decisions in other areas that what is known as the "single publication rule" will apply. Under the single publication rule, if only one work (or message) is involved, its distribution constitutes a single publication on the date of the first publication of the message and gives rise to the cause of action at the time of that first publication. Thus, if an allegedly defamatory message is posted by subscriber "A" onto a bulletin board on January 1, 1996, the cause of action will accrue on that date. No new cause of action will accrue if on January 1, 1997 subscriber "B" first accesses that message and reads it. Similarly, no new cause of action will accrue against A if on January 1, 1997, B finds the statement sufficiently interesting that she decides to re–post it onto another bulletin board. However, this event may give rise to a separate cause of action for libel against B.

It is not yet clear whether a new statute of limitations period would begin to run if A, at a later time, republished her own message by transferring it to a new bulletin board or by reposting it on the same board.   Current case law reflects that a single edition or issue of a publication constitutes one publication even though it is distributed (or read) over a period of time, while a new edition constitutes a second publication.   A libel plaintiff would no doubt argue that the re–posting constitutes a new publication because it was the result of a separate independent decision to republish the message.[39]   This argument has considerable support in the case law, but its resolution is not yet clear.

ENDNOTES

1. For a considerably more extended discussion of the law of defamation, two of the best treatises on that subject are R. Sack and S. Baron, *Libel, Slander, and Related Problems* (2d Ed. 1994) and R. Smolla, *Law of Defamation* (1994).

2. *Cubby, Inc. v. CompuServe, Inc.*, 776 F. Supp. 135, 19 Med.L.Rptr. (B.N.A.) 1525 (S.D.N.Y. 1991); *Stratton Oakmont, Inc. v. Prodigy Services Co.*, 23 Med.L.Rptr. (BNA) 1794 (Sup. Ct. Nassau Co. 1995).

3. Prosser, *Torts*, Section III at 739 (4th Ed. 1971).

4. *Gertz v. Robert Welch, Inc.*, 418 U.S. 323, 339-40 (1974).

5. *Milkovich v. Lorain Journal Co.*, 497 U.S. 1 (1990).

6. *Gertz*, 418 U.S. at 345, 344.

7. Uploading involves transmitting data in the form of either a private e-mail message or public by accessible posting from a local source or personal computer onto a multiple access host or server, *e.g.*, the process of transferring data from one's personal computer to an electronic bulletin board.

8. *See, e.g., Cubby, Inc. v. Compuserve, Inc.*, 776 F. Supp. 135, 139, 19 Med.L.Rptr.1525, 1527 (S.D.N.Y. 1991) (Leisure, J.), and cases cited therein.

9. In *It's In The Cards, Inc. v. Fuschetto*, 535 N.W.2d I I (Wisc.Ct.App. 1995), the Wisconsin Court of Appeals addressed the issue of whether the SportsNet online service is a "periodical" under the Wisconsin statute requiring a request for a retraction as a condition precedent to the filing of a libel suit. While the Court concluded that SportsNet was not a periodical, this ruling is likely to have limited applicability. The Court relied exclusively on the "ordinary meaning" of the word periodical, which is defined in *Webster's Third New*

International Dictionary as: "a magazine or other publication of which the issues appear at stated or regular intervals. " The Court also noted that previous Wisconsin cases had interpreted the retraction statute to apply only to the print media and not the broadcast media. The Court concluded by observing that there was no cyberspace at the time the statute was enacted and that any expansion of the retraction statute must be accomplished by legislative action. *See also Medphone v. Denigris,* Civil Action No. 92-3785 (D.N.J.) (defamation action, now settled, arising from allegedly defamatory statements made on Prodigy's "Money Line" by private investor).

10. 776 F. Supp. 135, 139-41, 19 Med.L.Rptr. (BNA) 1525 (S.D.N.Y. 1991) (Leisure, J.).

11. 361 U.S. 147, 152-53 (1959).

12. 776 F. Supp. at 141, 19 Med.L.Rptr. at 1529.

13. 776 F. Supp. at 143, 19 Med.L.Rptr. at 1531.

14. *Id.*

15. *Id.*

16. 23 Med.L.Rptr. (BNA) 1794 (Sup. Ct. Nassau Co. 1995).

17. 23 Med.L.Rptr. (BNA) at 1797.

18. *See* generally R. Sack and S. Baron, *Libel, Slander and Related Problems* at 368 (2nd Ed. 1994).

19. Another potentially relevant area is lawsuits brought against print media publishers for statements that appear in their classified advertising sections. In the non-defamation context, the courts have discussed extensively the liability of *Soldier of Fortune* magazine for violent acts committed by persons who advertised their services in the magazine. *Compare Braun v. Soldier of Fortune Magazine, Inc.,* 968 F.2d 11 10, 20 Med. L. Rptr (BNA) 1777 (11th Cir. 1992), *cert. denied* 113 S. Ct. 1028 (1993) (holding that the magazine could be

sued for wrongful death based on the publication of a classified ad which listed an assassin-for-hire, and which led to a murder, where the Court determined that the classified ad, on its face, presented a clearly identifiable and substantial danger of harm to the public) with *Eimann v. Soldier of Fortune Magazine, Inc.*, 880 F.2d 830, 16 Med. L. Rptr. (BNA) 2148 (5th Cir. 1989), *cert. denied* 493 U.S. 1024 (1990) (no liability because the ad was not specific enough to indicate any illegal intent).

20. 800 F. Supp. 928, 20 Med.L.Rptr. (BNA) 1361 (E.D.Wash. 1992).

21. 20 Med.L.Rptr. at 1363

22. *See, e.g., Lerman v. Chuckleberry Publishing, Inc.*, 521 F. Supp. 228, 235, 7 Med.L.Rptr. (BNA) 2282, 2287 (S.D.N.Y. 1981); *Cubby*, 776 F. Supp. at 139, 19 Med.L.Rptr. (BNA) at 1527.

23. Libel plaintiffs may also argue (in reliance on *Harte-Hanks Communications, Inc. v. Connaughton*, 491 U.S. 657 (1989)) that such a policy suggests a "deliberate effort to avoid the truth."

24. For example, a traditional media entity that operates an on-line site for interactive communications between its writers or editors and the public might not feel comfortable posting such messages because the mere presence of those messages would detract from their reputations as careful journalists.

25. See G. Robertson and A. Nichols, *Media Law*, 56 (2nd Ed. 1990).

26. R. Smolla, *Law of Defamation* at Section 1.03[3].

27. *See also* Handman & Balin, *Bachchan v. India Abroad: Non Recognition of British Libel Judgments: The American Revolution Revisited*, 10 Comm. Law, No. 3, at 1, 22 (Fall 1992).

28. *See New York Times Co. v. Sullivan*, 376 U.S. 254 (1964) (Black, J., concurring).

29. 376 U.S. 254 (1964).

30. This lawsuit is described in the excellent work by Anthony Lewis, *Make No Law, The Sullivan Case And The First Amendment.*

31. *See, e.g., Keeton v. Hustler Magazine, Inc.*, 465 U.S. 770, 781 (1984).

32. "SLAPP" is the acronym for Strategic Lawsuit Against Public Participation. A SLAPP suit is litigation without merit to punish or dissuade the exercise of First Amendment rights. Some states allow the defendant in such a suit to recover certain damages.

33. *Keeton v. Hustler Magazine, Inc.*, 465 U.S. 770 (1984); Calder v. Jones, 465 U.S. 783 (1984).

34. *Keeton*, 465 U.S. at 781.

35. *See, e.g., Gonzales v. Atlanta Constitution*, 4 Med.L.Rptr. (BNA) 2146 (N.D.Ill. 1979) (daily circulation of *Atlanta Constitution* in Illinois of 37 newspapers constituting less than 0.001% of total circulation could not meet constitutional test for jurisdiction); *Church of Scientology v. Adams*, 584 F.2d 893 (9th Cir. 1978) (0.04% of circulation insufficient to meet constitutional standards); *Sipple v. DeMoines Register and Tribune Co.*, 82 Cal.App. 3d 143, 147 Cal.Rptr. 59 (1978) (0.3% circulation not sufficient to meet constitutional standards); *Buckley v. New York Post Corp.*, 373 F.2d 175 (2d Cir. 1967) (circulation of 2000 copies per day in Connecticut is sufficient to meet constitutional standards); *Akbar v. New York Magazine Co.*, 490 F. Supp. 60, 1059 (D.D.C. 1980) (0.7% of circulation in District of Columbia *is* sufficient for jurisdiction). Additional cases concerning the issue of jurisdictional sufficiency may be found in R. Sack and S. Baron, *Libel, Slander, and Related Problems* (2d Ed. 1994) at 743-45.

36. 23 Med.L.Rptr. (BNA) 1367 (D.D.C. 1995).

37. *See also Bachchan v. India Abroad Publications, Inc.*, 154 Misc. 2d 228, 585 N.Y.S. 2d 661 (Sup. Ct. N.Y. Co. 1992).

38. A U.S. defendant sued abroad is always free to argue to the foreign

court that there is no *in personam* jurisdiction; that the case should be dismissed and refiled, if the plaintiff so chooses, in the U.S. *(forum non-conveniens)*; or that U.S. law should apply. The success of these arguments will obviously vary depending upon the facts, the independence of the forum country's judiciary and the identity of the plaintiff. Such defendants should also consider whether international tribunals may be utilized.

39. *See, e.g., Rinaldi v. Viking Penguin, Inc.*, 52 N.Y.2d 422, 420 N.E.2d 377, 438 N.Y.S.2d 496 (1981).

Appendix 1

Sample Form: U.S. Copyright Office Forms:
<u>Form TX</u>

■Filling Out Application Form TX

Detach and read these instructions before completing this form.
Make sure all applicable spaces have been filled in before you return this form.

BASIC INFORMATION

When to Use This Form: Use Form TX for registration of published or unpublished non-dramatic literary works, excluding periodicals or serial issues. This class includes a wide variety of works: fiction, nonfiction, poetry, textbooks, reference works, directories, catalogs, advertising copy, compilations of information, and computer programs. For periodicals and serials, use Form SE.

Deposit to Accompany Application: An application for copyright registration must be accompanied by a deposit consisting of copies or phonorecords representing the entire work for which registration is to be made. The following are the general deposit requirements as set forth in the statute:

Unpublished Work: Deposit one complete copy (or phonorecord).

Published Work: Deposit two complete copies (or one phonorecord) of the best edition.

Work First Published Outside the United States: Deposit one complete copy (or phonorecord) of the first foreign edition.

Contribution to a Collective Work: Deposit one complete copy (or phonorecord) of the best edition of the collective work.

The Copyright Notice: For works first published on or after March 1, 1989, the law provides that a copyright notice in a specified form "may be placed on all publicly distributed copies from which the work can be visually per-

ceived." Use of the copyright notice is the responsibility of the copyright owner and does not require advance permission from the Copyright Office. The required form of the notice for copies generally consists of three elements: (1) the symbol "©," or the word "Copyright," or the abbreviation "Copr."; (2) the year of first publication; and (3) the name of the owner of copyright. For example: "© 1993 Jane Cole." The notice is to be affixed to the copies "in such manner and location as to give reasonable notice of the claim of copyright." Works first published prior to March 1, 1989, must carry the notice or risk loss of copyright protection.

For information about notice requirements for works published before March 1, 1989, or other copyright information, write: Information Section, LM-401, Copyright Office, Library of Congress, Washington, D.C. 20559.

PRIVACY ACT ADVISORY STATEMENT Required by the Privacy Act of 1974 (Public Law 93-579)	PRINCIPAL USES OF REQUESTED INFORMATION • Establishment and maintenance of a public record
AUTHORITY FOR REQUESTING THIS INFORMATION • Title 17 U.S.C. Secs 409 and 410	• Examination of the application for compliance with legal requirements
FURNISHING THE REQUESTED INFORMATION IS • Voluntary	OTHER ROUTINE USES • Public inspection and copying • Preparation of public indexes • Preparation of public catalogs of copyright registrations
BUT IF THE INFORMATION IS NOT FURNISHED • It may be necessary to delay or refuse registration • You may not be entitled to certain relief, remedies, and benefits provided in chapters 4 and 5 of title 17 U.S.C.	• Preparation of search reports upon request NOTE • No other advisory statement will be given you in connection with this application • Please keep this statement and refer to it if we communicate with you regarding this application

LINE-BY-LINE INSTRUCTIONS

Please type or print using black ink.

1 SPACE 1: Title

Title of This Work: Every work submitted for copyright registration must be given a title to identify that particular work. If the copies or phonorecords of the work bear a title or an identifying phrase that could serve as a title, transcribe that wording *completely and exactly* on the application. Indexing of the registration and future identification of the work will depend on the information you give here.

Previous or Alternative Titles: Complete this space if there are any additional titles for the work under which someone searching for the registration might be likely to look or under which a document pertaining to the work might be recorded.

Publication as a Contribution: If the work being registered is a contribution to a periodical, serial, or collection, give the title of the contribution in the "Title of this Work" space. Then, in the line headed "Publication as a Contribution," give information about the collective work in which the contribution appeared.

2 SPACE 2: Author(s)

General Instructions: After reading these instructions, decide who are the "authors" of this work for copyright purposes. Then, unless the work is a "collective work," give the requested information about every "author" who contributed any appreciable amount of copyrightable matter to this version of the work. If you need further space, request Continuation sheets. In the case of a collective work such as an anthology, collection of essays, or encyclopedia, give information about the author of the collective work as a whole.

Name of Author: The fullest form of the author's name should be given. Unless the work was "made for hire," the individual who actually created the work is its "author." In the case of a work made for hire, the statute provides that "the employer or other person for whom the work was prepared is considered the author."

What is a "Work Made for Hire"? A "work made for hire" is defined as (1) "a work prepared by an employee within the scope of his or her employment"; or (2) "a work specially ordered or commissioned for use as a contribution to a collective work, as a part of a motion picture or other audiovisual work, as a translation, as a supplementary work, as a compilation, as an instructional text, as a test, as answer material for a test, or as an atlas, if the parties expressly agree in a written instrument signed by them that the works shall be considered a work made for hire." If you have checked "Yes" to indicate that the work was "made for hire," you must give the full legal name of the employer (or other person for whom the work was prepared). You may also include the name of the employee along with the name of the employer (for example: "Elster Publishing Co., employer for hire of John Ferguson").

"Anonymous" or "Pseudonymous" Work: An author's contribution to a work is "anonymous" if that author is not identified on the copies or phonorecords of the work. An author's contribution to a work is "pseudonymous" if that author is identified on the copies or phonorecords under a fictitious name. If the work is "anonymous" you may: (1) leave the line blank; or (2) state "anonymous" on the line; or (3) reveal the author's identity. If the work is "pseudonymous" you may: (1) leave the line blank; or (2) give the pseudonym and identify it as such (for example: "Huntley Haverstock, pseudonym"); or (3) reveal the author's name, making clear which is the real name and which is the pseudonym (for example: "Judith Barton, whose pseudonym is Madeline Elster"). However, the citizenship or domicile of the author must be given in all cases.

Dates of Birth and Death: If the author is dead, the statute requires that the year of death be included in the application unless the work is anonymous or pseudonymous. The author's birth date is optional but is useful as a form of identification. Leave this space blank if the author's contribution was a "work made for hire."

192

Author's Nationality or Domicile: Give the country of which the author is a citizen or the country in which the author is domiciled. Nationality or domicile must be given in all cases.

Nature of Authorship: After the words "Nature of Authorship," give a brief general statement of the nature of this particular author's contribution to the work. Examples: "Entire text", "Coauthor of entire text"; "Chapters 11-14", "Editorial revision", Compilation and English translation"; "New text".

3 SPACE 3: Creation and Publication

General Instructions: Do not confuse "creation" with "publication." Every application for copyright registration must state " the year in which creation of the work was completed." Give the date and nation of first publication only if the work has been published.

Creation: Under the statute, a work is "created" when it is fixed in a copy or phonorecord for the first time. Where a work has been prepared over a period of time, the part of the work existing in fixed form on a particular date constitutes the created work on that date. The date you give here should be the year in which the author completed the particular version for which registration is now being sought, even if other versions exist or if further changes or additions are planned.

Publication: The statute defines "publication" as " the distribution of copies or phonorecords of a work to the public by sale or other transfer of ownership or by rental, lease, or lending; a work is also "published" if there has been an " offering to distribute copies or phonorecords to a group of persons for purposes of further distribution, public performance or public display." Give the full date (month, day, year) when, and the country where, publication first occurred. If first publication took place simultaneously in the United States and other countries it is sufficient to state "U.S.A."

4 SPACE 4: Claimant(s)

Name(s) and Address(es) of Copyright Claimant(s): Give the name(s) and address(es) of the copyright claimant(s) in this work even if the claimant is the same as the author. Copyright in a work belongs initially to the author of the work (including, in the case of a work made for hire, the employer or other person for whom the work was prepared) The copyright claimant is either the author of the work, or a person or organization to whom the copyright initially belonging to the author has been transferred

Transfer: The statute provides that, if the copyright claimant is not the author, the application for registration must contain a brief statement of how the claimant obtained ownership of the copyright." if any copyright claimant named in space 4 is not an author named in space 2 give a brief statement explaining how the claimant(s) obtained ownership of the copyright. Examples: "By written contract"; "Transfer of all rights by author"; "Assignment"; "By will." Do not attach transfer documents or other attachments or riders

5 SPACE 5: Previous Registration

General Instructions: The questions in space 5 are intended to show whether an earlier registration has been made for this work and, if so, whether there is any basis for a new registration. As a general rule only one basic copyright registration can be made for the same version of a particular work

Same Version: If this version is substantially the same as the work covered by a previous registration, a second registration is not generally possible unless: (1) the work has been registered in unpublished form and a second registration is now being sought to cover this first published edition; or (2) someone other than the author is identified as copyright claimant in the earlier registration and the author is now seeking registration in his or her own name If either of these two exceptions apply, check the appropriate box and give the earlier registration number and date. Otherwise, do not submit Form TX; instead write the Copyright Office for information about supplementary registration or recordation of transfers of copyright ownership

Changed Version: If the work has been changed and you are now seeking registration to cover the additions or revisions, check the last box in space 5 give the earlier registration number and date and complete both parts of space 6 in accordance with the instructions below

Previous Registration Number and Date: If more than one previous registration has been made for the work, give the number and date of the latest registration

6 SPACE 6: Derivative Work or Compilation

General Instructions: Complete space 6 if this work is a "changed version" "compilation" or "derivative work" and it it incorporates one or more earlier works that have already been published or registered for copyright or that have fallen into the public domain A compilation is defined as " a work formed by the collection and assembling of preexisting materials or of data that are selected, coordinated or arranged in such a way that the resulting work as a whole constitutes an original work of authorship " A "derivative work" is " a work based on one or more preexisting works." Examples of derivative works include translations, fictionalizations, abridgments, condensations, or any other form in which a work may be recast, transformed, or adapted " Derivative works also include works consisting of editorial revisions, annotations, or other modifications which these changes, as a whole represent an original work of authorship

Preexisting Material (space 6a): For derivative works, complete this space and space 6b In space 6a identify the preexisting work that has been recast transformed, or adapted An example of preexisting material might be "Russian version of Goncharov's 'Oblomov'" Do not complete space 6a for compilations

Material Added to This Work (space 6b): Give a brief, general statement of the new material covered by the copyright claim for which registration is sought Derivative work examples include: "Foreword, editing, critical annotations" "Translation" "Chapters 11-17." If the work is a compilation describe both the compilation itself and the material that has been compiled Example "Compilation of certain 1917 speeches by Woodrow Wilson. A work may be both a derivative work and compilation, in which case a sample statement might be: "Compilation and additional new material."

7 SPACE 7: Manufacturing Provisions

Due to the expiration of the Manufacturing Clause of the copyright law on June 30, 1986, this space has been deleted.

8 SPACE 8: Reproduction for Use of Blind or Physically Handicapped Individuals

General Instructions: One of the major programs of the Library of Congress is to provide Braille editions and special recordings of works for the exclusive use of the blind and physically handicapped. In an effort to simplify and speed up the copyright licensing procedures that are a necessary part of this program section 710 of the copyright statute provides for the establishment of a voluntary licensing system to be tied in with copyright registration Copyright Office regulations provide that you may grant a license for such reproduction and distribution solely for the use of persons who are certified by competent authority as unable to read normal printed material as a result of physical limitations The license is entirely voluntary, nonexclusive, and may be terminated upon 90 days notice

How to Grant the License: If you wish to grant it, check one of the three boxes in space 8 Your check in one of these boxes together with your signature in space 10 will mean that the Library of Congress can proceed to reproduce and distribute under the license without further paperwork For further information, write for Circular 63

9,10,11 SPACE 9,10,11: Fee, Correspondence, Certification, Return Address

Fee: The Copyright Office has the authority to adjust fees at 5-year intervals based on changes in the Consumer Price Index The next adjustment is due in 1996. Please contact the Copyright Office after July 1995 to determine the actual fee schedule

Deposit Account: If you maintain a Deposit Account in the Copyright Office identify it in space 9 Otherwise leave the space blank and send the fee of $5 with your application and deposit

Correspondence (space 9) This space should contain the name address, area code, and telephone number of the person to be consulted if correspondence about this application becomes necessary

Certification (space 10) The application can not be accepted unless it bears the date and the handwritten signature of the author or other copyright claimant, or of the owner of exclusive rights, or of the duly authorized agent of author, claimant or owner of exclusive rights

Address for Return of Certificate (space 11) The address box must be completed legibly since the certificate will be returned in a window envelope

FORM TX
For a Literary Work
UNITED STATES COPYRIGHT OFFICE

REGISTRATION NUMBER

_____ TX _____ TXU

EFFECTIVE DATE OF REGISTRATION

Month   Day   Year

DO NOT WRITE ABOVE THIS LINE. IF YOU NEED MORE SPACE, USE A SEPARATE CONTINUATION SHEET.

1

TITLE OF THIS WORK ▼

PREVIOUS OR ALTERNATIVE TITLES ▼

PUBLICATION AS A CONTRIBUTION If this work was published as a contribution to a periodical, serial, or collection, give information about the collective work in which the contribution appeared.   **Title of Collective Work ▼**

If published in a periodical or serial give   Volume ▼   Number ▼   Issue Date ▼   On Pages ▼

---

2   a

NAME OF AUTHOR ▼

DATES OF BIRTH AND DEATH
Year Born ▼   Year Died ▼

Was this contribution to the work a "work made for hire"?
☐ Yes
☐ No

AUTHOR'S NATIONALITY OR DOMICILE
Name of Country
OR { Citizen of ▶ _____
     Domiciled in ▶ _____

WAS THIS AUTHOR'S CONTRIBUTION TO THE WORK
Anonymous? ☐ Yes ☐ No
Pseudonymous? ☐ Yes ☐ No
If the answer to either of these questions is "Yes," see detailed instructions.

NATURE OF AUTHORSHIP Briefly describe nature of material created by this author in which copyright is claimed ▼

NOTE
Under the law, the "author" of a "work made for hire" is generally the employer, not the employee (see instructions). For any part of this work that was "made for hire" check "Yes" in the space provided, give the employer (or other person for whom the work was prepared) as "Author" of that part, and leave the space for dates of birth and death blank.

b

NAME OF AUTHOR ▼

DATES OF BIRTH AND DEATH
Year Born ▼   Year Died ▼

Was this contribution to the work a "work made for hire"?
☐ Yes
☐ No

AUTHOR'S NATIONALITY OR DOMICILE
Name of Country
OR { Citizen of ▶ _____
     Domiciled in ▶ _____

WAS THIS AUTHOR'S CONTRIBUTION TO THE WORK
Anonymous? ☐ Yes ☐ No
Pseudonymous? ☐ Yes ☐ No
If the answer to either of these questions is "Yes," see detailed instructions.

NATURE OF AUTHORSHIP Briefly describe nature of material created by this author in which copyright is claimed ▼

c

NAME OF AUTHOR ▼

DATES OF BIRTH AND DEATH
Year Born ▼   Year Died ▼

Was this contribution to the work a "work made for hire"?
☐ Yes
☐ No

AUTHOR'S NATIONALITY OR DOMICILE
Name of Country
OR { Citizen of ▶ _____
     Domiciled in ▶ _____

WAS THIS AUTHOR'S CONTRIBUTION TO THE WORK
Anonymous? ☐ Yes ☐ No
Pseudonymous? ☐ Yes ☐ No
If the answer to either of these questions is "Yes," see detailed instructions.

NATURE OF AUTHORSHIP Briefly describe nature of material created by this author in which copyright is claimed ▼

---

3   a

YEAR IN WHICH CREATION OF THIS WORK WAS COMPLETED This information must be given in all cases.

b Complete this information Month ▶ _____ Day ▶ _____ Year ▶ _____ ◀ Nation
ONLY if this work has been published.

DATE AND NATION OF FIRST PUBLICATION OF THIS PARTICULAR WORK

4

See instructions before completing this space.

COPYRIGHT CLAIMANT(S) Name and address must be given even if the claimant is the same as the author given in space 2 ▼

TRANSFER If the claimant(s) named here in space 4 is (are) different from the author(s) named in space 2, give a brief statement of how the claimant(s) obtained ownership of the copyright ▼

APPLICATION RECEIVED

ONE DEPOSIT RECEIVED

TWO DEPOSITS RECEIVED

FUNDS RECEIVED

DO NOT WRITE HERE OFFICE USE ONLY

MORE ON BACK ▶ • Complete all applicable spaces (numbers 5-11) on the reverse side of this page.
• See detailed instructions.   • Sign the form at line 8.

DO NOT WRITE HERE
Page 1 of _____ pages

EXAMINED BY

CHECKED BY

☐ CORRESPONDENCE
Yes

FORM TX

FOR
COPYRIGHT
OFFICE
USE
ONLY

DO NOT WRITE ABOVE THIS LINE. IF YOU NEED MORE SPACE, USE A SEPARATE CONTINUATION SHEET.

PREVIOUS REGISTRATION Has registration for this work, or for an earlier version of this work, already been made in the Copyright Office?
☐ Yes ☐ No If your answer is "Yes" why is another registration being sought? (Check appropriate box) ▼
a. ☐ This is the first published edition of a work previously registered in unpublished form.
b. ☐ This is the first application submitted by this author as copyright claimant.
c. ☐ This is a changed version of the work, as shown by space 6 on this application.
If your answer is "Yes" give: **Previous Registration Number** ▼   **Year of Registration** ▼

5

DERIVATIVE WORK OR COMPILATION Complete both space 6a and 6b for a derivative work; complete only 6b for a compilation.
a. **Preexisting Material** Identify any preexisting work or works that this work is based on or incorporates. ▼

b. **Material Added to This Work** Give a brief general statement of the material that has been added to this work and in which copyright is claimed. ▼

6

See instructions
before completing
this space

— space deleted —

7

REPRODUCTION FOR USE OF BLIND OR PHYSICALLY HANDICAPPED INDIVIDUALS A signature on this form at space 10 and a check in one
of the boxes here in space 8 constitutes a non-exclusive grant of permission to the Library of Congress to reproduce and distribute solely for the blind and physically
handicapped and under the conditions and limitations prescribed by the regulations of the Copyright Office: (1) copies of the work identified in space 1 of this
application in Braille or similar tactile symbols; or (2) phonorecords embodying a fixation of a reading of that work; or (3) both.

a ☐ Copies and Phonorecords   b ☐ Copies Only   c ☐ Phonorecords Only

8

See instructions

DEPOSIT ACCOUNT If the registration fee is to be charged to a Deposit Account established in the Copyright Office, give name and number of Account.
Name ▼   **Account Number** ▼

9

CORRESPONDENCE Give name and address to which correspondence about this application should be sent.   Name/Address/Apt/City/State/ZIP ▼

Area Code and Telephone Number ▶

Be sure to
give your
daytime phone
◀ number

CERTIFICATION* I, the undersigned, hereby certify that I am the
check only one ▶
☐ author
☐ other copyright claimant
☐ owner of exclusive rights
☐ authorized agent of
Name of author or other copyright claimant, or owner of exclusive rights ▲

of the work identified in this application and that the statements made
by me in this application are correct to the best of my knowledge.

10

Typed or printed name and date ▼ If this application gives a date of publication in space 3, do not sign and submit it before that date.
                                                                    date ▶

☐ Handwritten signature (X) ▼

**MAIL
CERTIFI-
CATE TO**

Certificate
will be
mailed in
window
envelope

Name ▼

Number/Street/Apartment Number ▼

City/State/ZIP ▼

YOU MUST:
• Complete all necessary spaces
• Sign your application in space 10

**SEND ALL 3 ELEMENTS
IN THE SAME PACKAGE:**
1. Application form
2. Nonrefundable $20 filing fee
   in check or money order
   payable to Register of Copyrights
3. Deposit material

MAIL TO:
Register of Copyrights
Library of Congress
Washington, D.C. 20559-6000

11

The Copyright Office
has the authority to ad-
just fees at 5-year intervals, based on changes
in the Consumer Price
Index. The next adjust-
ment is due in 1996.
Please contact the
Copyright Office after
July 1995 to determine
the actual fee schedule.

*17 U.S.C. § 506(e): Any person who knowingly makes a false representation of a material fact in the application for copyright registration provided for by section 409, or in any written statement filed in connection
with the application, shall be fined not more than $2,500.

April 1993—300,000   ♻ PRINTED ON RECYCLED PAPER   U.S. GOVERNMENT PRINTING OFFICE: 1993-342-582/80,019

Sample Form: U.S. Copyright Office Forms:
Form SR

Filling Out Application Form SR

Detach and read these instructions before completing this form.
Make sure all applicable spaces have been filled in before you return this form.

BASIC INFORMATION

When to Use This Form: Use Form SR for copyright registration of published or unpublished sound recordings. It should be used when the copyright claim is limited to the sound recording itself, and it may also be used where the same copyright claimant is seeking simultaneous registration of the underlying musical, dramatic, or literary work embodied in the phonorecord.

With one exception, "sound recordings" are works that result from the fixation of a series of musical, spoken, or other sounds. The exception is for the audio portions of audiovisual works, such as a motion picture soundtrack or an audio cassette accompanying a filmstrip; these are considered a part of the audiovisual work as a whole.

Deposit to Accompany Application: An application for copyright registration of a sound recording must be accompanied by a deposit consisting of phonorecords representing the entire work for which registration is to be made.

Unpublished Work: Deposit one complete phonorecord.

Published Work: Deposit two complete phonorecords of the best edition, together with "any printed or other visually perceptible material" published with the phonorecord.

Work First Published Outside the United States: Deposit one complete phonorecord of the first foreign edition.

Contribution to a Collective Work: Deposit one complete phonorecord of the best edition of the collective work.

The Copyright Notice: For sound recordings first published on or after March 1, 1989, the law provides that a copyright notice in a specified form "may be placed on all publicly distributed phonorecords of the sound recording." Use of the copyright notice is the responsibility of the copyright owner and does not require advance permission from the Copyright Office. The required form of the notice for phonorecords of sound recordings consists of three elements: (1) the symbol P (the letter "P" in a circle); (2) the year of first publication of the sound recording; and (3) the name of the owner of copyright. For example: "℗ 1993 XYZ Record Co." The notice is to be "placed on the surface of the phonorecord, or on the label or container, in such manner and location as to give reasonable notice of the claim of copyright." Works first published prior to March 1, 1989, must carry the notice or risk loss of copyright protection.

For information about notice requirements for works published before March 1, 1989, or other copyright information, write. Information Section, LM-401, Copyright Office, Library of Congress, Washington, D.C. 20559.

PRIVACY ACT ADVISORY STATEMENT Required by the Privacy Act of 1974 (P.L. 93-679)
The authority for requesting this information is title 17 U.S.C. secs. 409 and 410. Furnishing the requested information is voluntary. But if the information is not furnished it may be necessary to delay or refuse registration and you may not be entitled to certain relief, remedies, and benefits provided in chapters 4 and 5 of title 17, U.S.C.

The principal uses of the requested information are the establishment and maintenance of a public record and the examination of the application for compliance with legal requirements.

Other routine uses include public inspection and copying, preparation of public indexes, preparation of public catalogs of copyright registrations, and preparation of search reports upon request.

NOTE No other advisory statement will be given in connection with this application. Please keep this statement and refer to it if we communicate with you regarding this application.

LINE-BY-LINE INSTRUCTIONS

Please type or print using black ink.

1 SPACE 1: Title

Title of This Work: Every work submitted for copyright registration must be given a title to identify that particular work. If the phonorecords or any accompanying printed material bear a title (or an identifying phrase that could serve as a title), transcribe that wording completely and exactly on the application. Indexing of the registration and future identification of the work may depend on the information you give here.

Nature of Material Recorded: Indicate the general type or character of the works or other material embodied in the recording. The box marked "Literary" should be checked for nondramatic spoken material of all sorts, including narration, interviews, panel discussions, and training material. If the material recorded is not musical, dramatic, or literary in nature, check "Other" and briefly describe the type of sounds fixed in the recording. For example: "Sound Effects"; "Bird Calls"; "Crowd Noises."

Previous or Alternative Titles: Complete this space if there are any additional titles for the work under which someone searching for the registration might be likely to look or under which a document pertaining to the work might be recorded.

2 SPACE 2: Author(s)

General Instructions: After reading these instructions, decide who are the "authors" of this work for copyright purposes. Then, unless the work is a "collective work," give the requested information about every "author" who contributed any appreciable amount of copyrightable matter to this version of the work. If you need further space, request additional Continuation Sheets. In the case of a collective work such as a collection of previously published or registered sound recordings, give information about the author of the collective work as a whole. If you are submitting this Form SR to cover the recorded musical, dramatic, or literary work as well as the sound recording itself, it is important for space 2 to include full information about the various authors of all of the material covered by the copyright claim, making clear the nature of each author's contribution.

Name of Author: The fullest form of the author's name should be given. Unless the work was "made for hire," the individual who actually created the work is its "author." In the case of a work made for hire, the statute provides that "the employer or other person for whom the work was prepared is considered the author."

What is a "Work Made for Hire"? A "work made for hire" is defined as: (1) a work prepared by an employee within the scope of his or her employment"; or (2) "a work specially ordered or commissioned for use as a contribution to a collective work, as a part of a motion picture or other audiovisual work, as a translation, as a supplementary work, as a compilation, as an instructional text, as a test, as answer material for a test, or as an atlas, if the parties expressly agree in a written instrument signed by them that the work shall be considered a work made for hire." If you have checked "Yes" to indicate that the work was "made for hire," you must give the full legal name of the employer (or other person for whom the work was prepared). You may also include the name of the employee along with the name of the employer (for example: "Elster Record Co., employer for hire of John Ferguson").

"Anonymous" or "Pseudonymous" Work: An author's contribution to a work is "anonymous" if that author is not identified on the copies or phonorecords of the work. An author's contribution to a work is "pseudonymous" if that author is identified on the copies or phonorecords under a fictitious name. If the work is "anonymous" you may: (1) leave the line blank; or (2) state "anonymous" on the line; or (3) reveal the author's identity. If the work is "pseudonymous" you may: (1) leave the line blank; or (2) give the pseudonym and identify it as such (for example: "Huntley Haverstock, pseudonym"); or (3) reveal the author's name, making clear which is the real name and which is the pseudonym (for example: "Judith Barton, whose pseudonym is Madeline Elster"). However the citizenship or domicile of the author must be given in all cases.

Dates of Birth and Death: If the author is dead, the statute requires that the year of death be included in the application unless the work is anonymous or pseudonymous. The author's birth date is optional, but is useful as a form of identification. Leave this space blank if the author's contribution was a "work made for hire."

Author's Nationality or Domicile: Give the country in which the author is a citizen, or the country in which the author is domiciled. Nationality or domicile must be given in all cases.

Nature of Authorship: Give a brief general statement of the nature of this particular author's contribution to the work. If you are submitting this Form SR to cover both the sound recording and the underlying musical, dramatic, or literary work, make sure that the precise nature of each author's contribution is reflected here. Examples where the authorship pertains to the recording: "Sound Recording"; "Performance and Recording"; "Compilation and Remixing of Sounds." Examples where the authorship pertains to both the recording and the underlying work: "Words, Music, Performance, Recording"; "Arrangement of Music and Recording"; "Compilation of Poems and Reading."

3 SPACE 3: Creation and Publication

General Instructions: Do not confuse "creation" with "publication." Every application for copyright registration must state "the year in which creation of the work was completed." Give the date and nation of first publication only if the work has been published.

Creation: Under the statute, a work is "created" when it is fixed in a copy or phonorecord for the first time. Where a work has been prepared over a period of time, the part of the work existing in fixed form on a particular date constitutes the created work on that date. The date you give here should be the year in which the author completed the particular version for which registration is now being sought, even if other versions exist or if further changes or additions are planned.

Publication: The statute defines "publication" as "the distribution of copies or phonorecords of a work to the public by sale or other transfer of ownership or by rental, lease, or lending"; a work is also "published" if there has been an "offering to distribute copies or phonorecords to a group of persons for purposes of further distribution, public performance, or public display." Give the full date (month, date, year) when, and the country where, publication first occurred. If first publication took place simultaneously in the United States and other countries, it is sufficient to state "U.S.A."

4 SPACE 4: Claimant(s)

Name(s) and Address(es) of Copyright Claimant(s): Give the name(s) and address(es) of the copyright claimant(s) in the work even if the claimant is the same as the author. Copyright in a work belongs initially to the author of the work (including, in the case of a work made for hire, the employer or other person for whom the work was prepared). The copyright claimant is either the author of the work or a person or organization to whom the copyright initially belonging to the author has been transferred.

Transfer: The statute provides that, if the copyright claimant is not the author, the application for registration must contain "a brief statement of how the claimant obtained ownership of the copyright." If any copyright claimant named in space 4 is not an author named in space 2, give a brief statement explaining how the claimant(s) obtained ownership of the copyright. Examples: "By written contract"; "Transfer of all rights by author"; "Assignment"; "By will." Do not attach transfer documents or other attachments or riders.

5 SPACE 5: Previous Registration

General Instructions: The questions in space 5 are intended to show whether an earlier registration has been made for this work and, if so, whether there is any basis for a new registration. As a rule, only one basic copyright registration can be made for the same version of a particular work.

Same Version: If this version is substantially the same as the work covered by a previous registration, a second registration is not generally possible unless: (1) the work has been registered in unpublished form and a second registration is now being sought to cover this first published edition; or (2) someone other than the author is identified as copyright claimant in the earlier registration and the author is now seeking registration in his or her own name. If either of these two exceptions apply, check the appropriate box and give the earlier registration number and date. Otherwise, do not submit Form SR; instead write the Copyright Office for information about supplementary registration or recordation of transfers of copyright ownership.

Changed Version: If the work has been changed and you are now seeking registration to cover the additions or revisions, check the last box in space 5, give the earlier registration number and date, and complete both parts of space 6 in accordance with the instructions below.

Previous Registration Number and Date: If more than one previous registration has been made for the work, give the number and date of the latest registration.

6 SPACE 6: Derivative Work or Compilation

General Instructions: Complete space 6 if this work is a "changed version," "compilation," or "derivative work," and if it incorporates one or more earlier works that have already been published or registered for copyright, or that have fallen into the public domain, or sound recordings that were fixed before February 15, 1972. A "compilation" is defined as "a work formed by the collection and assembling of preexisting materials or of data that are selected, coordinated, or arranged in such a way that the resulting work as a whole constitutes an original work of authorship." A "derivative work" is "a work based on one or more preexisting works." Examples of derivative works include recordings reissued with substantial editorial revisions or abridgments of the recorded sounds, and recordings republished with new recorded material, or any other form in which a work may be recast, transformed, or adapted." Derivative works also include works "consisting of editorial revisions, annotations, or other modifications" if these changes, as a whole, represent an original work of authorship.

Preexisting Material (space 6a): Complete this space and space 6b for derivative works. In this space identify the preexisting work that has been recast, transformed, or adapted. For example, the preexisting material might be: "1970 recording by Sperrvalle Symphony of Bach Double Concerto." Do not complete this space for compilations.

Material Added to This Work (space 6b): Give a brief, general statement of the additional new material covered by the copyright claim for which registration is sought. In the case of a derivative work, identify this new material. Examples: "Recorded performances on bands 1 and 3"; "Remixed sounds from original multitrack sound sources"; "New words, arrangement, and additional sounds." If the work is a compilation, give a brief, general statement describing both the material that has been compiled and the compilation itself. Example: "Compilation of 1930s Recordings by various swing bands."

7,8,9 SPACE 7,8,9: Fee, Correspondence, Certification, Return Address

Fee: The Copyright Office has the authority to adjust fees at 5-year intervals, based on changes in the Consumer Price Index. The next adjustment is due in 1996. Please contact the Copyright Office after July 1995 to determine the actual fee schedule.

Deposit Account: If you maintain a Deposit Account in the Copyright Office, identify it in space 7. Otherwise leave the space blank and send the fee of $20 with your application and deposit.

Correspondence (space 7): This space should contain the name, address, area code, and telephone number of the person to be consulted if correspondence about this application become necessary.

Certification (space 8): This application cannot be accepted unless it bears the date and the handwritten signature of the author or other copyright claimant, or of the owner of exclusive right(s), or of the duly authorized agent of the author, claimant, or owner of exclusive right(s).

Address for Return of Certificate (space 9): The address box must be completed legibly since the certificate will be returned in a window envelope.

MORE INFORMATION

"Works": "Works" are the basic subject matter of copyright; they are what authors create and copyright protects. The statute draws a sharp distinction between the "work" and "any material object in which the work is embodied."

"Copies" and "Phonorecords": These are the two types of material objects in which works are embodied. In general, "copies" are objects from which a work can be read or visually perceived, directly or with the aid of a machine or device, such as manuscripts, books, sheet music, film, and videotape. "Phonorecords" are objects embodying fixations of sounds, such as audio tapes and phonograph disks. For example, a song (the "work") can be reproduced in sheet music ("copies") or phonograph disks ("phonorecords") or both.

"Sound Recordings": These are "works," not "copies" or "phonorecords." "Sound recordings" are works that result from the fixation of a series of musical, spoken, or other sounds, but not including the sounds accompanying a motion picture or other audiovisual work. Example: When a record company issues a new release, the release will typically involve two distinct "works": the "musical work" that has been recorded, and the "sound recording" as a separate work in itself. The material objects that the recorded content sends out are "phonorecords"—physical reproductions of both the "musical work" and the "sound recording."

Should You File More Than One Application? If your work consists of a recorded musical, dramatic, or literary work and if both that "work" and the sound recording as a separate "work" are eligible for registration, the application form you should file depends on the following:

File Only Form SR if: The copyright claimant is the same for both the musical, dramatic, or literary work and for the sound recording, and you are seeking a single registration to cover both of these "works."

File Only Form PA (or Form TX) if: You are seeking to register only the musical, dramatic, or literary work, not the sound recording. Form PA is appropriate for works of the performing arts; Form TX is for nondramatic literary works.

Separate Applications Should Be Filed on Form PA (or Form TX) and on Form SR if: (1) The copyright claimant for the musical, dramatic, or literary work is different from the copyright claimant for the sound recording; or (2) You prefer to have separate registrations for the musical, dramatic, or literary work and for the sound recording.

FORM SR
For a Sound Recording
UNITED STATES COPYRIGHT OFFICE

REGISTRATION NUMBER

SR   SRU

EFFECTIVE DATE OF REGISTRATION

Month   Day   Year

DO NOT WRITE ABOVE THIS LINE. IF YOU NEED MORE SPACE, USE A SEPARATE CONTINUATION SHEET.

1

TITLE OF THIS WORK ▼

PREVIOUS OR ALTERNATIVE TITLES ▼

NATURE OF MATERIAL RECORDED ▼ See instructions
☐ Musical   ☐ Musical-Dramatic
☐ Dramatic   ☐ Literary
☐ Other _____

2   **a**

NAME OF AUTHOR ▼

DATES OF BIRTH AND DEATH
Year Born ▼   Year Died ▼

Was this contribution to the work a "work made for hire"?
☐ Yes
☐ No

AUTHOR'S NATIONALITY OR DOMICILE
Name of Country
OR { Citizen of ▶ _____
Domiciled in ▶ _____

WAS THIS AUTHOR'S CONTRIBUTION TO THE WORK
Anonymous?   ☐ Yes ☐ No
Pseudonymous?   ☐ Yes ☐ No
If the answer to either of these questions is "Yes" see detailed instructions.

NATURE OF AUTHORSHIP Briefly describe nature of material created by this author in which copyright is claimed ▼

NOTE

Under the law the "author" of a "work made for hire" is generally the employer, not the employee (see instructions). For any part of this work that was "made for hire" check "Yes" in the space provided, give the employer (or other person for whom the work was prepared) as "Author" of that part, and leave the space for dates of birth and death blank.

b

NAME OF AUTHOR ▼

DATES OF BIRTH AND DEATH
Year Born ▼   Year Died ▼

Was this contribution to the work a "work made for hire"?
☐ Yes
☐ No

AUTHOR'S NATIONALITY OR DOMICILE
Name of Country
OR { Citizen of ▶ _____
Domiciled in ▶ _____

WAS THIS AUTHOR'S CONTRIBUTION TO THE WORK
Anonymous?   ☐ Yes ☐ No
Pseudonymous?   ☐ Yes ☐ No
If the answer to either of these questions is "Yes" see detailed instructions.

NATURE OF AUTHORSHIP Briefly describe nature of material created by this author in which copyright is claimed ▼

c

NAME OF AUTHOR ▼

DATES OF BIRTH AND DEATH
Year Born ▼   Year Died ▼

Was this contribution to the work a "work made for hire"?
☐ Yes
☐ No

AUTHOR'S NATIONALITY OR DOMICILE
Name of Country
OR { Citizen of ▶ _____
Domiciled in ▶ _____

WAS THIS AUTHOR'S CONTRIBUTION TO THE WORK
Anonymous?   ☐ Yes ☐ No
Pseudonymous?   ☐ Yes ☐ No
If the answer to either of these questions is "Yes" see detailed instructions.

NATURE OF AUTHORSHIP Briefly describe nature of material created by this author in which copyright is claimed ▼

3   **a**

YEAR IN WHICH CREATION OF THIS WORK WAS COMPLETED This information must be given ◀ Year in all cases.

b DATE AND NATION OF FIRST PUBLICATION OF THIS PARTICULAR WORK
Complete this information Month ▶ ___ Day ▶ ___ Year ▶ ___
ONLY if this work has been published   ◀ Nation

4

See instructions before completing this space.

COPYRIGHT CLAIMANT(S) Name and address must be given even if the claimant is the same as the author given in space 2 ▼

TRANSFER If the claimant(s) named here in space 4 is (are) different from the author(s) named in space 2, give a brief statement of how the claimant(s) obtained ownership of the copyright ▼

APPLICATION RECEIVED

ONE DEPOSIT RECEIVED

TWO DEPOSITS RECEIVED

REMITTANCE NUMBER AND DATE

DO NOT WRITE HERE OFFICE USE ONLY

MORE ON BACK ▶ • Complete all applicable spaces (numbers 5-9) on the reverse side of this page
• See detailed instructions.   • Sign the form at line 8

DO NOT WRITE HERE
Page 1 of ___ pages

EXAMINED BY	FORM SR
CHECKED BY	
☐ CORRESPONDENCE ☐ Yes	FOR COPYRIGHT OFFICE USE ONLY

DO NOT WRITE ABOVE THIS LINE. IF YOU NEED MORE SPACE, USE A SEPARATE CONTINUATION SHEET.

PREVIOUS REGISTRATION Has registration for this work, or for an earlier version of this work, already been made in the Copyright Office?

☐ Yes ☐ No If your answer is "Yes," why is another registration being sought? (Check appropriate box) ▼

a ☐ This is the first published edition of a work previously registered in unpublished form

b ☐ This is the first application submitted by this author as copyright claimant

c ☐ This is a changed version of the work, as shown by space 6 on this application

If your answer is "Yes" give: **Previous Registration Number** ▼ **Year of Registration** ▼

5

DERIVATIVE WORK OR COMPILATION Complete both space 6a and 6b for a derivative work; complete only 6b for a compilation

a **Preexisting Material** Identify any preexisting work or works that this work is based on or incorporates ▼

b **Material Added to This Work** Give a brief, general statement of the material that has been added to this work and in which copyright is claimed ▼

6

See instructions before completing this space

DEPOSIT ACCOUNT If the registration fee is to be charged to a Deposit Account established in the Copyright Office, give name and number of Account

Name ▼ **Account Number** ▼

7

CORRESPONDENCE Give name and address to which correspondence about this application should be sent Name/Address/Apt/City/State/ZIP ▼

Area Code and Telephone Number ►

Be sure to give your daytime phone ◄ number

CERTIFICATION* I the undersigned, hereby certify that I am the

check only one ▼

☐ author

☐ other copyright claimant

☐ owner of exclusive right(s)

☐ authorized agent of _____

Name of author or other copyright claimant, or owner of exclusive right(s) ▲

of the work identified in this application and that the statements made by me in this application are correct to the best of my knowledge.

Typed or printed name and date ▼ If this application gives a date of publication in space 3, do not sign and submit it before that date

date ►

Handwritten signature (X) ▼

8

MAIL CERTIFICATE TO

Name ▼

Number/Street/Apartment Number ▼

City/State/ZIP ▼

Certificate will be mailed in window envelope

YOU MUST
· Complete all necessary spaces
· Sign your application in space 8

SEND ALL 3 ELEMENTS IN THE SAME PACKAGE:
1. Application form
2. Nonrefundable $20 filing fee in check or money order payable to Register of Copyrights
3. Deposit material

MAIL TO:
Register of Copyrights
Library of Congress
Washington D.C. 20559

The Copyright Office has the authority to adjust fees at 5-year intervals, based on changes in the Consumer Price Index. The next adjustment is due in 1996. Please contact the Copyright Office after July 1995 to determine the actual fee schedule.

9

December 1993—75,000

☉U.S. GOVERNMENT PRINTING OFFICE: 1993-301-241/80,051

Sample Form: U.S. Copyright Office Forms:
Form VA

▨Filling Out Application Form VA

Detach and read these instructions before completing this form.
Make sure all applicable spaces have been filled in before you return this form.

BASIC INFORMATION

When to Use This Form: Use Form VA for copyright registration of published or unpublished works of the visual arts. This category consists of "pictorial, graphic, or sculptural works " including two-dimensional and three-dimensional works of fine, graphic, and applied art, photographs, prints and art reproductions, maps, globes, charts, technical drawings, diagrams, and models.

What Does Copyright Protect? Copyright in a work of the visual arts protects those pictorial, graphic, or sculptural elements that, either alone or in combination, represent an "original work of authorship." The statute declares: "In no case does copyright protection for an original work of authorship extend to any idea, procedure, process, system, method of operation, concept, principle, or discovery, regardless of the form in which it is described, explained, illustrated, or embodied in such work."

Works of Artistic Craftsmanship and Designs: "Works of artistic craftsmanship" are registrable on Form VA, but the statute makes clear that protection extends to "their form" and not to "their mechanical or utilitarian aspects." The "design of a useful article is considered copyrightable "only if, and only to the extent that, such design incorporates pictorial, graphic, or sculptural features that can be identified separately from, and are capable of existing independently of, the utilitarian aspects of the article."

Labels and Advertisements: Works prepared for use in connection with the sale or advertisement of goods and services are registrable if they contain "original work of authorship." Use Form VA if the copyrightable material in the work you are registering is mainly pictorial or graphic; use Form TX if it consists mainly of text. NOTE: Words and short phrases such as names, titles, and slogans cannot be protected by copyright, and the same is true of standard symbols, emblems, and other commonly used graphic designs that are in the public domain. When used commercially, material of that sort can sometimes be protected under state laws of unfair competition or under the Federal trademark laws. For information about trademark registration, write to the Commissioner of Patents and Trademarks, Washington, D.C. 20231

Architectural Works: Copyright protection extends to the design of buildings created for the use of human beings. Architectural works created on or after December 1, 1990, or that on December 1, 1990, were unconstructed and embodied only in unpublished plans or drawings are eligible. Request Circular 41 for more information.

Deposit to Accompany Application: An application for copyright registration must be accompanied by a deposit consisting of copies representing the entire work for which registration is to be made.

Unpublished Work: Deposit one complete copy.

Published Work: Deposit two complete copies of the best edition.

Work First Published Outside the United States: Deposit one complete copy of the first foreign edition.

Contribution to a Collective Work: Deposit one complete copy of the best edition of the collective work.

The Copyright Notice: For works first published on or after March 1, 1989, the law provides that a copyright notice in a specified form "may be placed on all publicly distributed copies from which the work can be visually perceived." Use of the copyright notice is the responsibility of the copyright owner and does not require advance permission from the Copyright Office. The required form of the notice for copies generally consists of three elements: (1) the symbol "©", or the word "Copyright," or the abbreviation "Copr."; (2) the year of first publication; and (3) the name of the owner of copyright. For example: "© 1991 Jane Cole." The notice is to be affixed to the copies "in such manner and location as to give reasonable notice of the claim of copyright." Works first published prior to March 1, 1989, must carry the notice or risk loss of copyright protection.

For information about notice requirements for works published before March 1, 1989, or other copyright information, write: Information Section, LM-401, Copyright Office, Library of Congress, Washington, D.C. 20559-6000.

LINE-BY-LINE INSTRUCTIONS

Please type or print using black ink.

1 SPACE 1: Title

Title of This Work: Every work submitted for copyright registration must be given a title to identify that particular work. If the copies of the work bear a title (or an identifying phrase that could serve as a title), transcribe that wording *completely* and *exactly* on the application. Indexing of the registration and future identification of the work will depend on the information you give here. For an architectural work that has been constructed, add the date of construction after the title; if unconstructed at this time, add "not yet constructed."

Previous or Alternative Titles: Complete this space if there are any additional titles for the work under which someone searching for the registration might be likely to look, or under which a document pertaining to the work might be recorded.

Publication as a Contribution: If the work being registered is a contribution to a periodical, serial, or collection, give the title of the contribution in the "Title of This Work" space. Then, in the line headed "Publication as a Contribution," give information about the collective work in which the contribution appeared.

Nature of This Work: Briefly describe the general nature or character of the pictorial, graphic, or sculptural work being registered for copyright. Examples: "Oil Painting"; "Charcoal Drawing"; "Etching"; "Sculpture"; "Map"; "Photograph"; "Scale Model"; "Lithographic Print"; "Jewelry Design"; "Fabric Design."

2 SPACE 2: Author(s)

General Instruction: After reading these instructions, decide who are the "authors" of this work for copyright purposes. Then, unless the work is a "collective work," give the requested information about every "author" who contributed any appreciable amount of copyrightable matter to this version of the work. If you need further space, request Continuation Sheets. In the case of a collective work, such as a catalog of paintings or collection of cartoons by various authors, give information about the author of the collective work as a whole.

Name of Author: The fullest form of the author's name should be given. Unless the work was "made for hire," the individual who actually created the work is its "author." In the case of a work made for hire, the statute provides that "the employer or other person for whom the work was prepared is considered the author."

What is a "Work Made for Hire"? A "work made for hire" is defined as: (1) "a work prepared by an employee within the scope of his or her employment"; or (2) "a work specially ordered or commissioned for use as a contribution to a collective work, as a part of a motion picture or other audiovisual work, as a translation, as a supplementary work, as a compilation, as an instructional text, as a test, as answer material for a test, or as an atlas, if the parties expressly agree in a written instrument signed by them that the work shall be considered a work made for hire." If you have checked "Yes" to indicate that the work was "made for hire," you must give the full legal name of the employer (or other person for whom the work was prepared). You may also include the name of the employee along with the name of the employer (for example: "Elster Publishing Co., employer for hire of John Ferguson")

"Anonymous" or "Pseudonymous" Work: An author's contribution to a work is "anonymous" if that author is not identified on the copies or phonorecords of the work. An author's contribution to a work is "pseudonymous" if that author is identified on the copies or phonorecords under a fictitious name. If the work is "anonymous" you may: (1) leave the line blank; or (2) state "anonymous" on the line; or (3) reveal the author's identity. If the work is "pseudonymous" you may: (1) leave the line blank; or (2) give the pseudonym and identify it as such (for example: "Huntley Haverstock, pseudonym"); or (3) reveal the author's name, making clear which is the real name and which is the pseudonym (for example: "Henry Leek, whose pseudonym is Enam Farrel"). However, the citizenship or domicile of the author must be given in all cases

Dates of Birth and Death: If the author is dead, the statute requires that the year of death be included in the application unless the work is anonymous or pseudonymous. The author's birth date is optional but is useful as a form of identification. Leave this space blank if the author's contribution was a "work made for hire."

Author's Nationality or Domicile: Give the country of which the author is a citizen or the country in which the author is domiciled. Nationality or domicile must be given in all cases

Nature of Authorship: Categories of pictorial, graphic and sculptural authorship are listed below. Check the box(es) that best describe(s) each author's contribution to the work.

3-Dimensional sculptures: fine art sculptures, toys, dolls, scale models, and sculptural designs applied to useful articles

2-Dimensional artwork: watercolor and oil paintings; pen and ink drawings; logo illustrations; greeting cards; collages; stencils; patterns; computer graphics; graphics appearing in screen displays; artwork appearing on posters, calendars, games, commercial prints and labels, and packaging, as well as 2-dimensional artwork applied to useful articles

Reproductions of works of art: reproductions of preexisting artwork made by, for example, lithography, photoengraving, or etching

Maps: cartographic representations of an area such as state and county maps, atlases, marine charts, relief maps, and globes

Photographs: pictorial photographic prints and slides and holograms

Jewelry designs: 3-dimensional designs applied to rings, pendants, earrings, necklaces, and the like

Designs on sheetlike materials: designs reproduced on textiles, lace, and other fabrics; wallpaper; carpeting; floor tile; wrapping paper; and clothing

Technical drawings: diagrams illustrating scientific or technical information in linear form such as architectural blueprints or mechanical drawings

Text: textual material that accompanies pictorial, graphic or sculptural works such as comic strips, greeting cards, games rules, commercial prints or labels, and maps

Architectural works: designs of buildings, including the overall form as well as the arrangement and composition of spaces and elements of the design. NOTE: Any registration for the underlying architectural plans must be applied for on a separate Form VA, checking the box "Technical drawing"

3 SPACE 3: Creation and Publication

General Instructions: Do not confuse "creation" with "publication." Every application for copyright registration must state "the year in which creation of the work was completed." Give the date and nation of first publication only if the work has been published

Creation: Under the statute, a work is "created" when it is fixed in a copy or phonorecord for the first time. Where a work has been prepared over a period of time, the part of the work existing in fixed form on a particular date constitutes the created work on that date. The date you give here should be the year in which the author completed the particular version for which registration is now being sought, even if other versions exist or if further changes or additions are planned

Publication: The statute defines "publication" as "the distribution of copies or phonorecords of a work to the public by sale or other transfer of ownership, or by rental, lease or lending." A work is also "published" if there has been an "offering to distribute copies or phonorecords to a group of persons for purposes of further distribution, public performance, or public display." Give the full date (month, day, year) when, and the country where, publication first occurred. If first publication took place simultaneously in the United States and other countries, it is sufficient to state "U.S.A."

4 SPACE 4: Claimant(s)

Name(s) and Address(es) of Copyright Claimant(s): Give the name(s) and address(es) of the copyright claimant(s) in this work even if the claimant is the same as the author. Copyright in a work belongs initially to the author of the work (including, in the case of a work made for hire, the employer or other person for whom the work was prepared) The copyright claimant is either the author of the work or a person or organization to whom the copyright initially belonging to the author has been transferred

Transfer: The statute provides that if the copyright claimant is not the author, the application for registration must contain "a brief statement of how the claimant obtained ownership of the copyright." If any copyright claimant named in space 4 is not an author named in space 2, give a brief statement explaining how the claimant(s) obtained ownership of the copyright Examples: "By written contract"; "Transfer of all rights by author"; "Assignment"; "By will" Do not attach transfer documents or other attachments or riders

5 SPACE 5: Previous Registration

General Instructions: The questions in space 5 are intended to find out whether an earlier registration has been made for this work and, if so, whether

there is any basis for a new registration. As a rule only one basic copyright registration can be made for the same version of a particular work

Same Version: If this version is substantially the same as the work covered by a previous registration, a second registration is not generally possible unless: (1) the work has been registered in unpublished form and a second registration is now being sought to cover this first published edition; or (2) someone other than the author is identified as a copyright claimant in the earlier registration, and the author is now seeking registration in his or her own name. If either of these two exceptions apply, check the appropriate box and give the earlier registration number and date. Otherwise, do not submit Form VA; instead, write the Copyright Office for information about supplementary registration or recordation or transfers of copyright ownership

Changed Version: If the work has been changed and you are now seeking registration to cover the additions or revisions, check the last box in space 5, give the earlier registration number and date, and complete both parts of space 6 in accordance with the instruction below.

Previous Registration Number and Date: If more than one previous registration has been made for the work, give the number and date of the latest registration.

6 SPACE 6: Derivative Work or Compilation

General Instructions: Complete space 6 if this work is a "changed version," "compilation," or "derivative work," and if it incorporates one or more earlier works that have already been published or registered for copyright, or that have fallen into the public domain. A "compilation" is defined as "a work formed by the collection and assembling of preexisting material, or of data that are selected, coordinated, or arranged in such a way that the resulting work as a whole constitutes an original work of authorship." A "derivative work" is "a work based on one or more preexisting works." Examples of derivative works include reproductions of works of art, sculptures based on drawings, lithographs based on paintings, maps based on previously published sources, or "any other form in which a work may be recast, transformed, or adapted." Derivative works also include works "consisting of editorial revisions, annotations, or other modifications" if these changes, as a whole, represent an original work of authorship

Preexisting Material (space 6a): Complete this space and space 6b for derivative works. In this space identify the preexisting work that has been recast, transformed, or adapted. Examples of preexisting material might be "Grunewald Altarpiece" or "19th century quilt design" Do not complete this space for compilations

Material Added to This Work (space 6b): Give a brief, general statement of the additional new material covered by the copyright claim for which registration is sought. In the case of a derivative work, identify this new material. Examples: "Adaptation of design and additional artistic work"; "Reproduction of painting by photolithography"; "Additional cartographic material"; "Compilation of photographs" If the work is a compilation, give a brief, general statement describing both the material that has been compiled and the compilation itself. Example: "Compilation of 19th century political cartoons"

7,8,9 SPACE 7,8,9: Fee, Correspondence, Certification, Return Address

Fee: The Copyright Office has the authority to adjust fees at 5-year intervals, based on changes in the Consumer Price Index. The next adjustment is due in 1996. Please contact the Copyright Office after July 1995 to determine the actual fee schedule.

Deposit Account: If you maintain a Deposit Account in the Copyright Office, identify it in space 7. Otherwise leave the space blank and send the fee of $20 with your application and deposit

Correspondence (space 7): This space should contain the name, address, area code and telephone number of the person to be consulted if correspondence about this application becomes necessary

Certification (space 8): The application cannot be accepted unless it bears the date and the handwritten signature of the author or other copyright claimant, or of the owner of exclusive rights, or of the duly authorized agent of the author, claimant, or owner of exclusive rights

Address for Return of Certificate (space 9): The address box must be completed legibly since the certificate will be returned in a window envelope

PRIVACY ACT ADVISORY STATEMENT Required by the Privacy Act of 1974 (P.L. 93 - 579)
The authority for requesting this information is title 17 U.S.C. secs. 409 and 410. Furnishing the requested information is voluntary. But if the information is not furnished, it may be necessary to delay or refuse registration and you may not be entitled to certain relief, remedies and benefits provided in chapters 4 and 5 of title 17 U.S.C.

The principal uses of the requested information are the establishment and maintenance of a public record and the examination of the application for compliance with legal requirements.

Other routine uses include public inspection and copying, preparation of public indexes, preparation of public catalogs of copyright registrations, and preparation of search reports upon request.

NOTE: No other advisory statement will be given you in connection with this application. Please keep this statement and refer to it if we communicate with you regarding this application.

FORM VA
For a Work of the Visual Arts
UNITED STATES COPYRIGHT OFFICE

REGISTRATION NUMBER

VA   VAU
EFFECTIVE DATE OF REGISTRATION

Month   Day   Year

DO NOT WRITE ABOVE THIS LINE. IF YOU NEED MORE SPACE, USE A SEPARATE CONTINUATION SHEET.

1

TITLE OF THIS WORK ▼   NATURE OF THIS WORK ▼ See instructions

PREVIOUS OR ALTERNATIVE TITLES ▼

PUBLICATION AS A CONTRIBUTION If this work was published as a contribution to a periodical, serial, or collection, give information about the collective work in which the contribution appeared.   **Title of Collective Work ▼**

If published in a periodical or serial give   **Volume ▼**   **Number ▼**   **Issue Date ▼**   **On Pages ▼**

2

a

NAME OF AUTHOR ▼   DATES OF BIRTH AND DEATH
                                                    Year Born ▼   Year Died ▼

Was this contribution to the work   AUTHOR'S NATIONALITY OR DOMICILE   WAS THIS AUTHOR'S CONTRIBUTION TO
made for hire?   Name of Country   THE WORK   If the answer to either
☐ Yes   OR { Citizen of ▶   Anonymous?   ☐ Yes   ☐ No   of these questions is
☐ No   { Domiciled in ▶   Pseudonymous?   ☐ Yes   ☐ No   'Yes' see detailed instructions

NATURE OF AUTHORSHIP Check appropriate boxes) **See instructions**
☐ 3-Dimensional sculpture   ☐ Map   ☐ Technical drawing
☐ 2-Dimensional artwork   ☐ Photograph   ☐ Text
☐ Reproduction of work of art   ☐ Jewelry design   ☐ Architectural work
☐ Design on sheetlike material

NOTE

Under the law, the 'author' of a 'work made for hire' is generally the employer, not the employee (see instructions) For any part of this work that was made for hire check 'Yes' in the space provided, give the employer (or other person for whom the work was prepared) as 'Author' of that part, and leave the space for dates of birth and death blank.

b

NAME OF AUTHOR ▼   DATES OF BIRTH AND DEATH
                                                    Year Born ▼   Year Died ▼

Was this contribution to the work   AUTHOR'S NATIONALITY OR DOMICILE   WAS THIS AUTHOR'S CONTRIBUTION TO
made for hire?   Name of Country   THE WORK   If the answer to either
☐ Yes   OR { Citizen of ▶   Anonymous?   ☐ Yes   ☐ No   of these questions is
☐ No   { Domiciled in ▶   Pseudonymous?   ☐ Yes   ☐ No   'Yes' see detailed instructions

NATURE OF AUTHORSHIP Check appropriate boxes) **See instructions**
☐ 3-Dimensional sculpture   ☐ Map   ☐ Technical drawing
☐ 2-Dimensional artwork   ☐ Photograph   ☐ Text
☐ Reproduction of work of art   ☐ Jewelry design   ☐ Architectural work
☐ Design on sheetlike material

3

a

YEAR IN WHICH CREATION OF THIS   DATE AND NATION OF FIRST PUBLICATION OF THIS PARTICULAR WORK
WORK WAS COMPLETED This information   Complete this information   Month ▶   Day ▶   Year ▶
must be given   ONLY if this work
◀ Year in all cases   has been published   ◀ Nation

4

See instructions before completing this space

COPYRIGHT CLAIMANT(S) Name and address must be given even if the claimant is the same as the author given in space 2 ▼

TRANSFER If the claimant(s) named here in space 4 is (are) different from the author(s) named in space 2, give a brief statement of how the claimant(s) obtained ownership of the copyright ▼

APPLICATION RECEIVED

ONE DEPOSIT RECEIVED

TWO DEPOSITS RECEIVED

FUNDS RECEIVED

DO NOT WRITE HERE
OFFICE USE ONLY

MORE ON BACK ▶   • Complete all applicable spaces (numbers 5-9) on the reverse side of this page.   DO NOT WRITE HERE
    • See detailed instructions.   • Sign the form at line 8.   Page 1 of   pages

EXAMINED BY

CHECKED BY

CORRESPONDENCE
Yes

FORM VA

FOR
COPYRIGHT
OFFICE
USE
ONLY

DO NOT WRITE ABOVE THIS LINE. IF YOU NEED MORE SPACE, USE A SEPARATE CONTINUATION SHEET.

PREVIOUS REGISTRATION Has registration for this work, or for an earlier version of this work, already been made in the Copyright Office?
☐ Yes ☐ No If your answer is "Yes," why is another registration being sought? (Check appropriate box) ▼
a. ☐ This is the first published edition of a work previously registered in unpublished form
b. ☐ This is the first application submitted by this author as copyright claimant
c. ☐ This is a changed version of the work, as shown by space 6 on this application

If your answer is "Yes," give: **Previous Registration Number** ▼   **Year of Registration** ▼

5

DERIVATIVE WORK OR COMPILATION Complete both space 6a and 6b for a derivative work; complete only 6b for a compilation
a. **Preexisting Material** Identify any preexisting work or works that this work is based on or incorporates ▼

b. **Material Added to This Work** Give a brief, general statement of the material that has been added to this work and in which copyright is claimed ▼

6

See instructions
before completing
this space

DEPOSIT ACCOUNT If the registration fee is to be charged to a Deposit Account established in the Copyright Office, give name and number of Account
Name ▼   **Account Number** ▼

7

CORRESPONDENCE Give name and address to which correspondence about this application should be sent   Name/Address/Apt/City/State/ZIP ▼

Area Code and Telephone Number ▶

Be sure to
give your
daytime phone
◀ number

CERTIFICATION* I, the undersigned, hereby certify that I am the
check only one ▼
☐ author
☐ other copyright claimant
☐ owner of exclusive right(s)
☐ authorized agent of _____
             Name of author or other copyright claimant, or owner of exclusive right(s) ▲

of the work identified in this application and that the statements made
by me in this application are correct to the best of my knowledge.

Typed or printed name and date ▼ If this application gives a date of publication in space 3, do not sign and submit it before that date.
                                                                Date ▶

Handwritten signature (X) ▼

8

MAIL CERTIFICATE TO

Name ▼

Number/Street/Apt ▼

City/State ZIP ▼

Certificate
will be
mailed in
window
envelope

YOU MUST:
• Complete all necessary spaces
• Sign your application in space 8
SEND ALL 3 ELEMENTS
IN THE SAME PACKAGE
1. Application form
2. Nonrefundable $20 filing fee
   in check or money order
   payable to Register of Copyrights
3. Deposit material
MAIL TO:
Register of Copyrights
Library of Congress
Washington, D C 20559-6000

The Copyright Office
has the authority to adjust fees at 5-year intervals, based on changes
in the Consumer Price
Index. The next adjustment is due in 1996.
Please contact the
Copyright Office after
July 1995 to determine
the actual fee schedule.

9

*17 U.S.C. § 506(e): Any person who knowingly makes a false representation of a material fact in the application for copyright registration provided for by section 409, or in any written statement filed in connection
with the application, shall be fined not more than $2,500

Jun 1993—300,000   ♻ PRINTED ON RECYCLED PAPER   ☆ U.S. GOVERNMENT PRINTING OFFICE 1993 342-582/80 021

Sample Form: U.S. Copyright Office Forms:
Form PA

Filling Out Application Form PA

Detach and read these instructions before completing this form.
Make sure all applicable spaces have been filled in before you return this form.

BASIC INFORMATION

When to Use This Form: Use Form PA for registration of published or unpublished works of the performing arts. This class includes works prepared for the purpose of being performed directly before an audience or indirectly by means of any device or process. Works of the performing arts include: (1) musical works including any accompanying words; (2) dramatic works, including any accompanying music; (3) pantomimes and choreographic works; and (4) motion pictures and other audiovisual works.

Deposit to Accompany Application: An application for copyright registration must be accompanied by a deposit consisting of copies or phonorecords representing the entire work for which registration is made. The following are the general deposit requirements as set forth in the statute:

Unpublished Work: Deposit one complete copy (or phonorecord).

Published Work: Deposit two complete copies (or one phonorecord) of the best edition.

Work First Published Outside the United States: Deposit one complete copy (or phonorecord) of the first foreign edition.

Contribution to a Collective Work: Deposit one complete copy (or phonorecord) of the best edition of the collective work.

Motion Pictures: Deposit *both* of the following: (1) a separate written description of the contents of the motion picture; and (2) for a published work, one complete copy of the best edition of the motion picture; or, for an unpublished work, one complete copy of the motion picture or identifying material. Identifying material may be either an audiorecording of the entire soundtrack or one frame enlargement or similar visual print from each 10-minute segment.

The Copyright Notice: For works first published on or after March 1, 1989, the law provides that a copyright notice in a specified form "may be placed on all publicly distributed copies from which the work can be visually perceived." Use of the copyright notice is the responsibility of the copyright owner and does not require advance permission from the Copyright Office. The required form of the notice for copies generally consists of three elements: (1) the symbol "©", or the word "Copyright," or the abbreviation "Copr."; (2) the year of first publication; and (3) the name of the owner of copyright. For example: "© 1993 Jane Cole." The notice is to be affixed to the copies "in such manner and location as to give reasonable notice of the claim of copyright." Works first published prior to March 1, 1989, must carry the notice or risk loss of copyright protection.

For information about requirements for works published before March 1, 1989, or other copyright information, write: Information Section, LM-401, Copyright Office, Library of Congress, Washington, D.C. 20559.

PRIVACY ACT ADVISORY STATEMENT Required by the Privacy Act of 1974 (P.L. 93-579)
The authority for requesting this information is title 17, U.S.C. secs. 409 and 410. Furnishing the requested information is voluntary. But if the information is not furnished, it may be necessary to delay or refuse registration and you may not be entitled to certain relief, remedies, and benefits provided in chapters 4 and 5 of the 17 U.S.C.
The principal uses of the requested information are the establishment and maintenance of a public record and the examination of the application for compliance with legal requirements.
Other routine uses include public inspection and copying, preparation of public indexes, preparation of public catalogs of copyright registrations, and preparation of search reports upon request.
NOTE: No other advisory statement will be given in connection with this application. Please keep this statement and refer to it if we communicate with you regarding this application.

LINE-BY-LINE INSTRUCTIONS
Please type or print using black ink

1 SPACE 1: Title

Title of This Work: Every work submitted for copyright registration must be given a title to identify that particular work. If the copies or phonorecords of the work bear a title (or an identifying phrase that could serve as a title), transcribe that wording completely and exactly on the application. Indexing of the registration and future identification of the work will depend on the information you give here. If the work you are registering is an entire collective work (such as a collection of plays or songs), give the overall title of the collection. If you are registering one or more individual contributions to a collective work, give the title of each contribution, followed by the title of the collection. Example: "A Song for Elinda" in *Old and New Ballads for Old and New People*."

Previous or Alternative Titles: Complete this space if there are any additional titles for the work under which someone searching for the registration might be likely to look, or under which a document pertaining to the work might be recorded.

Nature of This Work: Briefly describe the general nature or character of the work being registered for copyright. Examples: "Music"; "Song Lyrics"; "Words and Music"; "Drama"; "Musical Play"; "Choreography"; "Pantomime"; "Motion Picture"; "Audiovisual Work."

2 SPACE 2: Author(s)

General Instructions: After reading these instructions, decide who are the "authors" of this work for copyright purposes. Then, unless the work is a "collective work," give the requested information about every author who contributed any appreciable amount of copyrightable matter to this version of the work. If you need further space, request additional Continuation Sheets. In the case of a collective work, such as a songbook or a collection of plays, give the information about the author of the collective work as a whole.

Name of Author: The fullest form of the author's name should be given. Unless the work was "made for hire," the individual who actually created the work is its "author." In the case of a work made for hire, the statute provides that "the employer or other person for whom the work was prepared is considered the author."

What is a "Work Made for Hire"? A "work made for hire" is defined as: (1) "a work prepared by an employee within the scope of his or her employment"; or (2) "a work specially ordered or commissioned for use as a contribution to a collective work, as a part of a motion picture or other audiovisual work, as a translation, as a supplementary work, as a compilation, as an instructional text, as a test, as answer material for a test, or as an atlas, if the parties expressly agree in a written instrument signed by them that the work shall be considered a work made for hire." If you have checked "Yes" to indicate that the work was "made for hire," you must give the full legal name of the employer (or other person for whom the work was prepared). You may also include the name of the employee along with the name of the employer (for example: "Elster Music Co., employer for hire of John Ferguson")

"Anonymous" or "Pseudonymous" Work: An author's contribution to a work is 'anonymous" if that author is not identified on the copies or phonorecords of the work. An author's contribution to a work is "pseudonymous" if that author is identified on the copies or phonorecords under a fictitious name. If the work is anonymous you may: (1) leave the line blank; or (2) state 'anonymous" on the line; or (3) reveal the author's identity. If the work is "pseudonymous" you may: (1) leave the line blank; or (2) give the pseudonym and identify it as such (example: "Huntley Haverstock, pseudonym"); or (3) reveal the author's name, making clear which is the real name and which is the pseudonym (for example: "Judith Barton whose pseudonym is Madeline Elster") However, the citizenship or domicile of the author must be given in all cases.

Dates of Birth and Death: If the author is dead, the statute requires that the year of death be included in the application unless the work is anonymous or pseudonymous. The author's birth date is optional, but is useful as a form of identification. Leave this space blank if the author's contribution was a "work made for hire."

Author's Nationality or Domicile: Give the country of which the author is a citizen, or the country in which the author is domiciled. Nationality or domicile must be given in all cases.

Nature of Authorship: Give a brief general statement of the nature of this particular author's contribution to the work. Examples: "Words"; "Co-Author of Music"; "Words and Music"; "Arrangement"; "Co-Author of Book and Lyrics"; "Dramatization"; "Screen Play"; "Compilation and English Translation"; "Editorial Revisions."

3 SPACE 3: Creation and Publication

General Instructions: Do not confuse "creation" with "publication." Every application for copyright registration must state "the year in which creation of the work was completed." Give the date and nation of first publication only if the work has been published

Creation: Under the statute, a work is "created" when it is fixed in a copy or phonorecord for the first time. Where a work has been prepared over a period of time, the part of the work existing in fixed form on a particular date constitutes the created work on that date. The date you give here should be the year in which the author completed the particular version for which registration is now being sought, even if other versions exist or if further changes or additions are planned

Publication: The statute defines "publication" as 'the distribution of copies or phonorecords of a work to the public by sale or other transfer of ownership, or by rental, lease, or lending"; a work is also "published" if there has been an "offering to distribute copies or phonorecords to a group of persons for purposes of further distribution, public performance, or public display." Give the full date (month, day, year) when, and the country where, publication first occurred. If first publication took place simultaneously, in the United States and other countries, it is sufficient to state "U.S.A."

4 SPACE 4: Claimant(s)

Name(s) and Address(es) of Copyright Claimant(s): Give the name(s) and address(es) of the copyright claimant(s) in this work even if the claimant is the same as the author. Copyright in a work belongs initially to the author of the work (including, in the case of a work made for hire, the employer or other person for whom the work was prepared). The copyright claimant is either the author of the work or a person or organization to whom the copyright initially belonging to the author has been transferred.

Transfer: The statute provides that, if the copyright claimant is not the author, the application for registration must contain "a brief statement of how the claimant obtained ownership of the copyright." If any copyright claimant named in space 4 is not an author named in space 2, give a brief statement explaining how the claimant(s) obtained ownership of the copyright. Examples: "By written contract"; "Transfer of all rights by author"; "Assignment"; "By will." Do not attach transfer documents or other attachments or riders.

5 SPACE 5: Previous Registration

General Instructions: The questions in space 5 are intended to show whether an earlier registration has been made for this work and, if so, whether there is any basis for a new registration. As a general rule only one basic copyright registration can be made for the same version of a particular work

Same Version: If this version is substantially the same as the work covered by a previous registration, a second registration is not generally possible unless: (1) the work has been registered in unpublished form and a second registration is now being sought to cover this first published edition; or (2) someone other than the author is identified as copyright claimant in the earlier registration, and the author is now seeking registration in his or her own name. If either of these two exceptions apply, check the appropriate box and give the earlier registration number and date. Otherwise, do not submit Form PA; instead, write the Copyright Office for information about supplementary registration or recordation of transfers of copyright ownership.

Changed Version: If the work has been changed, and you are now seeking registration to cover the additions or revisions, check the last box in space 5, give the earlier registration number and date, and complete both parts of space 6 in accordance with the instructions below

Previous Registration Number and Date: If more than one previous registration has been made for the work, give the number and date of the latest registration

6 SPACE 6: Derivative Work or Compilation

General Instructions: Complete space 6 if this work is a "changed version," "compilation," or "derivative work," and if it incorporates one or more earlier works that have already been published or registered for copyright or that have fallen into the public domain. A "compilation" is defined as "a work formed by the collection and assembling of preexisting materials or of data that are selected, coordinated, or arranged in such a way that the resulting work as a whole constitutes an original work of authorship." A "derivative work" is "a work based on one or more preexisting works." Examples of derivative works include musical arrangements, dramatizations, translations, abridgments, condensations, motion picture versions, or "any other form in which a work may be recast, transformed, or adapted." Derivative works also include works "consisting of editorial revisions, annotations, or other modifications" if these changes, as a whole, represent an original work of authorship.

Preexisting Material (space 6a): Complete this space and space 6b for derivative works. In this space identify the preexisting work that has been recast, transformed, or adapted. For example, the preexisting material might be: "French version of Hugo's 'Le Roi s'amuse.'" Do not complete this space for compilations

Material Added to This Work (space 6b): Give a brief, general statement of the additional new material covered by the copyright claim for which registration is sought. In the case of a derivative work, identify this new material. Examples: "Arrangement for piano and orchestra"; "Dramatization for television"; "New film version"; "Revisions throughout: Act III completely new." If the work is a compilation, give a brief, general statement describing both the material that has been compiled and the compilation itself. Example: "Compilation of 19th Century Military Songs."

7,8,9 SPACE 7, 8, 9: Fee, Correspondence, Certification, Return Address

Fee: The Copyright Office has the authority to adjust fees at 5-year intervals, based on changes in the Consumer Price Index. The next adjustment is due in 1996. Please contact the Copyright Office after July 1995 to determine the actual fee schedule

Deposit Account: If you maintain a Deposit Account in the Copyright Office, identify it in space 7. Otherwise leave the space blank and send the fee of $20 with your application and deposit

Correspondence (space 7): This space should contain the name, address, area code, and telephone number of the person to be consulted if correspondence about this application becomes necessary

Certification (space 8): The application cannot be accepted unless it bears the date and the handwritten signature of the author or other copyright claimant, or of the owner of exclusive rights, or of the duly authorized agent of the author, claimant, or owner of exclusive right(s)

Address for Return of Certificate (space 9): The address box must be completed legibly since the certificate will be returned in a window envelope

MORE INFORMATION

How to Register a Recorded Work: If the musical or dramatic work that you are registering has been recorded (as a tape, disk, or cassette), you may choose either copyright application Form PA (Performing Arts) or Form SR (Sound Recordings) depending on the purpose of the registration

Form PA should be used to register the underlying musical composition or dramatic work. Form SR has been developed specifically to register a "sound recording" as defined by the Copyright Act—a work resulting from the "fixation of a series of sounds," separate and distinct from the underlying musical or dramatic work. Form SR should be used when the copyright claim is limited to the sound recording itself. (In one instance, Form SR may also be used to file for a copyright registration for both kinds of works—see (4) below.) Therefore

(1) File Form PA if you are seeking to register the musical or dramatic work, not the sound recording, even though what you deposit for copyright purposes may be in the form of a phonorecord

(2) File Form PA if you are seeking to register the audio portion of an audiovisual work, such as a motion picture soundtrack, these are considered integral parts of the audiovisual work

(3) File Form SR if you are seeking to register the "sound recording" itself, that is, the work that results from the fixation of a series of musical, spoken, or other sounds, but not the underlying musical or dramatic work

(4) File Form SR if you are the copyright claimant for both the underlying musical or dramatic work and the sound recording, and you prefer to register both on the same form

(5) File both forms PA and SR if the copyright claimant for the underlying work and sound recording differ or you prefer to have separate registration for them

"Copies" and "Phonorecords": To register for copyright, you are required to deposit "copies" or "phonorecords." These are defined as follows.

Musical compositions may be embodied (fixed) in "copies," objects from which a work can be read or visually perceived, directly or with the aid of a machine or device, such as manuscripts, books, sheet music, film and videotape. They may also be fixed in "phonorecords," objects embodying fixations of sounds such as tapes and phonograph disks, commonly known as phonograph records. For example, a song the work to be registered can be reproduced in sheet music ("copies") or phonograph records ("phonorecords") or both

FORM PA
For a Work of the Performing Arts
UNITED STATES COPYRIGHT OFFICE

REGISTRATION NUMBER

PA   PAU

EFFECTIVE DATE OF REGISTRATION

Month   Day   Year

DO NOT WRITE ABOVE THIS LINE. IF YOU NEED MORE SPACE, USE A SEPARATE CONTINUATION SHEET.

1

TITLE OF THIS WORK ▼

PREVIOUS OR ALTERNATIVE TITLES ▼

NATURE OF THIS WORK ▼ See instructions

2

a

NAME OF AUTHOR ▼

DATES OF BIRTH AND DEATH
Year Born ▼   Year Died ▼

Was this contribution to the work a "work made for hire"?
☐ Yes
☐ No

AUTHOR'S NATIONALITY OR DOMICILE
Name of Country
OR { Citizen of ▶
Domiciled in ▶

WAS THIS AUTHOR'S CONTRIBUTION TO THE WORK
Anonymous? ☐ Yes ☐ No
Pseudonymous? ☐ Yes ☐ No
If the answer to either of these questions is "Yes," see detailed instructions

NATURE OF AUTHORSHIP Briefly describe nature of material created by this author in which copyright is claimed ▼

NOTE

Under the law, the "author" of a "work made for hire" is generally the employer, not the employee (see instructions). For any part of this work that was "made for hire" check "Yes" in the space provided, give the employer (or other person for whom the work was prepared) as "Author" of that part, and leave the space for dates of birth and death blank.

b

NAME OF AUTHOR ▼

DATES OF BIRTH AND DEATH
Year Born ▼   Year Died ▼

Was this contribution to the work a "work made for hire"?
☐ Yes
☐ No

AUTHOR'S NATIONALITY OR DOMICILE
Name of Country
OR { Citizen of ▶
Domiciled in ▶

WAS THIS AUTHOR'S CONTRIBUTION TO THE WORK
Anonymous? ☐ Yes ☐ No
Pseudonymous? ☐ Yes ☐ No
If the answer to either of these questions is "Yes," see detailed instructions

NATURE OF AUTHORSHIP Briefly describe nature of material created by this author in which copyright is claimed ▼

c

NAME OF AUTHOR ▼

DATES OF BIRTH AND DEATH
Year Born ▼   Year Died ▼

Was this contribution to the work a "work made for hire"?
☐ Yes
☐ No

AUTHOR'S NATIONALITY OR DOMICILE
Name of Country
OR { Citizen of ▶
Domiciled in ▶

WAS THIS AUTHOR'S CONTRIBUTION TO THE WORK
Anonymous? ☐ Yes ☐ No
Pseudonymous? ☐ Yes ☐ No
If the answer to either of these questions is "Yes," see detailed instructions

NATURE OF AUTHORSHIP Briefly describe nature of material created by this author in which copyright is claimed ▼

3

a YEAR IN WHICH CREATION OF THIS WORK WAS COMPLETED This information must be given ◀ Year in all cases

b DATE AND NATION OF FIRST PUBLICATION OF THIS PARTICULAR WORK
Complete this information Month ▶ _____ Day ▶ _____ Year ▶ _____
ONLY if this work has been published ◀ Nation

4

See instructions before completing this space

COPYRIGHT CLAIMANT(S) Name and address must be given even if the claimant is the same as the author given in space 2 ▼

TRANSFER If the claimant(s) named here in space 4 is (are) different from the author(s) named in space 2, give a brief statement of how the claimant(s) obtained ownership of the copyright ▼

APPLICATION RECEIVED

ONE DEPOSIT RECEIVED

TWO DEPOSITS RECEIVED

FUNDS RECEIVED

DO NOT WRITE HERE OFFICE USE ONLY

MORE ON BACK ▶ • Complete all applicable spaces (numbers 5-9) on the reverse side of this page
• See detailed instructions   • Sign the form at line 8

DO NOT WRITE HERE

Page 1 of _____ pages

EXAMINED BY	FORM PA
CHECKED BY	
CORRESPONDENCE Yes	FOR COPYRIGHT OFFICE USE ONLY

DO NOT WRITE ABOVE THIS LINE. IF YOU NEED MORE SPACE, USE A SEPARATE CONTINUATION SHEET.

PREVIOUS REGISTRATION Has registration for this work, or for an earlier version of this work, already been made in the Copyright Office?

☐ Yes ☐ No If your answer is "Yes" why is another registration being sought? (Check appropriate box) ▼

a. ☐ This is the first published edition of a work previously registered in unpublished form

b. ☐ This is the first application submitted by this author as copyright claimant

c. ☐ This is a changed version of the work, as shown by space 6 on this application

If your answer is "Yes" give: **Previous Registration Number** ▼   **Year of Registration** ▼

5

DERIVATIVE WORK OR COMPILATION Complete both space 6a and 6b for a derivative work; complete only 6b for a compilation

a. **Preexisting Material** Identify any preexisting work or works that this work is based on or incorporates ▼

b. **Material Added to This Work** Give a brief, general statement of the material that has been added to this work and in which copyright is claimed ▼

6

See instructions
before completing
this space

DEPOSIT ACCOUNT If the registration fee is to be charged to a Deposit Account established in the Copyright Office give name and number of Account
Name ▼   **Account Number** ▼

CORRESPONDENCE Give name and address to which correspondence about this application should be sent   Name/Address/Apt/City/State/ZIP ▼

Area Code and Telephone Number ▶

7

Be sure to
give your
daytime phone
◀ number

CERTIFICATION* I, the undersigned, hereby certify that I am the

Check only one ▼

☐ author

☐ other copyright claimant

☐ owner of exclusive right(s)

☐ authorized agent of _____

Name of author or other copyright claimant, or owner of exclusive right(s) ▲

of the work identified in this application and that the statements made
by me in this application are correct to the best of my knowledge.

Typed or printed name and date ▼ If this application gives a date of publication in space 3, do not sign and submit it before that date

date ▶

☞ Handwritten signature (X) ▼

8

**MAIL
CERTIFI-
CATE TO**

Name ▼

Number/Street/Apartment Number ▼

City/State/ZIP ▼

**Certificate
will be
mailed in
window
envelope**

YOU MUST:
• Complete all necessary spaces
• Sign your application in space 8

**SEND ALL 3 ELEMENTS
IN THE SAME PACKAGE:**

1 Application form
2 Nonrefundable $20 filing fee
  in check or money order
  payable to Register of Copyrights
3 Deposit material

MAIL TO
Register of Copyrights
Library of Congress
Washington, D.C. 20559-6000

9

The Copyright Office
has the authority to ad-
just fees at 5-year intervals, based on changes
in the Consumer Price
Index. The next adjust-
ment is due in 1996.
Please contact the
Copyright Office after
July 1995 to determine
the actual fee schedule.

*17 U.S.C. § 506(e): Any person who knowingly makes a false representation of a material fact in the application for copyright registration provided for by section 409, or in any written statement filed in connection
with the application, shall be fined not more than $2,500.

July 1993—300,000   ♲ PRINTED ON RECYCLED PAPER   ⋆U.S. GOVERNMENT PRINTING OFFICE: 1993-342-582/80,017

Appendix 2

U.S. Patent And Trademark Office Form:
Application For Federal Registration

TRADEMARK/SERVICE MARK APPLICATION, PRINCIPAL REGISTER, WITH DECLARATION	MARK (Word(s) and/or Design)	CLASS NO. (If known)

TO THE ASSISTANT SECRETARY AND COMMISSIONER OF PATENTS AND TRADEMARKS:

APPLICANT'S NAME:

APPLICANT'S BUSINESS ADDRESS: _____
(Display address exactly as
it should appear on registration) _____
_____

APPLICANT'S ENTITY TYPE: (Check one and supply requested information)

Individual - Citizen of (Country):

Partnership - State where organized (Country, if appropriate): _____
Names and Citizenship (Country) of General Partners: _____

Corporation - State (Country, if appropriate) of Incorporation:

Other (Specify Nature of Entity and Domicile):

GOODS AND/OR SERVICES:

Applicant requests registration of the trademark/service mark shown in the accompanying drawing in the United States Patent and Trademark Office on the Principal Register established by the Act of July 5, 1946 (15 U.S.C. 1051 et. seq., as amended) for the following goods/services (SPECIFIC GOODS AND/OR SERVICES MUST BE INSERTED HERE):
_____
_____
_____
_____

BASIS FOR APPLICATION: (Check boxes which apply, but never both the first AND second boxes, and supply requested information related to each box checked.)

[ ] Applicant is using the mark in commerce on or in connection with the above identified goods/services. (15 U.S.C. 1051(a), as amended.) Three specimens showing the mark as used in commerce are submitted with this application.
• Date of first use of the mark in commerce which the U.S. Congress may regulate (for example, interstate or between the U.S. and a foreign country): _____
• Specify the type of commerce: _____
(for example, interstate or between the U.S. and a specified foreign country)
• Date of first use anywhere (the same as or before use in commerce date): _____
• Specify manner or mode of use of mark on or in connection with the goods/services: _____
(for example, trademark is applied to labels, service mark is used in advertisements)

[ ] Applicant has a bona fide intention to use the mark in commerce on or in connection with the above identified goods/services. (15 U.S.C. 1051(b), as amended.)
• Specify intended manner or mode of use of mark on or in connection with the goods/services: _____
(for example, trademark will be applied to labels, service mark will be used in advertisements)

[ ] Applicant has a bona fide intention to use the mark in commerce on or in connection with the above identified goods/services, and asserts a claim of priority based upon a foreign application in accordance with 15 U.S.C. 1126(d), as amended.
• Country of foreign filing _____ • Date of foreign filing: _____

[ ] Applicant has a bona fide intention to use the mark in commerce on or in connection with the above identified goods/services and, accompanying this application, submits a certification or certified copy of a foreign registration in accordance with 15 U.S.C. 1126(e), as amended.
• Country of registration: _____ • Registration number: _____

NOTE: Declaration, on Reverse Side, MUST be Signed

DECLARATION

The undersigned being hereby warned that willful false statements and the like so made are punishable by fine or imprisonment, or both, under 18 U.S.C. 1001, and that such willful false statements may jeopardize the validity of the application or any resulting registration, declares that he/she is properly authorized to execute this application on behalf of the applicant; he/she believes the applicant to be the owner of the trademark/service mark sought to be registered, or, if the application is being filed under 15 U.S.C. 1051(b), he/she believes applicant to be entitled to use such mark in commerce; to the best of his/her knowledge and belief no other person, firm, corporation, or association has the right to use the above identified mark in commerce, either in the identical form thereof or in such near resemblance thereto as to be likely, when used on or in connection with the goods/services of such other person, to cause confusion, or to cause mistake, or to deceive; and that all statements made of his/her own knowledge are true and that all statements made on information and belief are believed to be true.

_____   _____
DATE   SIGNATURE

_____   _____
TELEPHONE NUMBER   PRINT OR TYPE NAME AND POSITION

INSTRUCTIONS AND INFORMATION FOR APPLICANT

TO RECEIVE A FILING DATE, THE APPLICATION MUST BE COMPLETED AND SIGNED BY THE APPLICANT AND SUBMITTED ALONG WITH:

1. The prescribed **FEE** (**$245.00**) for each class of goods/services listed in the application;
2. A **DRAWING PAGE** displaying the mark in conformance with 37 CFR 2.52;
3. If the application is based on use of the mark in commerce, **THREE** (3) **SPECIMENS** (evidence) of the mark as used in commerce for each class of goods/services listed in the application. All three specimens may be in the nature of: (a) labels showing the mark which are placed on the goods; (b) photographs of the mark as it appears on the goods; (c) brochures or advertisements showing the mark as used in connection with the services.
4. An **APPLICATION WITH DECLARATION** (this form) - The application must be signed in order for the application to receive a filing date. Only the following person may sign the declaration, depending on the applicant's legal entity: (a) the individual applicant; (b) an officer of the corporate applicant; (c) one general partner of a partnership applicant; (d) all joint applicants.

SEND APPLICATION FORM, DRAWING PAGE, FEE, AND SPECIMENS (IF APPROPRIATE) TO:

U.S. DEPARTMENT OF COMMERCE
Patent and Trademark Office, Box TRADEMARK
Washington, D.C. 20231

Additional information concerning the requirements for filing an application is available in a booklet entitled **Basic Facts About Trademarks**, which may be obtained by writing to the above address or by calling: (703) 308-HELP.

Appendix 3

International Classification Of Goods/Services

RULES OF PRACTICE

Part 6 -- CLASSIFICATION OF GOODS AND SERVICES UNDER THE TRADEMARK ACT

6.1 International schedule of classes of goods and services.

GOODS

1. Chemical products used in industry, science, photography, agriculture, horticulture, forestry; artificial and synthetic resins; plastics in the form of powders, liquids or pastes, for industrial use: manures (natural and artificial); fire extinguishing compositions; tempering substances and chemical preparations for soldering; chemical substances for preserving foodstuffs; tanning substances; adhesive substances used in industry.

2. Paints, varnishes, lacquers; preservatives against rust and against deterioration of wood; coloring matters, dyestuffs; mordants; natural resins; metals in foil and powder form for painters and decorators.

3. Bleaching preparations and other substances for laundry use; cleaning, polishing, scouring and abrasive preparations; soaps; perfumery, essential oils, cosmetics, hair lotions; dentifrices.

4. Industrial oils and greases (other than oils and fats and essential oils); lubricants; dust laying and absorbing compositions; fuels (including motor spirit) and illuminants; candles, tapers, night lights and wicks.

5. Pharmaceutical, veterinary, and sanitary substances; infants' and invalids' foods; plasters, material for bandaging; material for stopping teeth, dental wax, disinfectants; preparations for killing weeds and destroying vermin.

6. Unwrought and partly wrought common metals and their alloys; anchors, anvils, bells, rolled and cast building materials; rails and other metallic materials for railway tracks; chains (except driving chains for vehicles); cables and wires (nonelectric); locksmiths' work; metallic pipes and tubes; safes and cash boxes; steel balls; horseshoes; nails and screws; other goods in nonprecious metal not included in other classes; ores.

7. Machines and machine tools; motors (except for land vehicles); machine couplings and belting (except for land vehicles); large size agricultural implements; incubators.

8. Hand tools and instruments; cutlery, forks, and spoons; side arms.

9. Scientific, nautical, surveying and electrical apparatus and instruments (including wireless), photographic, cinematographic, optical, weighing, measuring, signalling, checking (supervision), life-saving and teaching apparatus and instruments; coin or counterfreed apparatus; talking machines; cash registers; calculating machines; fire extinguishing apparatus.

10. Surgical, medical, dental, and veterinary instruments and apparatus (including artificial limbs, eyes, and teeth).

11. Installations for lighting, heating, steam generating, cooking, refrigerating, drying, ventilating, water supply, and sanitary purposes.

12. Vehicles; apparatus for locomotion by land, air, or water.

13. Firearms; ammunition and projectiles; explosive substances; fireworks.

14. Precious metals and their alloys and goods in precious metals or coated therewith (except cutlery, forks and spoons); jewelry, precious stones; horological and other chronometric instruments.

15. Musical instruments (other than talking machines and wireless apparatus).

TRADEMARK MANUAL OF EXAMINING PROCEDURE

16. Paper and paper articles, cardboard and cardboard articles; printed matter, newspaper and periodicals, books; bookbinding material; photographs; stationery, adhesive materials (stationery); artists' materials; paint brushes; typewriters and office requisites (other than furniture); instructional and teaching material (other than apparatus); playing cards; printers' type and cliches (stereotype).

17. Gutta percha, india rubber, balata and substitutes, articles made from these substances and not included in other classes; plastics in the form of sheets, blocks and rods, being for use in manufacture; materials for packing, stopping or insulating; asbestos, mica and their products; hose pipes (nonmetallic).

18. Leather and imitations of leather, and articles made from these materials and not included in other classes; skins, hides; trunks and travelling bags; umbrellas, parasols and walking sticks; whips, harness and saddlery.

19. Building materials, natural and artificial stone, cement, lime, mortar, plaster and gravel; pipes of earthenware or cement; roadmaking materials; asphalt, pitch and bitumen; portable buildings; stone monuments; chimney pots.

20. Furniture, mirrors, picture frames; articles (not included in other classes) of wood, cork, reeds, cane, wicker, horn, bone, ivory, whalebone, shell, amber, mother-of-pearl, meerschaum, celluloid, substitutes for all these materials, or of plastics.

21. Small domestic utensils and containers (not of precious metals, or coated therewith); combs and sponges; brushes (other than paint brushes); brushmaking materials; instruments and material for cleaning purposes; steel wool; unworked or semiworked glass (excluding glass used in building); glassware, porcelain and earthenware, not included in other classes.

22. Ropes, string, nets, tents, awnings, tarpaulins, sails, sacks; padding and stuffing materials (hair, kapok, feathers, seaweed, etc.); raw fibrous textile materials.

23. Yarns, threads.

24. Tissues (piece goods); bed and table covers; textile articles not included in other classes.

25. Clothing, including boots, shoes and slippers.

26. Lace and embroidery, ribands and braid; buttons, press buttons, hooks and eyes, pins and needles; artificial flowers.

27. Carpets, rugs, mats and matting; linoleums and other materials for covering existing floors; wall hangings (nontextile).

28. Games and playthings; gymnastic and sporting articles (except clothing); ornaments and decorations for Christmas trees.

29. Meats, fish, poultry and game; meat extracts; preserved, dried and cooked fruits and vegetables; jellies, jams; eggs, milk and other dairy products; edible oils and fats; preserves, pickles

30. Coffee, tea, cocoa, sugar, rice, tapioca, sago, coffee substitutes; flour, and preparations made from cereals; bread, biscuits, cakes, pastry and confectionery, ices; honey, treacle; yeast, baking powder; salt, mustard, pepper, vinegar, sauces, spices; ice.

31. Agricultural, horticultural and forestry products and grains not included in other classes; living animals; fresh fruits and vegetables; seeds; live plants and flowers; foodstuffs for animals, malt.

32. Beer, ale and porter; mineral and aerated waters and other nonalcoholic drinks; syrups and other preparations for making beverages.

33. Wines, spirits and liqueurs.

34. Tobacco, raw or manufactured; smokers' articles; matches.

RULES OF PRACTICE

SERVICES

35. Advertising and business.
36. Insurance and financial.
37. Construction and repair.
38. Communication.
39. Transportation and storage.
40. Material treatment.
41. Education and entertainment.
42. Miscellaneous.

6.2 Prior U.S. schedule of classes of goods and services.

GOODS

Class	Title
1	Raw or partly prepared materials.
2	Receptacles.
3	Baggage, animal equipments, portfolios, and pocket books.
4	Abrasives and polishing materials.
5	Adhesives.
6	Chemicals and chemical compositions.
7	Cordage.
8	Smokers' articles, not including tobacco products.
9	Explosives, firearms, equipments, and projectiles.
10	Fertilizers.
11	Inks and inking materials.
12	Construction materials.
13	Hardware and plumbing and steamfitting supplies.
14	Metals and metal castings and forgings.
15	Oils and greases.
16	Protective and decorative coatings.
17	Tobacco products.
18	Medicines and pharmaceutical preparations.
19	Vehicles.
20	Linoleum and oiled cloth.
21	Electrical apparatus, machines, and supplies.
22	Games, toys, and sporting goods.
23	Cutlery, machinery, and tools, and parts thereof.
24	Laundry appliances and machines.
25	Locks and safes.
26	Measuring and scientific appliances.
27	Horological instruments.
28	Jewelry and precious-metal ware.
29	Brooms, brushes, and dusters.
30	Crockery, earthenware, and porcelain.
31	Filters and refrigerators.
32	Furniture and upholstery.
33	Glassware
34	Heating, lighting, and ventilating apparatus.
35	Belting, hose, machinery packing, and nonmetallic tires.
36	Musical instruments and supplies.
37	Paper and stationery.

TRADEMARK MANUAL OF EXAMINING PROCEDURE

38	Prints and publications.
39	Clothing.
40	Fancy goods, furnishings, and notions.
41	Canes, parasols, and umbrellas.
42	Knitted, netted, and textile fabrics, and substitutes therefor.
43	Thread and yarn.
44	Dental, medical, and surgical appliances.
45	Soft drinks and carbonated waters.
46	Foods and ingredients of foods.
47	Wines.
48	Malt beverages and liquors.
49	Distilled alcoholic liquors.
50	Merchandise not otherwise classified.
51	Cosmetics and toilet preparations.
52	Detergents and soaps.

SERVICES

100	Miscellaneous.
101	Advertising and business.
102	Insurance and financial.
103	Construction and repair.
104	Communication.
105	Transportation and storage.
106	Material treatment.
107	Education and entertainment.

6.3 Schedule for certification marks.

In the case of certification marks, all goods and services are classified in two classes as follows:

A. Goods
B. Services

6.4 Schedule for collective membership marks.

All collective membership marks are classified as follows:

Class	Title
200	Collective Membership.

Appendix 4

Sample Form: Assignment Of All Rights In
<u>Works, Including Copyright Rights</u>

WHEREAS, _____, an individual with an address at _____ _____ (hereinafter "Assignor") is the author of the works depicted and/or listed in Exhibit A hereto (hereinafter collectively referred to as "The Works");

WHEREAS, Assignor is desirous of assigning to _____, a corporation organizing and existing under the laws of the State of ____ _, with an address at _____ (hereinafter referred to as "Assignee"), and Assignee is desirous of acquiring all of Assignor's right, title and interest in and to the Works, including, but not limited to, all of Assignor's copyright rights in and to the Works, all possible copyright registrations, patents, trademarks, all possible applications for and any renewals and/or extensions of any of the foregoing and any other intangible intellectual property embodied in the Works, including all rights to recover for past infringement;

NOW, THEREFORE, in consideration of the sum of $1.00 plus other good and valuable consideration, the receipt and adequacy of which is hereby acknowledged, Assignor hereby assigns unto Assignee all of Assignor's right, title and interest in and to the Works, including, but not limited to, all of Assignor's copyright rights therein, all possible copyright registrations, patents, trademarks, all possible applications for and any renewals and any extensions of any of the foregoing and any other intangible intellectual property embodied in the Works, including all rights to recover for past infringement, which interest and rights shall be held until the full end of the term for which any of the foregoing (or any renewals and/or extensions thereof) is or may be granted.

Without limiting the foregoing, Assignor hereby waives any and all claims that Assignor may now or hereafter have in any jurisdiction to so--called "moral rights" or rights of "droit morale" with respect to the Works.

Assignor also agrees to execute such further instruments as Assignee may request to establish, maintain, or protect Assignee's right, title or interest in and to the Works.

IN WITNESS WHEREOF, Assignor has executed this Agreement on the date set forth below.

[ASSIGNOR]

By:_____
   (signature)

_____
   (typed name, title)

State of _____)
)   ss:
County of _____)

   This _____ day of _____, before me personally came the above–named _____, to me personally known as the individual who executed the foregoing assignment, who acknowledged to me that he executed the same of his own free will for the purposes therein set forth.

_____
My commission expires:

[ASSIGNEE]

By:_____

    (signature)

_____

    (typed name, title)

State of _____)

)   ss:

County of _____)

    This _____ day of _____, before me personally came the above–named _____, to me personally known as the individual who executed the foregoing assignment, who acknowledged to me that he executed the same of his own free will for the purposes therein set forth.

_____

               My commission expires:

Appendix 5

<u>Sample Form: Assignment Of Trademark Registration</u>

WHEREAS, _____, a _____ corporation with an address at _____ ("Assignor") has adopted and is using the mark _____ which is registered in the United States Patent and Trademark Office, Registration No. _____, dated _____ (the "Mark and Registration"); and

WHEREAS, _____, a _____ corporation with an address at _____ ("Assignee") is desirous of acquiring the Mark and the Registration thereof;

NOW, THEREFORE, for good and valuable consideration, the receipt and adequacy which is hereby acknowledged, Assignor does hereby assign unto said Assignee all right, title and interest in and to the Mark, together with all rights with past infringement and the goodwill of the business symbolized by the Mark, and the Registration thereof.

IN WITNESS WHEREOF, the parties hereto have caused this Agreement to be executed as of the day and year first above written.

[ASSIGNOR]

By:_____
   (signature)

_____
   (typed name, title)

State of _____)
)   ss:
County of _____)

    This _____ day of _____, before me personally came the above–named _____, to me personally known as the individual who executed the foregoing assignment, who acknowledged to me that he executed the same of his own free will for the purposes therein set forth.

                                 _____

                                   My commission expires:

[ASSIGNEE]

By:_____
    (signature)

_____
    (typed name, title)

State of _____)
)   ss:
County of _____)

    This _____ day of _____, before me personally came the above–named _____, to me personally known as the individual who executed the foregoing assignment, who acknowledged to me that he executed the same of his own free will for the purposes therein set forth.

                                   _____

                                   My commission expires:

Appendix 6

Sample Form: Basic Trademark License Agreement

THIS LICENSE AGREEMENT (the "Agreement"), effective as of this _____ day of _____, 19__, is by and between _____ _____, a _____ corporation, located at _____ ("LICENSOR") and _____ ___, a _____ corporation, located at _____ _____ ("LICENSEE").

WHEREAS, LICENSOR is the owner of the trade names, trademarks and service marks (hereinafter referred to as the "Names and Marks") and registrations thereof listed on and contained in the attached Exhibit A; and

WHEREAS, LICENSEE is desirous of using the Names and Marks in connection with [insert goods/services] for a period of five years from the date of execution of this Agreement;

WHEREAS, the "Territory" in this Agreement shall mean the United States and all its possessions and territories.

NOW, THEREFORE, for good and valuable consideration, the receipt and adequacy of which is hereby acknowledged and in consideration of the mutual promises set forth herein, the parties agree as follows:

GRANT OF LICENSE

1. LICENSOR grants to LICENSEE a nonexclusive, nontransferable license to use the Names and Marks in the Territory in connection with the goods and services covered by the registrations referred to in Exhibit A for [insert goods/services] for a period of five years from the effective date of this Agreement.

OWNERSHIP OF MARKS

2. LICENSEE acknowledges that ownership of the Names and Marks is in LICENSOR and LICENSEE agrees it will do nothing inconsistent with such ownership and that all use of the Names and Marks by LICENSEE shall inure to the benefit of and be on behalf of LICENSOR. LICENSEE agrees that nothing in this Agreement shall give LICENSEE any right, title or interest in or to the Names and Marks other than the right to use the Names and Marks in accordance with this Agreement and LICENSEE agrees that it will not attack the title of LICENSOR to the Names and Marks or attack the validity of this Agreement. LICENSEE agrees that all rights in the Names and Marks and the goodwill connected therewith shall at all times remain the property of LICENSOR.

QUALITY STANDARDS AND MAINTENANCE

3. LICENSEE agrees that the nature and quality of all goods and services being sold and/or rendered by LICENSEE under the Names and Marks and all related advertising, promotional and other related uses of the Names and Marks shall conform to the standards set by and be under the control of LICENSOR.

4. LICENSEE agrees to cooperate with LICENSOR in facilitating LICENSOR's control of the nature and quality of all goods and services sold and/or rendered by LICENSEE and all related

advertising, promotional and related uses of the Names and Marks and to permit reasonable inspection of LICENSEE's operations, to supply LICENSOR with samples of all goods sold under the Names and Marks upon request by LICENSOR and to supply LICENSOR with samples of all advertising, promotional and related uses of the Names and Marks prior to dissemination of such materials to others.

5. LICENSEE shall comply with all applicable laws and regulations and obtain all appropriate government approvals pertaining to the sale, distribution and advertising of goods and services covered by this Agreement.

FORM OF USE

6. LICENSEE agrees to use the Names and Marks only in the form and manner and with appropriate legends as prescribed by LICENSOR as and shown in the copy of sample packaging material attached at Exhibit B hereto, and not to use any other trade name, trademark or service mark in combination with any of the Names and Marks without prior written approval of LICENSOR.

INFRINGEMENT PROCEEDINGS

7. LICENSEE agrees to notify LICENSOR of any unauthorized use of the Names and Marks by others as reasonably soon as possible after it comes to LICENSEE's attention. LICENSOR shall have the sole right and discretion to bring infringement or unfair competition proceedings involving the Names and Marks.

TERM

8. This Agreement shall continue in force and effect for [e.g., five years] from the effective date of this Agreement unless sooner terminated as provided for herein.

TERMINATION FOR CAUSE

9. LICENSOR shall have the right to terminate this Agreement upon thirty (30) days written notice to LICENSEE in the event of any affirmative act of insolvency by LICENSEE, or upon the appointment of any receiver or trustee to take possession of the properties of LICENSEE or upon the winding–up, sale, consolidation, merger or any sequestration by governmental authority of LICENSEE, or upon breach of any of the provisions hereof by LICENSEE.

EFFECT OF TERMINATION

10. Upon termination of this Agreement, LICENSEE agrees to immediately discontinue all use of the Names and Marks and any term confusingly similar thereto and to destroy or return to LICENSOR all remaining printed materials bearing any of the Names and Marks.

CHOICE OF LAW

11. It is agreed that this Agreement will be interpreted according to the laws of the State of _____, United States of America.

IN WITNESS WHEREOF, the parties hereto have caused this Agreement to be executed as of the day and year first above written.

[LICENSOR]

_____
(signature)

_____
(typed name, title)

State of _____)
)   ss:
County of _____)

This _____ day of _____, before me personally came the above–named _____, to me personally known as the individual who executed the foregoing assignment, who acknowledged to me that he executed the same of his own free will for the purposes therein set forth.

_____
My commission expires:

[LICENSEE]

_____
(signature)

_____
(typed name, title)

State of _____)
)   ss:
County of _____)

This _____ day of _____, before me personally came the above–named _____, to me personally known as the individual who executed the foregoing assignment, who acknowledged to me that he executed the same of his own free will for the purposes therein set forth.

_____
My commission expires:

Appendix 7

Sample Form: Work Made For Hire/Assignment Clause
In Independent Contractor-Type Agreement For Artwork

• • • •

Artist hereby acknowledges that Artist's work and services hereunder and all results and proceeds thereof, including, without limitation, the [insert previously defined work] are works done under Employer's direction and control and that all such works, services, results and proceeds shall be considered "works made for hire" (as that term is defined in the Copyright Statute). As between Artist and Employer, Employer shall be considered the author of the [insert previously defined work] for all purposes, and the sole and exclusive owner of all of the rights comprised in the copyright and of all possible copyright registrations, patents, trademarks, all applications for renewals of any of the foregoing, and any other intangible intellectual property embodied in the [insert previously defined work].

To the extent such rights do not vest in Employer as a "work made for hire" in any aspect of the [insert previously defined work]. Artist further grants, assigns and transfers to Employer all of Artist's right, title and interest in and to the [insert previously defined work] and all material contained therein or prepared therefor and the results and proceeds thereof, including, but not limited to, the copyright, all possible copyright registrations, patents, trademarks, all possible applications for or renewals of any of the foregoing, and any other intangible intellectual property embodied in the [insert previously defined work].

• • • •

Appendix 8

Sample Form: Confidentiality Agreement

THIS AGREEMENT made this _____ day of _____ 199_ is by and between _____, an individual with an address at _____ _____ (hereinafter "Author") and _____, a _____ corporation with a principal place of business at _____ _____ (hereinafter "Publisher");

WHEREAS, Publisher is in the business of developing, marketing and distributing software programs;

WHEREAS, Author has valuable proprietary and trade secret information consisting of product and marketing ideas and concepts and other proprietary business, marketing and product information concerning the design, marketing and sale of software, which material and information has not been disclosed or become known to the general public (hereinafter "Confidential Information");

[Alternative Clause: **WHEREAS**, Author has created software and associated materials identified in Appendix "A" hereto which constitute and contain proprietary trade secrets and Confidential Information and material, which has not been disclosed or become known to the general public (hereinafter "Confidential Information");]

WHEREAS, for the sole purpose of determining whether Publisher and Author mutually desire to enter into a business arrangement pertaining to the development and distribution of software derived for and based on the Confidential Information, Publisher desires to receive such Confidential Information while agreeing to maintain all such Confidential Information in strict confidence; and

WHEREAS, Author is willing to disclose the Confidential Information to Publisher for the sole purpose of determining whether Author and Publisher mutually desire to enter into a business arrangement pertaining to the Confidential Information so long as Publisher agrees to maintain all such Confidential Information in strict confidence.

NOW, THEREFORE, in consideration of the mutual promises expressed herein, Author and Publisher agree as follows:

(1)   Publisher agrees to treat the Confidential Information as secret and confidential and specifically agrees not to disclose the Confidential Information to any third party, nor to make copies of any writings concerning or embodying the Confidential Information, nor to make any commercial use of the Confidential Information, nor to use the Confidential Information in any way for its own benefit without the prior express written consent of Author.

(2)   The obligations of Publisher outlined above shall extend for a period of ten (10) years from the date of disclosure provided that the obligation shall not extend to any information which:

  (a)   was known to Publisher prior to disclosure by Author as evidenced by written records;

  (b)   is or shall become generally available to the public other than through any act or omission by Publisher; or

  (c)   was or is lawfully made available to Publisher by a third party not under an obligation of non–disclosure to Author.

(3)   Publisher shall not, by virtue of this Agreement alone, obtain any rights or license in or to the Confidential Information.

(4)   This Agreement constitutes the entire undertaking between the parties with respect to the subject matter hereof and this Agreement may not be modified except in writing signed by both parties.

(5)   This Agreement shall be binding on all Publisher's employees, successors and assigns.

(6)   This Agreement shall be construed according to the laws of the State of _____.

(7)   In the event that Publisher decides not to enter into any business relationship with Author, Publisher shall return all Confidential Information to Author by pre–paid certified mail, return receipt requested, or by such other delivery which requires written confirmation of receipt.

(8)   This Agreement shall not be construed as granting or confirming any rights other than as expressly stated herein.

IN WITNESS WHEREOF, the parties have set their signature below as of the date given above.

[PUBLISHER]   **[AUTHOR]**

By:_____   By:_____

_____   _____
(Typed Name)   (Typed Name)

_____
(Typed Title)

Appendix 9

Proposed [PTO] Examination Guidelines
For Computer-Implemented Invention

DEPARTMENT OF COMMERCE

Patent and Trademark Office

[Docket No. 95053144–5144–01]

RIN 0651–XX02

Request for Comments on Proposed Examination Guidelines for

Computer–Implemented Inventions

AGENCY: Patent and Trademark Office, Commerce

ACTION: Notice and request for public comments.

SUMMARY: The Patent and Trademark Office (PTO) requests comments from any interested member of the public on proposed internal guidelines to be used by Office personnel in their review of patent applications on computer–implemented inventions.   Because these guidelines govern internal practices, they are exempt from notice and comment rulemaking under 5 U.S.C. § 553(b)(A).

DATES: Written comments on the proposed guidelines will be accepted by the PTO until July 31, 1995.

ADDRESSES: Written comments should be addressed to the Commissioner of Patents and Trademarks, marked to the attention of Jeff Kushan. Comments submitted by mail should be sent to Commissioner of Patents and Trademarks, Box 4, Patent and Trademark Office, Washington, DC 20231. Comments may also be submitted by telefax at

(703) 305–8885 and by electronic mail through the Internet to comments–software@uspto.gov. Written comments should include the following information:

– name and affiliation of the individual responding;

– an indication of whether comments offered represent views of the respondent's organization or are the respondent's personal views; and

– if applicable, information on the respondent's organization, including the type of organization (e.g., business, trade group, university, non–profit organization) and general areas of interest.

Parties presenting written comments who wish to have their comments included in a publicly accessible electronic database of comments must provide their comments in machine–readable format. Such submissions may be provided in the form of an electronic mail message sent through the Internet, or on a 3.5" floppy disk formatted for use in either a Macintosh or MS–DOS based computer. Machine–readable submissions must be provided as unformatted text (e.g., ASCII or plain text).

All written comments, whether submitted on paper or in machine–readable form, will be available for public inspection no later than August 18, 1995, in Room 902 of Crystal Park Two, 2121 Crystal Drive, Arlington, Virginia. In addition, comments provided in machine–readable format will be available no later than August 18, 1995, through anonymous file transfer protocol (ftp) via the Internet (address: comments.uspto.gov) and through the World Wide Web (address: www.uspto.gov).

FOR FURTHER INFORMATION CONTACT: Jeff Kushan by telephone at (703) 305–9300, by fax at (703) 305–8885, by electronic mail at kushan@uspto.gov, or by mail marked to his attention addressed to the Commissioner of Patents and Trademarks, Box 4, Washington, DC 20231.

SUPPLEMENTARY INFORMATION

I.   Guidelines for Examination of Computer–Implemented Inventions

A.   General Considerations

The following guidelines have been developed to assist Office personnel in their review of applications drawn to computer–implemented inventions. These guidelines respond to recent changes in the law that governs the patentability of computer–implemented inventions, and set forth the official policy of the Office regarding inventions in this field of technology.

It is essential that patent applicants obtain a prompt yet complete examination of their applications. The Office can best achieve this goal by raising any issue that may affect patentability in the initial action on the merits. Under the principles of compact prosecution, each claim should be reviewed for compliance with every statutory requirement of patentability in the initial review of the application, even if one or more claims is found to be deficient with respect to one statutory requirement. Deficiencies should be explained clearly, particularly when they serve as a basis of a rejection. Where possible, examiners should indicate how rejections may be overcome and problems resolved. A failure to follow this approach can lead to unnecessary delays in the prosecution of the application.

B.   Procedures to be Followed When Evaluating
        Computer–Implemented Inventions

        The following procedures should be used when reviewing
applications drawn to computer–implemented inventions.

1.   Determine what the applicant has invented by reviewing the
written description and the claims.

(a)   Identify any specific embodiments of the invention that have been
disclosed, review the detailed description of the invention and note the
specific utility that has been asserted for the invention.

(b)   Analyze each claim carefully, correlating each claim element to
the relevant portion of the written description that describes that element.
Give claim elements their broadest reasonable interpretation that is
consistent with the written description.   If elements of a claimed
invention are defined in means plus function format, review the written
description to identify the specific structure, materials or acts that
correspond to each such element.

(c)   Considering each claim as a whole, classify the invention defined
by each claim as to its statutory category (i.e., process, machine,
manufacture or composition of matter).   Rely on the following
presumptions in making this classification.

(i)   A computer or other programmable apparatus whose actions are
directed by a computer program or other form of "software" is a
statutory "machine."

(ii)   A computer–readable memory that can be used to direct a
computer to function in a particular manner when used by the computer
[1] is a statutory "article of manufacture".

(iii)   A series of specific operational steps to be performed on or with the aid of a computer is a statutory "process".

A claim that clearly defines a computer–implemented process but is not cast as an element of a computer–readable memory or as implemented on a computer should be classified as a statutory "process." [2] If an applicant responds to an action of the Office based on this classification by asserting that subject matter claimed in this format is a machine or an article of manufacture, reject the claim under 35 U.S.C. § 112, second paragraph, for failing to recite at least one physical element in the claims that would otherwise place the invention in either of these two "product" categories. The Examiner should also object to the specification under 37 CFR 1.71(b) if such an assertion is made, as the complete invention contemplated by the applicant has not been cast precisely as being an invention within one of the statutory categories.

A claim that defines an invention as any of the following subject matter should be classified as non–statutory:

–   a compilation or arrangement of data, independent of any physical element;

–   a known machine–readable storage medium that is encoded with data representing creative or artistic expression (e.g., a work of music, art or literature)[3],[4];

–   a "data structure" independent of any physical element (i.e., not as implemented on a physical component of a computer such as a computer–readable memory to render that component capable of causing a computer to operate in a particular manner); or

–   a process that does nothing more than manipulate abstract ideas or concepts (e.g., a process consisting solely of the steps one would follow in solving a mathematical problem [5]).

Claims in this form are indistinguishable from abstract ideas, laws of nature and natural phenomena and may not be patented. Non–statutory claims should be handled in the manner described in section (2)(c) below.

2.   Analyze each claim to determine if it complies with § 112, second paragraph, and with § 112, first paragraph.

(a)   Determine if the claims particularly point out and distinctly claim the invention.   To do this, compare the invention as claimed to the invention as it has been described in the specification.   Pay particular attention to the specific utility contemplated for the invention—features or elements of the invention that are necessary to provide the specific utility contemplated for that invention must be reflected in the claims. If the claims fail to accurately define the invention, they should be rejected under § 112, second paragraph.   A failure to limit the claim to reflect features of the invention that are necessary to impart the specific utility contemplated may also create a deficiency under § 112, first paragraph.

If elements of a claimed invention are defined using "means plus function" language, but it is unclear what structure, materials or acts are intended to correspond to those elements, reject the claim under § 112, second paragraph. A rejection imposed on this basis shifts the burden to the applicant to describe the specific structure, material or acts that correspond to the means element in question, and to identify the precise location in the specification where a description of that means element can be found.   Interpretation of means elements for § 112, second paragraph purposes must be consistent with interpretation of such elements for §§ 102 and 103 purposes.

Computer program–related elements of a computer–implemented [6] invention may serve as the specific structure, material or acts that correspond to an element of an invention defined using a means plus function limitation. For example, a series of operations performed by a computer under the direction of a computer program may serve as "specific acts" that correspond to a means element. Similarly, a computer–readable memory encoded with data representing a computer program that can cause a computer to function in a particular fashion, or a component of a computer that has been reconfigured with a computer program to operate in a particular fashion, can serve as the "specific structure" corresponding to a means element.

Claims must be defined using the English language. See, 37 CFR 1.52(a). A computer programming language is not the English language, despite the fact that English words may be used in that language. Thus, an applicant may not use computer program code, in either source or object format, to define the metes and bounds of a claim. A claim which attempts to define elements of an invention using computer program code, rather than the functional steps which are to be performed, should be rejected under § 112, second paragraph, and should be objected to under 37 CFR 1.52(a).

(b)   Construe the scope of the claimed invention to determine if it is adequately supported by an enabling disclosure. Construe any element defined in means plus function language to encompass all reasonable equivalents of the specific structure, material or acts disclosed in the specification corresponding to that means element. Special care should be taken to ensure that each claim complies with the written description and enablement requirements of 35 U.S.C. § 112.

(c)   A claim as a whole that defines non–statutory subject matter is deficient under § 101, and under § 112, second paragraph. Determining the scope of a claim as a whole requires a clear understanding of what the applicant regards as the invention. The review performed in step 1 should be used to gain this understanding.

(i)   If the invention as disclosed in the written description is statutory, but the claims define subject matter that is not, the deficiency can be corrected by an appropriate claim amendment. Therefore, reject the claims under §§ 101 and 112, second paragraph, but identify the features of the invention that, if recited in the claim, would render the claimed subject matter statutory.

(ii)   If the invention, both as disclosed and as claimed, is not statutory subject matter, reject the claims under § 101 for being drawn to non–statutory subject matter, and under § 112, second paragraph, for failing to particularly point out and distinctly claim an invention entitled to protection under U.S. patent law.

An invention is not statutory if it falls within any of the non–statutory claim categories outlined in section (1)(c) above. Also, in rare situations, a claim classified as a statutory machine or article of manufacture may define non–statutory subject matter. Non–statutory subject matter (i.e., abstract ideas, laws of nature and natural phenomena) does not become statutory merely through a different form of claim presentation.

Such a claim will (a) define the "invention" not through characteristics of the machine or article of manufacture claimed but exclusively in terms of a non–statutory process that is to be performed on or using that machine or article of manufacture, and (b) encompass any product in the stated class (e.g., computer, computer–readable memory) configured in any manner to perform that process.

3.   Determine if the claimed invention is novel and nonobvious under §§ 102 and 103. When evaluating claims defined using "means plus function" language, refer to the specific guidance provided in the In re Donaldson guidelines [1162 OG 59] and section (2)(a) above.

C.   Notes on the Guidelines

[1]   Articles of manufacture encompassed by this definition consist of two elements: (1) a computer–readable storage medium, such as a memory device, a compact disc or a floppy disk, and (2) the specific physical configuration of the substrate of the computer–readable storage medium that represents data (e.g., a computer program), where the

storage medium so configured causes a computer to operate in a specific and predefined manner. The composite of the two elements is a storage medium with a particular physical structure and function (e.g., one that will impart the functionality represented by the data onto a computer).

[2]   For example, a claim that is cast as "a computer program" but which then recites specific steps to be implemented on or using a computer should be classified as a "process." A claim to simply a "computer program" that does not define the invention in terms of specific steps to be performed on or using a computer should not be classified as a statutory process.

[3]   The specific words or symbols that constitute a computer program represent the expression of the computer program and as such are a literary creation.

[4]   A claim in this format should also be rejected under ñ 103, as being obvious over the known machine–readable storage medium standing alone.

[5]   A claim to a method consisting solely of the steps necessary to converting one set of numbers to another set of numbers without reciting any computer–implemented steps would be a non–statutory claim under this definition.

[6]   This includes the software and any associated computer hardware that is necessary to perform the functions directed by the software.

II.   Additional Information

An analysis of the law supporting the examination guidelines for computer–implemented inventions is being prepared. Interested members of the public are invited to comment on this legal analysis. Copies of the legal analysis can be obtained from Jeff Kushan on or after June 23, 1995, who can be reached using the information indicated above.

Bruce A. Lehman   Date

Assistant Secretary of Commerce and
Commissioner of Patents and Trademarks

A

addresses
  digital signatures, 156-157
  domain names, 78-79
advertising
  false and/or misleading, 90-91
  infringement of rights of
    publicity, 92
America On-line (AOL), 173
answer texts, 11
antitrust issues, 153-156
architectural works, 13
artwork, 6
assignments, 12, 131-135 (*see also*
    licensing)
  copyrights, 42-43
  definition/description, 133-134
  examples of uses for, 131-132
  forms
    rights to a work, 214-216
    trademark registration,
      217-218
    work-for-hire, 225
  recordation of, 134-135
  trademarks, 82
  written requirements, 133
atlases, 11
audiovisual works, 6, 10, 13

B

Berne Convention, 28, 32, 44

C

case law, 87
CD-ROM (*see* multimedia works)
choreographic works, 13
Church of Scientology, 114, 177
clean room practice, 15
Clipper Chip, 157
collective works, 10

color depletion theory, 58
colors, trademarking, 58-59
commissioned works, 10-12
common carriers, defamation
    liability of, 164-170
common law, 55, 87
competition, unfair (*see* unfair
    competition)
compilations, 11
compulsory licensing, phonorecords,
    25-26
CompuServe, 166-167
computer hardware, patenting, 96-97
computer software
  clean room practice, 15
  freeware, 142
  games, 20
  licensing, 124
    shrinkwrap-type, 146-148
  multimedia works, 144-146
  patent protection, 106-110
    on The Internet, 110-111
  patenting, 96, 100
  reproduction rights, 24-25
  shareware, 142-143
  source code, 13, 117-118
Confidentiality Agreement, 123,
    127-129
  form, 226-228
  issues contained in, 128
contracts
  Confidentiality Agreement, 123,
    127-129, 226-228
  trade secret protection, 122-123
Copyright Act, 13, 14
  assignments and licensing,
    42-43
  computer programs and, 24-25
  copyright notice and, 30
  duration of copyright, 36-37

moral rights, 28-29
phonorecords and, 25-26
public domain and, 32-33
copyright infringement, 37-42
court cases
Bridge Publications Inc. v.
Vien, 42
Brown Bag Software v.
Symantec Corp., 38
Computer Associates Int'l v.
Altai Inc., 38
Data General Corp. v.
Grumman Data System
Corp., 40
Sega Enters. v. Maphia, 40
United States v.
LaMacchia, 42
definition/description, 37
fines, 41
liability, 39-40
proving, 39
remedies, 41
copyright notice, 29-31
displaying, 30-31
proper form of, 29-30
public domain and, 32-33
published works and, 31
Copyright Office, address, 34
Copyright Statute, 16
copyrightable works, 6
categories of, 13
copyrights, 6-48
area of protection, 3-4, 15-21
assignments, 12, 42-43
Constitutional basis for
protection of, 2
court cases
Apple Computer Inc. v.
Franklin Computer
Corp., 20

Baker v. Selden, 19-20
Bleistein v. Donaldson
Lithographing Co., 17
Community for Creative
Nonviolence v. Reid, 9
Computer Associates Int'l v.
Altai Inc., 20
Feist Publications v. Rural
Telephone Services
Co., 18
Lotus v. Borland, 16
Mazer v. Stein, 17
Whelan Associates Inc. v.
Jaslow Dental
Laboratory Inc.,
20
duration of, 36-37
forms
Application Form PA,
204-207
Application Form SR,
196-199
Application Form TX,
192-195
Application Form VA,
200-203
assignment of a work,
214-216
identifying/searching for rights-
holders, 43-44, 136-140
intellectual property and, 1-2
international considerations,
44-45
licensing, 25-26, 42-43, 135-
142
provisions involving,
140-142
material not protected, 15-21
originality and creativity
requirements, 14-19

owner/user rights, 21-29
    attribution and integrity, 28-29
    computer programs, 24-25
    copying/reproduction, 22
    fair use concept, 26-27
    phonorecords, 25-26
    right to make derivative works, 23-24
    right to reproduce a work, 23
ownership, 7-12
    commissioned works, 10-12
    independent contractors, 9
    joint works, 12
    works made for hire, 8-9
registering, 33-36
    address, 34
    fee, 35
    length of time, 35-36
    required forms for, 34
    required information for, 35
    time limit, 34
shareware, 143
subject matter of, 12-14
transferring rights, 139
court cases
    Akbar v. New York Magazine Co., 182
    Alpo Petfoods Inc. v. Ralston Purina Co., 92
    Apple Computer Inc. v. Franklin Computer Corp., 20
    Arizona Retail Systems Inc. v. The Software Link Inc., 147
    Auvil v. CBS 60 Minutes, 171
    Bachchan v. India Abroad Publications Inc., 179
    Baker v. Selden, 19-20
    Bleistein v. Donaldson Lithographing Co., 17
    Braun v. Soldier of Fortune Magazine Inc., 171
    Bridge Publications Inc. v. Vien, 42
    Brown Bag Software v. Symantec Corp., 38
    Buckley v. New York Post Corp., 182
    Church of Scientology v. Adams, 182
    Communications Satellite Corp. v. Comcet Inc., 80
    Community for Creative Nonviolence v. Reid, 9
    Computer Associates Int'l v. Altai Inc., 20, 38
    Cubby Inc. v. CompuServe Inc., 166-167, 170
    Data General Corp. v. Grumman Data Systems Corp., 40
    Den-Mat Corp. v. Block Drug Co. Inc., 80
    Distrionics Texas Inc. et al. v. Sony Corp. et al., 154
    E.R. Squib & Sons Inc. v. Princeton Pharmaceuticals Inc., 60
    Eimann v. Soldier of Fortune Magazine Inc., 171
    Estate of Elvis Presley v. Russen, 92
    Feist Publications v. Rural Telephone Services Co., 18
    Gale Group Inc. v. King City Indus Co. Ltd., 91
    Gertz v. Robert Welch Inc., 163
    Gonzalas v. Atlanta Constitution, 182

Hancock v. American Steel & Wire Co., 80
Harte-Hanks Communications Inc. v. Connaughton, 176
It's In The Cards Inc. v. Fuschetto, 166-167
Keeton v. Hustler Magazine Inc., 181, 182
Lerman v. Chuckleberry Publishing Inc., 176
Lotus v. Borland, 16
Matusevitch v. Telnikoff, 183
Mazer v. Stein, 17
McGraw-Hill Inc. v. Comstock Partners Inc., 61
Mechanical Plastics Corp. v. Titan Technologies, 57
Medphone v. Denigris, 166
Milkovich v. Lorain Journal Co., 163
MTV Networks v. Curry, 78
New York Times Co. v. Sullivan, 180
Norstrilla Software Inc. v. Lacie Ltd., 80
Qualitex Co. v. Jacobson Products Co., 59
Rinaldi v. Viking Penguin Inc., 186
Sega Enters. v. Maphia, 40
Sipple v. DeMoines Register and Tribune Co., 182
Skil Corp. v. Rockwell Int'l Corp., 91
Smith v. California, 167
Step-Saver Data Systems Inc. v. Wyse Technology, 147
Stratton Oakmont Inc. v. Prodigy Services Co., 162, 168, 170

Tse, Saiget, Watanabe and McClure Inc. v. Gentlecare Systems Inc., 60
U-Haul Int'l v. Jartran Inc., 91
United States of America v. Microsoft, 155
United States v. LaMacchia, 42
Vault Corp. v. Quaid Software Ltd., 147
Vidal Sassoon Inc. v. Bristol-Myers Co., 91
Warner Bros. Inc. v. Gay Toys Inc., 92
Weight Watchers Int'l Inc. v. Stouffer Corp., 61
Whelan Associates Inc. v. Jaslow Dental Laboratory Inc., 20
Wyatt Earp Enterprises Inc. v. Sackman Inc., 92
cryptography, 157

D

data encryption (*see* encryption)
defamation, 160-191
    advice to on-line service owners, 172-178
    court cases
        Akbar v. New York Magazine Co., 182
        Auvil v. CBS 60 Minutes, 171
        Bachchan v. India Abroad Publications Inc., 179
        Braun v. Soldier of Fortune Magazine Inc., 171
        Buckley v. New York Post Corp., 182
        Church of Scientology v. Adams, 182

Cubby Inc. v. CompuServe Inc., 166-167, 170
Eimann v. Soldier of Fortune Magazine Inc., 171
Gertz v. Robert Welch Inc., 163
Gonzalas v. Atlanta Constitution, 182
Harte-Hanks Communications Inc. v. Connaughton, 176
It's In The Cards Inc. v. Fuschetto, 166-167
Keeton v. Hustler Magazine Inc., 181, 182
Lerman v. Chuckleberry Publishing Inc., 176
Matusevitch v. Telnikoff, 183
Medphone v. Denigris, 166
Milkovich v. Lorain Journal Co., 163
New York Times Co. v. Sullivan, 180
Rinaldi v. Viking Penguin Inc., 186
Sipple v. DeMoines Register and Tribune Co., 182
Smith v. California, 167
Stratton Oakmont Inc. v. Prodigy Services Co., 162, 168, 170
definition/description, 162
example, 160-161
Internet messages and, 178-184
liability of
common carriers, 165-170
distributors, 164, 165-170
owners/operators of on-line services, 165-178
publishers, 164, 165-170
libel, 161-164, 185-186
principles, 161-164
radio shows and, 171
slander, 161-162
television programs, 171-172
derivative works, 23-24, 141
digital signature algorithm (DSA), 156
digital signatures, 156-157
distributors, defamation liability of, 164, 165-170
court cases
MTV Networks v. Curry, 78
use and registration of, 78-79
dramatic works, 13

E
E-mail, 120
encryption
Clipper Chip, 157
public-key, 156

F
Federal Rules of Civil Procedure, 182
Federal Trade Commission, 155
forms
assignment
rights to a work, 214-216
trademark registration, 217-218
Work-For-Hire, 225
Confidentiality Agreement, 226-228
copyright
Application Form PA, 204-207

Application Form SR,
196-199
Application Form TX,
192-195
Application Form VA,
200-203
licensing, trademark agreement,
219-224
patent
Application for Federal
Registration, 208-209
examination guidelines,
229-238
trademark, International
Classification of
Goods/Services,
210-213
freeware, 142

G
GATT Treaty, 32
government works, 21
graphics, 13

H
hardware (*see* computer hardware)

I
independent contractor, 9
instructional texts, 11
intellectual property
definition/description, 1
overview, 1-4
international interests
copyrights, 44-45
trademarks, 83-84
Internet
advice regarding material
content on, 172-178

defamation liability and,
165-178
defamation suits, 178-184
domain names (*see* domain
names)
patent protection and, 110-111
trade secret protection on,
125-127
inventions, 1 (*see also* patents)
unpatentable, 109

J
joint works, 12

L
Lanham Act, 52, 87
false and/or misleading
advertising, 90-91
infringement of rights of
publicity, 92
protection of unregistered
trademarks, 89-90
remedies for unfair competition,
91-92
wrongful acts proscribed by,
88-89
law
case, 87
common, 55, 87
statutory, 87
law of dilution, 93-94
libel, 161-164, 185-186, 180 (*see
also* defamation)
Library of Congress, 34
licensing, 131-159 (*see also*
assignments)
compulsory, 25-26
copyrights, 24-43, 135-142
provisions involving,
140-142

court cases
  Arizona Retail Systems Inc.
    v. The Software Link,
    Inc., 147
  Distrionics Texas Inc. et al.
    v. SonyCorp. et al., 154
  Step-Saver Data Systems
    Inc. v. Wyse Techno-
    logy, 147
  United States of America v.
    Microsoft, 155
  Vault Corp. v. Quaid
    Software Ltd., 147
cross-licensing agreements, 154
definition/description, 133-134
digital signatures, 156-157
examples of uses for, 131-132
forms, trademark agreement,
  219-224
multimedia works, 144-146
oral and/or implied, 134
patents, 151-156
shrinkwrap-type, 146-148
software, 124
trademarks, 82, 148-151
transferring rights, 139
literary works, 13
  definition, 13
litigation (*see* court cases)

M
Maxwell, Robert, 177-178, 179
moral rights, 28-29, 141
motion pictures (*see* audiovisual
  works)
multimedia works, licensing,
  144-146
musical works, 13

O
Office Action paper, 102
on-line services
  advice regarding material
  content,   172-178
  defamation liability of owners/
    operators, 165-178
ownership, transferring (*see*
  assignments)

P
pantomimes, 13
Patent and Trademark Office (PTO),
  55, 69-71
  examination guidelines,
    102-103, 229-238
  forms, Application For Federal
    Registration, 2, 192
  history, 97
  recordation of assignments, 134
patents, 96-112
  appealing decision, 103
  application for, 101
  area of protection, 3
  computer hardware and, 96-97
  computer software and, 96, 100,
    106-110
  Constitutional basis for
    protection of, 2
  costs, 100-101, 103, 104
  court cases
    Distrionics Texas Inc. et al.
      v. Sony Corp. et al.,
      154
  definition/description, 98-99
  duration of, 104
  enforcing, 104-105
  filing fee, 101, 103

infringement, 106
Internet and, 110-111
inventions that are unpatentable, 109
investigations and searches for existing, 105-106
licensing, 151-156
    antitrust issues, 153-156
    cross-licensing agreements, 154
    provisions, 151-152
    rights acquisition, 152-153
maintenance fees, 104
Notice of Allowance, 103
obtaining, 100-104
Office Action paper, 102
requirements
    procedural, 99-100
    substantive, 99
rights of, 103-104
pictorial works, 13
Prodigy, 168-170
public domain, 32-33
public-key encryption, 156
publicity (*see* advertising)
publishers, defamation liability of, 164-170

R
reproduction rights (*see also* copyrights)
    advertising and, 22
    commentaries and news reporting, 22
    computer programs, 24-25
    fair use concept, 26-27
    libraries and archiving, 22
    public performance by teachers/pupils, 22

secondary transmissions via satellite and cable TV, 22
reverse engineering, 124

S
sculptural works, 13
service mark, definition/description, 51-52
shareware, 142-143
signatures, digital, 156-157
slander, 161-162 (*see also* defamation; libel)
software (*see* computer software)
sound recordings, 13
    compulsory licensing for, 25-26
source code (*see* computer software)
statutory law, 87
Strategic Lawsuit Against Public Participation (SLAPP), 182
supplementary works, 10
symbols
    registered trademark, 72
    unregistered trademark, 73

T
tests, 11
The Internet (*see* Internet)
trade dress, infringement of, 90
trade names
    definition/description, 52
    infringement of, 90
trade secrets, 113-130
    definition/description, 114
    factors determining protectability, 116
    misappropriation claim elements, 120-121
    patent protection and, 115

protection
    by Confidentiality Agree-
       ment, 123, 127-129
    by contract, 122-123
    in businesses, 118-119
    on The Internet, 125-127
    requirements, 117-120
    reverse engineering, 124
    rights enforcement, 120-122
trademark infringement, 79-82
confusing similarities, 80
court cases
    *Communications Satellite
       Corp. v. Comcet Inc.*,
       80
    *Den-Mat Corp. v. Block
       Drug Co Inc.*, 80
    *Hancock v. American Steel
       & Wire Co.*, 80
    *Norstrilla Software Inc. v.
       Lacie Ltd.*, 80
filing, 81
law of dilution, 93-94
litigation, 79, 82
trademarks, 49-86
actual use of, 64
application process, 68-72
    applicant requirements,
       68-69
    examination/approval,
       69-70
    fee, 68
    length of time, 70
    opposition to and appeal
       board, 71
    publication in Official
       Gazette, 70
arbitrary terms and, 61
area of protection, 3, 56-58,
    89-90

assignment, 82
availability, 54-56
cancellation of, 75-76
choosing, 53-63
coined terms and, 61
colors as, 58-59
common law sources, 55
Constitutional basis for
    protection of, 2
constructive use of, 65
court cases
    *E.R. Squib & Sons Inc. v.
       P r i n c e t o n
       Pharmaceuticals
       Inc.*, 60
    *McGraw-Hill Inc. v.
       Comstock Partners
       Inc.*, 61
    *Mechanical Plastics Corp.
       v. Titan Technologies*,
       57
    MTV Networks v. Curry, 78
    *Qualitex Co. v. Jacobson
       Products Co.*, 59
    *Tse, Saiget, Watanabe and
       McClure Inc. v.
       Gentlecare
       Systems, Inc.*,
       60
    *Weight Watchers Int'l Inc.
       v. Stouffer Corp.*, 61
declaration of incontestability,
    75
declaration of use, 74
definition/description, 49-50
descriptive terms and, 60
duration of, 73-74
forms
    assignment, 217-218

International Classification of Goods/Services, 210-213
licensing, 219-224
generic designation of, 76-77
generic terms and, 59
importance of categories of, 62-63
international considerations, 83-84
law of dilution of, 93-94
licensing, 82, 148-151
maintaining usage of, 73-77
obtaining, 64-68
reapplying after cancellation of, 74
registering, 66-68
  Principal Register, 67
  Supplemental Register, 67
renewing, 74
scope of protection, 59
subject matter for, 56-58
suggestive terms and, 61
symbols
  registered, 72
  unregistered, 73
    protection of, 89-90
  using on the Internet, 77
value of, 52-53
transfer of ownership (*see* assignments)
translations, 10

U
unfair competition, 87-95
case law, 87
common law, 87
court cases
  Alpo Petfoods Inc. v. Ralston Purina Co., 92
  Estate of Elvis Presley v. Russen, 92
  Gale Group Inc. v. King City Indus. Co. Ltd., 91
  Skil Corp. v. Rockwell Int'l Corp., 91
  U-Haul Int'l v. Jartran Inc., 91
  Vidal Sassoon Inc. v. Bristol-Myers Co., 91
  Warner Bros. Inc. v. Gay Toys Inc., 92
  Wyatt Earp Enterprises Inc. v. Sackman Inc., 92
infringement of rights of publicity, 92
Lanham Act and, 88-93
law of dilution of trademarks, 93-94
protection of unregistered trademarks, 89-90
remedies, 91-92
statutory law, 87
Uniform Commercial Code (UCC), 147
Uniform Trade Secrets Act (UTSA), 113
United States Constitution
  copyright protection covered by, 2
  First Amendment, 27, 163
  patent protection covered by, 2
  trademark protection covered by, 2
United States Patent and Trademark Office (*see* Patent and Trademark Office)
Universal Copyright Convention, 44

W
work-for-hire
    doctrine, 8-9
    form, 225
works
    answer text, 11
    architectural, 13
    art, 6
    atlas, 11
    audiovisual, 6, 10, 13
    choreographic, 13
    collective, 10
    commissioned, 10-12
    compilation, 11
    copyrightable (*see* copyrightable
        works; copyrights)
    derivative, 23-24, 141
    dramatic, 13
    government, 21
    graphic, 13
    instructional text, 11
    joint, 12
    literary, 13
    made for hire, 8-9
    multimedia, 144-146
    musical, 13
    pantomimes, 13
    pictorial, 13
    protection upon creation, 6-7
    sculptural, 13
    sound recordings, 13, 25-26
    supplementary, 10
    test, 11
    translations, 10
    written, 6
World Trade Organization, 32
written works, 6

Government Institutes Mini-Catalog

PC #	ENVIRONMENTAL TITLES	Pub Date	Price
629	ABCs of Environmental Regulation: Understanding the Fed Regs	1998	$49
627	ABCs of Environmental Science	1998	$39
672	Book of Lists for Regulated Hazardous Substances, 9th Edition	1999	$79
579	Brownfields Redevelopment	1998	$79
4100 ◉	CFR Chemical Lists on CD ROM, 1998 Edition	1998	$125
4089 ⊟	Chemical Data for Workplace Sampling & Analysis, Single User Disk	1997	$125
512	Clean Water Handbook, 2nd Edition	1996	$89
581	EH&S Auditing Made Easy	1997	$79
673	E H & S CFR Training Requirements, 4th Edition	1999	$89
4082 ◉	EMMI-Envl Monitoring Methods Index for Windows-Network	1997	$537
4082 ◉	EMMI-Envl Monitoring Methods Index for Windows-Single User	1997	$179
525	Environmental Audits, 7th Edition	1996	$79
548	Environmental Engineering and Science: An Introduction	1997	$79
643	Environmental Guide to the Internet, 4rd Edition	1998	$59
650	Environmental Law Handbook, 15th Edition	1999	$89
353	Environmental Regulatory Glossary, 6th Edition	1993	$79
652	Environmental Statutes, 1999 Edition	1999	$79
4097 ◉	OSHA CFRs Made Easy (29 CFRs)/CD ROM	1998	$129
4102 ◉	1999 Title 21 Food & Drug CFRs on CD ROM-Single User	1999	$325
4099 ◉	Environmental Statutes on CD ROM for Windows-Single User	1999	$139
570	Environmentalism at the Crossroads	1995	$39
536	ESAs Made Easy	1996	$59
515	Industrial Environmental Management: A Practical Approach	1996	$79
510	ISO 14000: Understanding Environmental Standards	1996	$69
551	ISO 14001: An Executive Report	1996	$55
588	International Environmental Auditing	1998	$149
518	Lead Regulation Handbook	1996	$79
554	Property Rights: Understanding Government Takings	1997	$79
582	Recycling & Waste Mgmt Guide to the Internet	1997	$49
615	Risk Management Planning Handbook	1998	$89
603	Superfund Manual, 6th Edition	1997	$115
566	TSCA Handbook, 3rd Edition	1997	$95
534	Wetland Mitigation: Mitigation Banking and Other Strategies	1997	$75

PC #	SAFETY and HEALTH TITLES	Pub Date	Price
547	Construction Safety Handbook	1996	$79
553	Cumulative Trauma Disorders	1997	$59
663	Forklift Safety, 2nd Edition	1999	$69
539	Fundamentals of Occupational Safety & Health	1996	$49
612	HAZWOPER Incident Command	1998	$59
535	Making Sense of OSHA Compliance	1997	$59
589	Managing Fatigue in Transportation, ATA Conference	1997	$75
558	PPE Made Easy	1998	$79
598	Project Mgmt for E H & S Professionals	1997	$59
552	Safety & Health in Agriculture, Forestry and Fisheries	1997	$125
669	Safety & Health on the Internet, 3rd Edition	1999	$59
597	Safety Is A People Business	1997	$49
668	Safety Made Easy, 2nd Edition	1999	$59
590	Your Company Safety and Health Manual	1997	$79

Government Institutes

4 Research Place, Suite 200 • Rockville, MD 20850-3226
Tel. (301) 921-2323 • FAX (301) 921-0264
Email: giinfo@govinst.com • Internet: http://www.govinst.com

Please call our customer service department at (301) 921-2323 for a free publications catalog.

CFRs now available online.
Call (301) 921-2355 for info.

Government Institutes Order Form

4 Research Place, Suite 200 • Rockville, MD 20850-3226
Tel (301) 921-2323 • Fax (301) 921-0264
Internet: http://www.govinst.com • E-mail: giinfo@govinst.com

4 EASY WAYS TO ORDER

1. Tel: **(301) 921-2323**
Have your credit card ready when you call.

2. Fax: **(301) 921-0264**
Fax this completed order form with your company purchase order or credit card information.

3. Mail: **Government Institutes Division**
ABS Group Inc.
P.O. Box 846304
Dallas, TX 75284-6304   USA
Mail this completed order form with a check, company purchase order, or credit card information.

4. Online: **Visit http://www.govinst.com**

PAYMENT OPTIONS

❑ **Check** *(payable in US dollars to ABS Group Inc.*
Government Institutes Division)

❑ **Purchase Order** *(This order form must be attached to your company P.O. Note: All International orders must be prepaid.)*

❑ **Credit Card**   ❑ *VISA*   ❑ Master Card
Exp. ___ /____   ❑ AMERICAN EXPRESS
Credit Card No. _____
Signature _____

(Government Institutes' Federal I.D.# is 13-2695912)

CUSTOMER INFORMATION

Ship To: (Please attach your purchase order)

Name: _____
GI Account # (*7 digits on mailing label*): _____
Company/Institution: _____
Address: _____
(Please supply street address for UPS shipping)
_____
City: _____ State/Province: _____
Zip/Postal Code: _____ Country: _____
Tel: ( ) _____
Fax: ( ) _____
Email Address: _____

Bill To: (if different from ship-to address)

Name: _____
Title/Position: _____
Company/Institution: _____
Address: _____
(Please supply street address for UPS shipping)
_____
City: _____ State/Province: _____
Zip/Postal Code: _____ Country: _____
Tel: ( ) _____
Fax: ( ) _____
Email Address: _____

Qty.	Product Code	Title	Price

❑ **New Edition No Obligation Standing Order Program**
Please enroll me in this program for the products I have ordered. Government Institutes will notify me of new editions by sending me an invoice. I understand that there is no obligation to purchase the product. This invoice is simply my reminder that a new edition has been released.

15 DAY MONEY-BACK GUARANTEE
If you're not completely satisfied with any product, return it undamaged within 15 days for a full and immediate refund on the price of the product.

SOURCE CODE: BP01

Subtotal _____
MD Residents add 5% Sales Tax _____
Shipping and Handling (see box below) _____
Total Payment Enclosed _____

Shipping and Handling	Sales Tax	
Within U.S:	Maryland	5%
1-4 products: $6/product	Tennessee	6%
5 or more: $4/product	Texas	8.25%
Outside U.S:	Virginia	4.5%
Add $15 for each item (Global)		